AF762813

Judicial Anti-Corruption Campaigns

This book offers a comparative analysis of mass prosecutions for political corruption in Italy, Brazil, and Romania.

The book outlines how judicial showdowns with political corruption emerge, what consequences they create, and whether they can be considered legitimate judicial operations or coups orchestrated by political forces with the assistance of the judiciary. Due to the similarities exhibited in the legal, political, and economic spheres of the events, the book explores the Italian Mani Pulite, Brazilian Lava Jato, and Romanian judicial anti-corruption campaigns. These campaigns were simultaneously legal operations, narratives created by the media, and opportunities for the emergence of new political actors. The book demonstrates why judicial activity was a crucial tool for reducing and preventing corruption in these countries. In addition to investigating the key legal issues and narratives, the book explores the controversies of these campaigns and assesses whether they should be seen as judicial revolutions or cases of prosecutorial overreach.

Providing a holistic comparative assessment of judicial means as a tool for controlling corruption, this book will be of interest to academics in the fields of Corruption Studies, Law, Development Studies, and Political Science.

Nedim Hogic is a Postdoctoral Research Fellow with the University of Oslo. He researches and teaches on matters of comparative law and politics. He holds an LL.M. from Harvard Law School and Ph.D. from Sant' Anna School of Advanced Studies.

Routledge Corruption and Anti-Corruption Studies

The series features innovative and original research on the subject of corruption from scholars around the world. As well as documenting and analysing corruption, the series aims to discuss anti-corruption initiatives and endeavours, in an attempt to demonstrate ways forward for countries and institutions where the problem is widespread. The series particularly promotes comparative and interdisciplinary research targeted at a global readership.

In terms of theory and method, rather than basing itself on any one orthodoxy, the series draws broadly on the tool kit of the social sciences in general, emphasizing comparison, the analysis of the structure and processes, and the application of qualitative and quantitative methods.

Corruption and Development in Nigeria
Edited by Ọláyínká Àkànle and David O. Nkpe

Corruption Proofing in Africa
A Systems Thinking Approach
Edited by Dan Kuwali

Corruption, Ethics, and Governance in South Africa
Issues, Cases, and Interventions
Edited by Modimowabarwa Kanyane

Deconstructing Corruption in Africa
Edited by Ina Kubbe, Emmanuel Saffa Abbdulai and Michael Johnston

The Digitalisation of Anti-Corruption in Brazil
Scandals, Reforms, and Innovation
Fernanda Odilla

Judicial Anti-Corruption Campaigns
Prosecutions in Italy, Brazil and Romania
Nedim Hogic

For more information about this series, please visit: www.routledge.com/Routledge-Corruption-and-Anti-Corruption-Studies/book-series/RCACS

Judicial Anti-Corruption Campaigns

Prosecutions in Italy, Brazil and Romania

Nedim Hogic

Routledge
Taylor & Francis Group
LONDON AND NEW YORK

First published 2026
by Routledge
4 Park Square, Milton Park, Abingdon, Oxon, OX14 4RN

and by Routledge
605 Third Avenue, New York, NY 10158

Routledge is an imprint of the Taylor & Francis Group, an informa business

© 2026 Nedim Hogic

The right of Nedim Hogic to be identified as author of this work has been asserted in accordance with sections 77 and 78 of the Copyright, Designs and Patents Act 1988.

All rights reserved. No part of this book may be reprinted or reproduced or utilised in any form or by any electronic, mechanical, or other means, now known or hereafter invented, including photocopying and recording, or in any information storage or retrieval system, without permission in writing from the publishers.

Trademark notice: Product or corporate names may be trademarks or registered trademarks, and are used only for identification and explanation without intent to infringe.

British Library Cataloguing-in-Publication Data
A catalogue record for this book is available from the British Library

ISBN: 978-1-032-36905-1 (hbk)
ISBN: 978-1-032-36987-7 (pbk)
ISBN: 978-1-003-33481-1 (ebk)

DOI: 10.4324/9781003334811

Typeset in Times New Roman
by SPi Technologies India Pvt Ltd (Straive)

Contents

1 Corruption and how to fight it

1.1 Prologue

Although not dealing specifically with the country I come from, Bosnia and Herzegovina, this research is much motivated by the developments I witnessed between the 1990s and the 2010s. This is because, during that period, Bosnian society became not only more encroached by corruption but also more explained by corruption. Going beyond an anecdotal experience, this observation has consistently fascinated researchers. In a 2002 study, the United Nations Development Programme (UNDP) observed that when perceiving corruption, Bosnian citizens could not differentiate between domestic governments and the international organizations present on the ground. In a striking passage, the researchers explained this observation by claiming that "the citizens explained the world in terms of corruption."[1] Later, Professor Rothstein would use this passage to support his thesis—discussed in the first chapter of this book—that corruption is a collective action problem requiring a collective approach to reforms, necessary to foster a lasting change to the corruption equilibrium within a society.[2]

However, the explanation of the perception of my fellow citizens was much simpler. During the 1990s, Bosnia and Herzegovina was in the midst of aggression from its neighbors, Serbia and Croatia. This aggression turned into a bloody civil war that claimed more than 100,000 lives. The three main ethnic groups that were at war against each other expected support, sympathy, help, and aid from the international community. However, regardless of their political stance or allegiance, the war left the Bosnians with a bitter and cynical view of the international community. In response to how they perceive the international organizations in terms of corruption, they did not have in mind the organizational practices leading to the misuse of power for private gain. Instead, they projected their own sense of injustices, suffered and perceived in the misuse of public power, to international actors. They did so believing that the aid, support, and sympathy they deserved never came or was unevenly divided and that it did not do much or enough to prevent suffering or war.

DOI: 10.4324/9781003334811-1

In short, the reason Bosnians believed that the international organizations were corrupt was not based on their perception of what politics is but on their first-hand experience with what was, at the time, a decade-long engagement of the international community in and with Bosnia and Herzegovina.

Although we could dismiss this story as a classic case of cultural insensitivity, it is not the point I wish to make here. Throughout the travels that I have undertaken as a Ph.D. researcher, I encountered many people who told me how fascinated they were that I was researching corruption as if they knew exactly what I meant when I would utter the word "corruption." While corruption may have different meanings in different contexts, the very mention that I researched political corruption immediately won me sympathy from most audiences and claimed that it should be researched in their country. Thus, corruption is, regardless of the context something recognizable and perceived as existing.

However, this research is driven by the question of what can be explained by corruption. My own experience from work in development organizations made me realize that more than a name or a concept, corruption has become a way to explain the world, the failures of policies, the lack of responsibility of the political elites, and the injustices of the world. As I hoped that in my own country, people would move away from corruption as the prevalent explanation for the injustices of the world, an opposite trend was emerging: the world was explaining itself more and more similarly in the vernacular used by my fellow citizens.

This is why I have not focused on studying corruption and the challenges to the rule of law in my home country, where it would be much easier to gather the data, interview prominent judges and policymakers, and assess the impact of regulatory measures and the external influences to the fight against corruption. Instead, I want to capture a snapshot of the changes in perception, trust, and the quality of governance in three countries that had experienced a strong judicial and prosecutorial response to the cases of political corruption—Italy, Brazil, and Romania.

All three cases have been precedents of some sort. The Italian investigations that began as an inquiry into the breaches of party financing legislation dubbed the "Mani Pulite" ("Clean Hands") contributed to the collapse of the political system known as the "First Republic," the demise of the two most powerful parties in the country, and the emergence of both right- and left-wing populism. The Romanian political and legal landscape in the 2010s was marked by the anti-corruption investigations led by the independent prosecutorial office, the Anti-Corruption Directorate (herein: DNA), which has, at least in terms of the sheer number of prosecuted holders of political office, set the standards for many of the aspiring European Union member states as well as many of the so-called "old European Union member states." Finally, the most complex case is that of Brazil, where an anti-corruption investigation that started as an everyday inquiry into the workings of a currency exchange office became a showdown turned into a scandal that would lead the country to face a deeply embedded network of corrupt exchanges between the private and government sectors.

Far-reaching and unprecedented as they were, the three investigations were far from being clear victories for the rule of law and democratic accountability. They led to considerable mobilization of political opposition and to counternarratives of prosecutorial overreach and unfair targeting. In this book, I investigate what their reach has been in establishing corruption control in society. The main lessons to be learned, I feel, lie in the domain of socio-legal analysis, which focuses on the ability of the legal system to prevent and prosecute corruption. The book is an attempt to learn more about how the changes that led to the independence of the judicial and prosecutorial offices, enabling them to prosecute those responsible for political corruption, have led to or have failed to lead to a more trustworthy and just society based on the rule of law.

1.2 The problem of corruption

Legal systems of the world prosecute those who breach the law, and the duty to prosecute is a core aspect of every legal system in the world. While the principle of equality before the law is central to the legal system of most countries, the holders of public office often escape unpunished for the misuses that they exercise while holding office. Prosecuting these individuals demands a significant amount of courage from law enforcement agencies, prosecutors, and judges. In many instances, a significant amount of technical expertise and international co-operation is required before prosecutions leading to a conviction may occur.[3] Prosecuting holders or former holders of political office means acting against those who not only have power within a society but may also enjoy popular legitimacy.

These misuses can be different; they may be the acquirement of illicit gains for the performance of regular tasks of a holder of public office, creation of an unfair advantage for themselves, their kinship, cronies, or other connected individuals through public procurement, vote buying, or electoral frauds. They may take the form of appropriation of public funds or may include the kickbacks, that is, the funds that are paid to the holder of public office for (non-)performance of a certain action that favors another private or public entity. In some cases, no financial transaction will occur, but the holder of a public office will exercise undue influence to foster an undue advantage for another entity, and this favor will be reciprocally returned through another in which case we speak of influence trading. Depending on the forms that such illicit actions take, they may be classified as bribery, patronage, cronyism, nepotism, or influence trading. Corruption is thus a wide umbrella-like concept under which different forms of abuses of public power are lumped together.[4] Regarding the variations between the scales at which a corrupt act takes place, we speak of petty corruption, grand corruption, and state capture.[5] With regard to the sectors, corruption seems to be present in all sectors of human activity.

Table 1.1 Classification of corruption

Based on the scale	Petty corruption, grand corruption, state capture.
Based on the sectors where it occurs	Environmental, corruption in education, business corruption, judicial corruption, political corruption, construction, tax, health, energy, forestry, customs and immigration. bureaucratic corruption.
Based on the type of behavior involved	Cronyism—favoring, in particular through appointments, of friends and associates. Nepotism—favoring of relatives and family members. Embezzlement—The misappropriation of property or funds legally entrusted to someone in their formal position as an agent or guardian. Extortion—the unlawful extraction of money or property through intimidation. Patronage—favoring of individuals based on their political loyalty and not on merits. Clientelism—exchange of goods and services for political support, vote buying. Bribery—corrupt receipt, favor or solicitation of a private favor for private action. Kickback—a form of bribery in which a company that is awarded a contract, or from which a purchase is made, turns over a portion of the money received to an official or employee as a reward for helping to bring about the transaction. Kleptocracy—a system of government in which leaders use their position for private gain at the expense of the governed. It is typically correlated with autocratic regimes with no meaningful accountability mechanism, effectively allowing the leader to plunder the state and its citizens for personal enrichment and to entrench his hold on power. Influence trading—"intentionally, promising giving or offering, directly or indirectly, of any undue advantage to anyone who asserts or confirms to exert an improper influence over the decision making of any person, whether the undue advantage is for himself or herself or for anyone else, as well as the request, receipt or acceptance of the offer or the promise of such an advantage, in consideration of that influence."

(*Continued*)

Table 1.1 (Continued)

Based on the type of activities it may involve	Appointing personnel (e.g., in public administration), Buying things (procurement), Delivering programmes or services, making things (construction/manufacturing), rebuilding things (after a disaster), controlling activities (licensing, regulation, issuing of permits), administering (justice, for example).

Author, based on a model developed by Graycar, Corruption and the sources cited in notes above.

"Alternatively called "administrative" or "bureaucratic" corruption, the term refers to the everyday corruption that takes place when bureaucrats meet the public." Based on Glossary, U4 Anti-Corruption Resource Centre, https://www.u4.no/terms#petty-corruption

Perpetrated at the highest levels of government and usually involves both substantial benefits for the officials involved and significant losses for the state and its citizens. https://www.u4.no/terms#petty-corruption

State capture denotes a strong influence of a small number of private individuals over the legal and political sector of a state. Unlike other forms of corruption that just deteriorate the state, state capture can go so far as to legalize corruption making the distribution of resources flow in the direction of a group of individuals. See Fazekas M. & Toth I. J., From corruption to state capture: A new analytical framework with empirical application from Hungary, *Political Research Quarterly* 69(2), (2016), 320–334.

Based on Glossary, U4 Anti-Corruption Resource Centre https://www.u4.no/terms#embezzlement

Britannica, The Editors of Encyclopaedia. "extortion". *Encyclopedia Britannica*, 23 February 2016, https://www.britannica.com/topic/extortion. Accessed 25 April 2022.

James E. Clapp, Dictionary of the Law, (2000), 261.

Based on Glossary, U4 Anti-Corruption Resource Centre, https://www.u4.no/terms#kleptocracy

Based on Council of Europe Criminal Law Convention on Corruption, ETS 173, Article 12.

Clearly, there is a considerable overlap between the definitions of various types of corrupt behavior. All types of this behavior may not be recognized as criminal acts; legitimate lobbying may be close and similar to influence trading, and legitimate political measures that the executive branch of government undertakes may be hard to distinguish from clientelism. Therefore, while not every misuse of public office for private gain is necessarily defined as a criminal act recognized as such by the legislator, but every such misuse is often understood by the public to be political corruption.[6] In a case where the misuse is a criminal act recognized as such by the legislator, an action of the law enforcement bodies may lead to its sanctioning before the courts; where such criminalization is absent, the public may sanction the individual through a reputational loss. A good example of this is influence trading (influence peddling), which, while being increasingly criminalized in jurisdictions across the world, still remains a matter to be determined in each individual case that the prosecutor brings against an individual.[7] Favors done to the holder of public office or the favors that the public official offers to others may be of different nature, and so does their acceptability among different jurisdictions. There are two main reasons for this: one is the difference between the legal systems that occur due to different trajectories of their development[8] and the other is the different cultural understanding of corruption that may be present in different contexts. These different explanations may not necessarily mean that what is desirable in one jurisdiction may be a punishable offense in another, but rather that the behavior in which a holder of a public office misuses public power is more tolerable. Simply put, the concepts of corruption do not vary as much as does the tolerance.[9] While corrupt acts generally do not fare well within the public opinion in any territory,[10] the election of political candidates may not necessarily depend on their corruptness. One of the first European political parties that was held liable for corruption before the court, the Croatian HDZ, was voted back in power only several years after the judgment in which it was found to be liable for a money laundering scheme was passed. While being an important cleavage among different political parties that compete for power within a country, the stance toward corruption or previous corrupt behavior is not necessarily a predictor of a political outcome.[11]

This does not mean that some countries are more inclined to corruption. A cross-international survey has determined that countries with Protestant faith, common law legal tradition, or those that were colonized by the British Empire have a lower prevalence of corruption.[12] However, neither of these traits has made the societies with these traits less immune to the emergence of corrupt political actors or state capture.[13] In some cultures, however, a tradition of gift-giving and the importance of one's personal connections in society are important to one's personal success and wealth. These norms of reciprocity and of expectance of a return favor (quid pro quo) differ between and within societies.[14] Such diversity may lead to a different perception of corrupt behavior and create problems in assessing and fighting corruption, creating difficulties in the creation of a universal approach to corruption that produces equal and comparable results across different contexts.[15] Still, the distinction between a bribe and a gift exists insofar that while gifts include a vague expectation of future behavior, bribes have an explicit quid pro quo expectation.[16] How exactly this distinction evolved over the course of human history is not entirely clear. It seems that the earliest societies did not know the distinction between gift-giving and corruption; instead, the consolidation of religious traditions and the notions of morality this brought might have played a significant role.[17] The recent focus of corruption scholars on histories of anti-corruption activity presents us with evidence for the existence of this distinction in pre-modern states.[18] The bribe-gift distinction, however, is useful because it reminds us that at the root of corrupt acts lies an "interplay between primary human imperatives and an economic and social system trying to control and channel those imperatives."[19] Equally important is the fact that, while the levels of corruption and its perception may dramatically differ, the recognition of corrupt behavior exists across cultures.

The problems of the causes of corruption are differently treated across the disciplines. Relying on the sociological tradition stemming from Max Weber and Robert Putnam, Mungiu Pippidi as one of the leading contemporary authors in the field of corruption studies, sees corruption as a natural state of both individuals and societies, one that is rooted in reciprocity and favoritism.[20] Thus, she argues that we should study the emergence of universalistic norms in those societies which rely less on social connections but on universal norms of behavior.[21] Authors inspired by the economic theories see the causes of corruption in the failure of prevention of rent-seeking that may come as a result of weak enforcement of legislation due to a lack of quality of institutions and a large state apparatus.[22] Both economists and political scientists have focused on the type of political institutions that society uses[23] as well as on the quality of the bureaucracy, in particular public administration.[24]

1.3 Consequences of corruption

Corruption is correlated to economic development; the wealthier the nation, the less the chance that it will be corrupt.[25] Corruption lowers investment[26] and acts as an impediment to economic growth.[27] Nevertheless, the relationship between corruption and economic growth is far from being a one-way street. As examples of China, Vietnam, and Qatar in the last thirty years testify, corrupt states can have high levels of investment and growth. The relationship between investment and growth has been explained through the link between corruption and predictability—the existence of corrupt actors may increase predictability favored by the investors over instability as a variable that determines their willingness to invest.[28] To make matters more complicated, economic growth by itself may lead to a decrease in perceived corruption.[29] Known also as the "East Asian paradox" (the term "crony capitalism" is also used), this happens when small- and medium-sized enterprises are "taxed" by the corrupt state yet simultaneously benefit from its overall developmental policies.[30] While useful in the short run, as it has a beneficial effect on the supply and demand of labor and products within the state, in the long run, these policies run to a development of cartels of power.

In a much clearer way than with economic development, corruption is correlated to democratic accountability.[31] Democratic countries have a stronger mechanism of accountability for elected and appointed officials, which lowers their incentives to engage in corruption. Additionally, democratic countries develop systems of rewards for public administration that are merit-based and universalistic, thereby reducing the incentive to engage in nepotism, cronyism, and other forms of corrupt behavior. Consequentially, democratic backsliding, such as that experienced in many Eastern European democracies in the past decade, increases both perceived and real corruption, lowers legal responses to corruption, and can lead to state capture.[32] This is particularly visible in times of crisis (such as the COVID-19 global pandemic) that require fast responses and efficiency in the state's response to the crisis.[33]

Corruption works against democracy. As it privileges some while disfavoring others, it erodes trust in public institutions and governments. As such it is related to inequality with which it has a bidirectional relationship—corruption may both make inequality worse and may become worse due to inequality.[34] As we will see later in this chapter, this problem and its perception greatly shape the choice of tools that experts believe should be used against corruption. In societies with high levels of trust, corruption is lower,[35] and the public has more faith in the fairness of the judicial system.[36] The adverse effects of corruption are perhaps most salient in this domain. In corrupt countries, citizens do not believe in the impartiality of public institutions and fair outcomes of administrative, legislative, and judicial procedures. The system itself is viewed as favoring those who are "connected" with those in positions of political power.[37] Thus, corruption in these societies becomes a norm rather than a deviation from the societal norm. While empirical research suggests that the moral distinction between corrupt and non-corrupt behavior is maintained even under such circumstances,[38] corrupt behavior becomes the desired norm or a survival strategy, and honest behavior is a moral ideal to which it is difficult to strive. This increases the perception of corruption and leads to the behavior whose consequences I described in the Prologue to this book—that of explaining the world in terms of corruption. The consequences of such attitudes are far-reaching because they lead us to the conclusion that corruption is a self-reinforcing behavior.[39] As a result, corruption becomes self-perpetuating and pervasive, spreading from the field of politics to diverse sectors such as the environment[40] and education.

1.4 Measuring corruption

Global estimates of the funds due to corruption have been regularly published by influential think tanks and international organizations, such as, for example, the World Bank and the International Monetary Fund.[41] One such recent estimate puts the cost of global corruption at 2.6 trillion US dollars, or 5% of the global gross domestic product, of which 1 trillion alone has been paid in bribes. However, these numbers are to be understood as an educated guess; the institutions publishing them cannot make such calculations precisely, as they lack the data to do so.[42]

This is because, by its very nature, corruption is secretive and thus more difficult to measure than ordinary crimes. It is reported less frequently than ordinary crimes, and the very judicial bodies tasked with its suppression might be a part of the state capture project that fosters corruption. For this reason, measurements using judicial and prosecutorial statistics that consider the number of investigations and condemnations are not very reliable for determining the presence of corruption in society.[43] Thus, proxy indicators are often used as substitutes. These can be subjective, based on perception and experience, and objective, based on hard data. The most famous subjective index and the most popular index of corruption is the Corruption Perception Index[44] published by the global non-governmental organization Transparency International (TI), which measures the perception of corruption using expert assessments and surveys of businesspeople and the population. The same methodology is used for the Control of Corruption dataset of the Worldwide Governance Indicators[45] published by the World Bank and the World Justice Project's Rule of Law Index.[46] These two indices, while applying the same methodology, aim to measure not so much the presence of corruption, but rather its absence, by focusing on the quality of legal systems and experience of businesses with them as one of the variables. Large N-quantitative comparative studies operate with these and other indices, which are often used as proxies for corruption. As such, they use the indices to establish a correlation between a particular set of anti-corruption measures, such as perceived party corruption and the introduction of party financing legislation.[47] The correlation between the introduction of legislation and perceived party corruption then becomes an assessment of its effectiveness.

Experience-based indicators, as the second branch of subjective-based indicators (i.e., the Global Corruption Barometer of TI and Eurobarometer, produced by the European Commission or victimization surveys[48]) measure people's experience with corruption. By this, we infer the level of victimization due to petty corruption, as the cases of grand corruption or state capture are experienced by few.

Objective measures of corruption examine useful proxies for measuring trends in corrupt activities or activities related to corruption, such as public procurement. For example, in the aftermath of the *Mani pulite* campaign, a significant decrease in the cost of public work was recorded in Italy—a clear sign of fear of public exposure or prosecution of corrupt transactions.[49] This observation led Golden and Picci to suggest that, by comparing how much the state pays with how much is built, we can approximate how corrupt the state is. Such an approach inspired further measurements of public procurement, which suggest that an increase in single bidding tenders in public procurement is a proxy that raises an alarm bell for ongoing developments in state capture because it maps awards to those who perpetrate state capture.[50]

While the indicator-based approaches to the measurement of global governance trends remain widespread, some legal scholars refer to "governance by indicators," thus highlighting the importance of the approach.[51] Many remain skeptical about the limitations of such measurements. There is no doubt that these measurements have, due to media attention and the global outreach of their promotion, been useful in increasing awareness of corruption worldwide. However, the question remains: What exactly do these indices measure? Indices based on perceptions of corruption seem to measure not so much the actual level of corruption but rather a set of beliefs within a society that concern the society's fairness. In contrast, indices that focus on the quality of governance may be unable to clearly distinguish between concepts such as the absence of corruption and constraints on government power. This is the case for the World Justice Project Rule of Law Index and the regulatory quality and government effectiveness of the Worldwide Governance Index.[52] Further, the approach to measurement often uses countries as national units, which causes methodological problems, as not all areas of governance within a country may be equally susceptible to corruption.[53] Imperfect as they may be, these measures help us establish a trend and hypothesize about the (dis-)functionality of anti-corruption measures and track changes over a long period of time.[54]

1.5 Evolution of understanding and regulation of corruption

The international legal framework against corruption has been significantly strengthened in the past three decades. Legal instruments such as the Convention on Combating Bribery of Foreign Public Officials in International Business Transactions of the Organization for Economic Co-operation and Development (OECD), the United Nations (UN) Convention Against Corruption (UNCAC), and the Council of Europe's Civil and Criminal Law Conventions have greatly contributed to harmonizing legal solutions across jurisdictions.[55] Different important international organizations heavily conditioned both their founding members and those who wished to join them on strengthening a country's anti-corruption framework; thus, international integration that appeared in this period promoted anti-corruption.[56]

This harmonization and expansion of the anti-corruption regulation is a consequence of an expanding interest in the topic of corruption that began developing in the 1990s. The increased interest has been a result of several factors. First were the lessons learned from the failed economic development activities fostered by the World Bank and the International Monetary Fund in the prior decades of their work with underdeveloped countries. Believing that much of their borrowing and technical assistance eventually serves not to alleviate poverty but to maintain corrupt regimes, the World Bank decided to proclaim the fight against corruption as its top development priority and to amplify the voices of those economists who share similar attitudes.[57] This development colluded with several others. The Cold War ended, consequently ending outside support for many corrupt regimes and driving a wave of democratization across the world.[58] A remaking of the legal systems that followed as a part of the wider democratization process provided an excellent opportunity for the inclusion of many legal norms that were to act as incentives against corrupt behavior.[59] Second, an influential strain of thinking within the economic theory became focused on the study of the institutions and their quality as a precondition for economic development. Known as institutionalist theory, it would influence much of the development thinking in the 1990s and inform the views of influential policymakers.[60] This theory saw the quality of institutions as the key to lowering transaction costs[61] and thus making the economy more inefficient. Under this view, the quality of governance became as important as the abundance of resources or access to financial markets as an explanation of the country's rise and failure. Finally, globalization has led to an unprecedented rise in global investment and business-making activities, which has, in turn, led to a greater demand for universally accepted standards. The United States, which has, in 1977 and in the aftermath of the Watergate scandal, enacted the Foreign Corrupt Practices Act[62] (FCPA), an act that greatly limited the ability of US companies to bribe abroad, led the way in the global fight against bribery in the business environment.[63] Due to the expansive jurisdiction of the Securities Exchange Commission (SEC) and the proactive engagement of the US Department of Justice (DOJ), FCPA enforcement strengthened corporate compliance standards globally[64] and the spillover effect which stretched to the supply chains of many major multinational companies restricted the possibilities of undetected engagement in corrupt behavior.[65] As we will see in Chapter 4, such developments will become contested as imperialist and anti-competitive practices by those who find themselves on the receiving end of these activities.

The evolution that I have briefly described was a departure from the earlier understandings of corruption developed in the Cold War period, during which corruption was seen as a by-product of modernization. Underdeveloped political infrastructure and intra-party competition based on the control of resources—or, as we would today say, the ability to engage in state capture—were the primary explanatory factors of political corruption.[66] Corruption was viewed as not necessarily bad, as it was recognized that it could cut through the red tape and make bureaucracy more efficient by acting as a "grease in the wheels."[67] Part of the reasons explaining this distinction in views lies in particular conditions that existed during the 1990s, as I described earlier. There is also the fact that during this time, corruption was studied mostly by political scientists and less so by economists, or, at least, corruption did not have a central role in the economic theories that it would acquire later. This does not mean that the political scientists of the time considered corruption to be irrelevant—Huntington himself wrote that a high capacity for corruption means a high capacity for violence—but rather that corruption was viewed primarily as a crude, backward mode of governance.[68]

1.6 The fight against corruption

As the understanding of corruption has evolved, so has the approach to fighting against corruption. The primary means of fighting corruption was the regulation and enforcement of anti-corruption legislation. Traditionally, this term referred to the norms of the criminal code (and in common law countries, important precedents) regulating acts, such as undue influence, personal gains stemming out of the performance of public duty, and the embezzlement of public funds. Today, the term also includes the campaign finance legislation, lobbying regulation, rules, and codes of conduct for members of the parliament and electoral administration; special protection for those who report corruption (the so-called "whistleblowers"), and the specific strategic documents (often called "anti-corruption strategies") in which countries set out a detailed set of measures adopted at the national level.[69] Specific institutions dedicated primarily to fighting corruption have been founded in many states. Depending on the jurisdiction, these institutions may include specialized courts, prosecutorial bodies, anti-corruption agencies, specialized police units, ethical committees, quality control offices, and audit courts. There are also those institutions and regulations that, while not being specialized to fight against corruption, may have a role in its sanction or prevention. For example, in presidential political systems, legislative bodies may impeach the president for reasons that may include bribery. The same can be said for administrative procedure acts; while their role is generally to define the procedures that the various agencies of the executive branch of government, the consequence of the higher quality of these acts is transparency, which allows citizens not only a safeguard of their rights but also a higher degree of transparency and insight in the work of the governments.[70]

In many modern democracies, all governmental institutions are usually required to adopt an integrity plan or some other form of document that regulates the internal responsibilities for the procurement of goods and acts within the scope of entrusted responsibilities by the law. To curb corruption within the government and private entities, states and institutions introduce compliance programs that define the internal procedures for lowering the incentives and opportunities for engaging in corrupt behavior. This shows an important trend in the design of anti-corruption regulations and institutions today, which focuses on the codification of illegal behavior and its punishment but also on prevention both within the public and the private sector.

Although not a key part of the legislative framework, the work of civil society organizations and investigative journalists in the fight against corruption cannot be overstated. The work that nongovernmental organizations do in raising awareness and in advocacy for better regulation and transparency standards has contributed to the elevation of the status of corruption as one of the most important problems in the modern world.[71] Some of the biggest media leaks concerning corruption were published by independent networks of investigative journalists who have published data on offshore bank accounts, which unleashed a plethora of information not only about tax evasion but about transactions conducted via shell companies registered in jurisdictions where business information registers are secret, prompting a political and legal backlash against those engaged in such operations.[72]

Finally, political parties are the most important yet often overlooked actors in the anti-corruption struggle. Although ranked as institutions with the lowest degree of public trust and often studied as a corrupt actor, it is the opposition political parties that often rally behind anti-corruption efforts or try to expose the government as corrupt. Commitments to a certain party ideology may act as an incentive for lowering the corruption of public officials acting within a bureaucratic environment that is otherwise conducive to corruption.[73]

Although often exuding a populist zeal, the anti-corruption cry remains essential to the mobilization of political support in many countries around the world.[74] Coupled with a powerful media campaign, a populist anti-corruption drive may ride on the wave of support brought forward by the anti-corruption campaigns or actors. In that sense, anti-corruption may influence electoral volatility in different democracies in the world and may present the problem of corruption within a country as a leading problem of that country.[75]

1.7 Anti-corruption strategies and different understandings of the problem of corruption

As we have seen, many countries, international organizations, companies, and governmental agencies develop strategic documents that allow them a holistic approach in identifying and addressing the risks of corruption. However, the underlying approach of these attempts is often based on one of the two understandings of corruption: the understanding of corruption as a principal–agent problem and the understanding of corruption as a collective action problem. While not mutually exclusive,[76] the two approaches differ in the set and timing of measures they propose to be deployed as an effective remedy for curbing corruption.

Understanding of corruption as a principal–agent problem comes from the neo-institutionalist approach to economics,[77] whose increase in importance was paralleled with the elevation of corruption as a topic of global importance during the 1990s[78] and of which the principal–agent theory (or agency theory) is one of the key branches.[79] The neo-institutionalist approach to economics has, as one of its basic assumptions, the idea that rational actors strive to maximize their preferences that are ordered according to their priorities.[80] It is important to distinguish between principal–agent and rational choice theory; the latter comes from the neoclassical approach to the economy and has been an inspiration to the new institutional economics of which the principal–agent theory is a key tool. The principal–agent theory, instead, recognizes that the engagement of actors in a principal–agent relationship is based on their individual, rational choice but also that this rational choice may lead to maximizing one's gains at the expense of the other.[81] But, the institutions can constrain actors' choices so that the conscious design of institutions may help to overcome problems involved in the principal–agent relationship.[82]

In explaining the principal–agent relationship, a concept that is ever present in society, it is perhaps best to use an example. Such relationships exist in any situation when a certain task is entrusted to someone. By entrusting the taxi driver with the task of driving you to get somewhere or, to use another example, by ordering a lower-ranked civil servant to perform certain tasks on your behalf within a ministry you head, a principal–agent relation is established. This relationship does not need to be between individuals. The principal might also be the electorate that elects political leaders who, as agents, are to work on the delivery of public goods. However, the principals do not have an overview of all the interests of the agent or his opportunities to exploit the powers conferred upon him. The reason for this is the asymmetry of information; the principal, while retaining control over the agent, does not necessarily know everything that the agent knows. This may be because the agent is a specialist who possesses specialist knowledge about the task or because the task itself is so complex that the constant overview of the agent is extremely difficult. Without effective oversight or control, the agent has an opportunity to maximize the incentives for his illicit gains. Whether this opportunity will be used, in such cases, depends on his or her morality. As Vannucci warns, not all breaches of trust between the principal and the agent may be considered corruption, but only those where a violation of the formal or informal rules—which are aimed at preserving the principal's interest—occurs when the agent enters into another exchange with a corruptor, offering the discretionary power to take (or to abstain from) decision or to provide confidential information which assign or preserve rights over resources the corruptor would otherwise not be entitled to receiving money or other resources for that service.[83] Thus, information asymmetry in the principal–agent relationship creates a need for the limitations of incentives for the exploitation of this disbalance in the favor of the agent as well as a need for more transparency[84] and less discretion in agents' dealings. An example of one such limitation is the so-called general prevention, traditionally considered as the foundation for the punishment of many acts in criminal law.[85]

The principal–agent understanding of the problem of corruption leads to a simple expression that corruption equals monopoly plus discretion minus accountability.[86] Another limitation to engagement in corrupt acts is the enforcement of the norms, which, if efficient, reduces the risks of agents exploiting the principal's trust and the powers entrusted to him or her. Following this logic, regulatory capacity is the primary tool for the decrease of corruption because it directly impacts the equilibrium of corruption in society. This does not mean that all activities concerning the fight against corruption should be limited to prevention. Awareness-raising activities that are to be conducted by the media, NGOs, and the different actors dedicated to the fight against corruption also play a vital role in strengthening the integrity of public institutions. Through these activities, the asymmetry of information can be bypassed, and in combination with the preventive and repressive measures described herein, accountability as a primary precondition for corruption control can be achieved. The principal–agent approach to corruption emphasizes the choice of the individual to engage or not to engage in a corrupt activity.

Proponents of the collective action approach to corruption argue that the principal–agent theory misses three important elements concerning the importance of corruption in society. First, they claim that the principal–agent theory assumes the existence of a benevolent principal[87] and that many principals, especially in the cases of bureaucratic corruption, are not such. The principals do not necessarily have the willingness to investigate cases of corruption or to lower the incentives for corruption of their agents, and they do not necessarily have complete control over them. Second, they claim that the principal–agent theory relies too much on a neo-institutional approach to economics, which leads to the exclusion of structural inequality as not just a consequence but also a cause of corruption. Structural inequality is correlated with low social capital and low trust creating environments in which corrupt behavior is a rational response to everyday challenges.[88] In such environments, especially if a perception that the rich may ignore the rules exists, the problem of the fight against corruption will become purposeless for the majority of the population despite considerable investments in awareness raising or capacities.[89] Third, they claim that certain measures proposed are designed to fail because they ignore the collective mobilization that is needed to overcome the problem of the lack of social capital that might be necessary to implement many of the measures. Simply, they argue that in a society where the incentive is to cheat, honest behavior may be a deviation from the norm and that corruption might be a problem-solving behavior.[90] All or some of these shortcomings—it is argued—increase the likelihood that the countries following the principal–agent approach in the fight against corruption will remain with high levels of corruption despite taking numerous anti-corruption measures.[91] Therefore, much of this criticism came from the understanding that most interventions that happened in the past three decades were not designed with a collective action dimension of the corruption problem in mind[92] but were informed by a principal–agent framing of the problem. This has led to situations where many sophisticated legal solutions were introduced in societies where the respect for the rule of law was not high.[93] Instead, it is argued that interventions should be planned with a cultural view of corruption within the societies in mind.[94]

An example of the worries that the collective action theorists have in mind may be described as follows: presume that a European country, to increase its reputation by complying with GRECO recommendations, decides to tighten and enforce its campaign finance legislation with the intent of making political parties funding more transparent. The adoption of this measure in the parliament is smooth; no parties oppose it, and when it is passed, a body (perhaps a specialized committee appointed by the parliament, or the body in charge of organizing the elections whose chairpersons are appointed by the parliament) is tasked with its enforcement and is empowered to issue sanctions that may be subject to a judicial review. In a society where a considerable level of corruption exists, we may easily expect that either the judicial review, the appointment of the members, the interpretation of the legal norms, or the issuance of fines becomes tainted by undue political influence, which will lead to poor enforcement of the norms. Alternatively, it is possible that the whole system of political party financing is bypassed through rigged bidding in public contracts, which allows those who are awarded contracts to reciprocate with awards for party members who may either donate to the party or keep the funds received for their own illicit enrichment. Thus, the reform does not achieve its primary role, which is to limit and/or make contributions to the parties more transparent and known to citizens, and this failure may add to the disillusionment with the anti-corruption measures in general. Looking at each and every one of these principal–agent relationships that exist between different actors, we may run the risk—of using an overused metaphor—of not seeing the forest from the trees.

To overcome such situations of state capture (or reform capture), a "big-bang approach" to anti-corruption is proposed. This approach includes measures that target a wide area of policy but also include collective action that aims to achieve a shift in collective norms of behavior, either through direct, top-down measures[95] or through indirect measures, such as education[96] or grassroots social movements,[97] or a combination of all of them.[98] For the sake of clarity, it is important to emphasize that most researchers consider this set of big-bang measures synonymous with big-push reforms, another term often used as a synonym in the literature.[99] A middle-of-the-road approach in classification is used by Fisman and Golden, who recognize that the big-bang approach exists even when the action takes place within one sector of bureaucracy—they use the example of thorough police reform in Georgia—if such reform has a spillover potential.[100]

Contrary to this approach, those favoring incremental reforms claim that they have an effect and are not useless because, while not necessarily bringing immediate dramatic change on their own, they still change the corruption equilibrium within a society. Although every measure that seeks to limit corrupt behavior may not work at the time of its introduction, it still may lead to a change in a corruption equilibrium as the introduction of these measures accrues over time.[101] If we consider the previous example of the campaign finance reform, we may observe that this effect is precisely what has happened in Italy; the reforms that were to curb illicit party financing introduced in the 1970s have demonstrated no significant effect until the law was enforced during the dramatical crackdown in the "Mani pulite" campaign that began eighteen years after the introduction of this legislation.[102]

We should not understand the two approaches as exclusive of one another. For example, it cannot be said that someone in favor of lowering the incentives for corruption through legal and institutional measures would reject popular mobilization against corruption or that someone who argues for the importance of the collective action approach would argue that the regulatory capacity is irrelevant. Further, both approaches highlight the role that education may play in developing a stronger response to corruption.[103] Rather, the difference seems to lie in the diverse acknowledgments of the various structural elements within society that prevent or enable an adequate response to corruption. These differences are a result of different intellectual traditions and histories from which the two approaches have developed. The institutional theory of economics and the law and economics approach to legal science have greatly influenced the principal–agent approach and the design of anti-corruption measures in the last three decades.[104] With their reliance on sociological and anthropological insights, the collective action approach theorists tend to argue that these insights had been excluded from the design of anti-corruption measures.[105] Thus, we may conclude that while different, both of the responses to the challenges of designing a valid anti-corruption strategy are context-dependent.

1.8 Legal approaches to corruption

There are two main ways in which legal norms constrain corruption. The first one is punitive, usually reflected in criminal law, or some punitive measures in administrative law. The second is preventive, aiming to separate powers within the state, particularly the executive branch of government, to limit the opportunities for corrupt behavior. This distinction can be tracked across the history of government and is also represented in current legal policy documents such as the UNCAC, which represents the main tendency in the legal regulation of corruption.[106] This section addresses both of these approaches as well as how law correlates to the principal–agent and collective action approaches to anti-corruption.

1.8.1 Principal–agent and collective action in legal science

We have seen that the institutional approach to economics has forged much of the contemporary understanding of corruption in the social sciences. Its influence is felt in the domain of legal approaches to corruption as well, where many prominent authors have applied this approach and their own expertise to diverse corruption-related topics.[107] While useful for illumining the societal and economic relations behind corrupt exchanges for the legal profession, this concept bears a certain risk. With lawyers only interested in exploring the best ways to detect, regulate, and punish any corrupt exchange that occurs, they are demoted to the writers and enforcers of laws and not as definers of the field of corruption.

Those legal theorists who have been friendlier toward the collective action theories have come from the sociological approach to legal studies. Coming from the background of the "law and development"[108] and "law and society" movements originating in the US, these approaches were originally—during the 1970s and 1980s—focused on the transposition of legislation and legal institutions from the developed countries to the Global South.[109] Later, at the end of the 1990s and the early 21st century, they became more critical of such an enterprise, citing that it serves the global developmental agenda and not the interests of the states and peoples where it was promoted.[110] In so doing, they have inspired a strain of critical legal theory that sought to offer a critical re-examination of the anti-corruption enterprise.[111] Despite promising early efforts, further dwellings using this theoretical approach have failed to yield new results, at least in the field of legal science. However, inquiries with a similar focus existing in the field of anthropology have offered critical re-examinations of anti-corruption projects and practices.[112] Their value for legal science is that it contextualizes anti-corruption efforts by examining the social conditions under which they take place, exposing unstated assumptions concerning perception and implementation.[113]

These scholars primarily focus on the *qualitative* and not the *quantitative* side of the functioning of anti-corruption laws and legislation. While authors such as Soreide highlight the efficiency of criminal law measures,[114] works of authors such as David Nelken ask the question of the context in which the anti-corruption measures take place.[115] By legal culture, two things are meant: one is the theoretical approach, which seeks to contextualize the object of its research within a group of legal families (i.e., civil or common or socialist law) or national legal systems, and second is the actual set of beliefs, practices, and behaviors existing within a part or a whole of the legal profession, usually within a national legal system. In that sense, for example, we can talk about the culture of practicing lawyers or the culture of judges (judicial culture).[116]

They remain skeptical concerning the power of the qualitative approaches enshrined, for example, in the global indicators of corruption, to effectively portray the state and level of corruption in one country.[117] Although admitting that "legal culture" is a concept extremely difficult to define,[118] the authors sought to use it to reject the one-size-fits-all approaches often found in contemporary anti-corruption norm diffusion. However, with this, they walk on a tightrope; too much focus on the comparative legal approach and highlighting the role of legal culture may lead to claims that one country's legal system is impossible to compare with that of another country. While highlighting misconceptions of the existing comparisons is certainly useful, the sheer fact that we live in the age of comparisons will make their claims of incomparability obsolete. In this sense, it is perhaps more helpful to try to extrapolate the underlying political, societal, and other backgrounds that politicize the legal comparison.[119]

Certainly, the divide between the two approaches should not be viewed as absolute. Many contemporary authors coming from both legal and non-legal fields, such as, Luciano Violante and Diego Gambetta, seek to combine the two to properly identify the causes and cures for corruption.[120]

1.8.2 Corruption and the rule of law

As we have stated, the growing relevance of corruption has brought a plethora of new legislation, regulations, and institutions. However, while the debates I have previously described are relatively recent, corruption was a focus of the legal system, particularly constitutional and criminal law, as branches of public law, from a much earlier period. Corruption has always been recognized to stem from the application of unchecked power. As the increased awareness of the relevance of corruption gained ground, so did the linking of this concept to one of the classical legal concepts, the rule of law, and its continental contemporary, *das Rechtsstaat*. The two concepts differ, primarily in the role that they ascribe to the independence of the judiciary,[121] but the academics and practitioners from both backgrounds have identified corruption as a common cause for concern considering its power to remove the borders between the different branches of government.[122] This removal of the borders between the branch of government allows the exercise of unchecked power by the executive branch, as the two other branches—the parliamentary, which exercises control over the executive primarily by means of checking the value of the decisions made in terms of the interests of citizens and their representation, and the judiciary, which is concerned primarily with the legality of the decisions—are being made powerless. Thereby, corruption becomes more than an evil preventing the economic development and efficient use of resources but also a challenge to the rule of law.

Certainly, and as evidenced by events in many countries of the world, this is much more than a perception. Separation of powers between the branches of government as a key precondition of the rule of law demands an independent judiciary and a system of checks and balances between the different branches.[123] Any disruption of this power increases the probability of the corrupt exchange occurring, as there is less probability that the separate branches of government will establish accountability and constraints that would limit the concentration of power. Therefore, the checks and balances system itself may be considered a system of corruption control.[124] Inspired by this realization, many authors began to almost equate the presence of corruption and the absence of the rule of law.

Still, it seems that it would be wrong to conflate the presence of widespread corruption with the absence of the rule of law. It is possible that widespread corruption exists in nations where most of the features of the rule of law or the *Rechtsstaat* exist. Situations of a breakdown of social order or high rises of poverty may create opportunities for corrupt exchanges by straining law enforcement in such ways that enforcing the law becomes difficult. Therefore, high rates of corruption indicate significant challenges to the rule of law and not necessarily its absence. By contrast, the absence of the rule of law usually does mean that society is corrupt. Even in such circumstances, it is possible that advances in curbing corruption happen, as the contemporary examples of the Chinese bureaucracy[125] or Qatari judges demonstrate,[126] or as testified by the historical development of anti-corruption measures in Denmark[127] or France,[128] whose absolutist monarchs sought to make the country more efficient.

In a wider and historical sense, we could say that the nexus between corruption and the rule of law has been explored as a theme in the historical development of states and polities by both legal and political theory. In the historical debate over the fall of Rome, corruption is considered to be one of the reasons for its fall; however, the clarity over whether it was a cause or a consequence remains unresolved even today.[129] There is more clarity, however, over the conclusion that the reason why the republican organization of the state in both Rome and in the city-states of ancient Greece was successfully introduced was the belief that it would curb absolute power and, thereby, reduce corruption.[130] However, the main difference between the reduction of absolute power taken within the absolute monarchies as in the previously referred instances was that while temporarily efficient, they have not been sustainable as a basis for a permanent paradigm change.

While the awareness of corruption existed throughout history, it was the theoretical approach developed by Montesquieu in his classical treatise The Spirit of the Laws, published in 1747 that became understood as the expression of the separation of powers (classified as the three main functions of government) as a check to the unbounded rise of executive power.[131] Unlike the two other branches of power—the legislative and the judicial—the executive may operate without the others as it has the monopoly of physical coercion, which it can exercise.[132] Expanding upon these ideas, James Madison designed the basic principle of checks and balances, applying it to the US constitutional system.[133] This institutional preference for the balance of powers was accustomed to other factors, which all required a decrease in patronage, such as the increased specialization of the professions, emergence of tax services, professional bureaucracies, standing armies, and urbanization.[134] These developments led to a classification of differences between public and private interests, with the latter deemed as impure and, as such, to be removed from the public domain.[135] As a result, from the 1800s, the usage of the term corruption became more linked to bribery in public office rather than moral degeneration.[136] The demands for meritocracy in public service led to its modernization and gradual formalization of qualities needed from the civil servant for the performance of the functions in public administration. Together, these events increased the importance of the rule of law; but, paradoxically, precisely because of the relevance of the rule of law, the private interests were mobilized (i.e., in political parties) to influence the public sphere.[137]

The ideal of the separation of powers was hardly the only invention of the rule of law theorists. Conceptions of the rule of law developed by many theorists are—sometimes even without specific knowledge of those applying them—used by anti-corruption practitioners. Among these conceptions, those of Joseph Raz and Lon Fuller stand out, perhaps not because of their superiority over the others but because of their widespread use in the global context of assessment of legal systems. Speaking in the contemporary vernacular but without an intention to downplay their contributions, we could say that Fuller and Raz were the first to design a "checklist" of constitutive elements of what the rule of law is.[138] Fuller's checklist, which, as Palombella observed, focuses "on the features which law generally needs in order to rule,"[139] contains generality, clarity, public availability, stability, consistency between rules and behaviors, non-retroactivity, non-contradictory rules, and possibility to be performed.[140] Somewhat differently, Raz formulated the principles of the rule of law as clarity, stability, generality, independence of the judicial institutions and the judicial review, access to justice, limitations to the discretion of law enforcement agencies, and a certain foundation in the principles of natural justice.[141] These criteria of thin, formal legality are today a part of the quality of government and rule of law measurements issued by the Varieties of Democracy and World Justice Project's Rule of Law Index,[142] which anti-corruption practitioners widely use.[143]

At the end of this brief overview of the interconnectedness between the ideas of the rule of law and corruption, we must observe that the classical paradigm between the separation of powers and the prevention of corruption has become largely outdated. These new approaches to the independence of institutions drove the emergence of a whole new set of independent regulatory and oversight institutions that are usually appointed by the parliaments but which perform the functions traditionally reserved for the executive branches that some theorists classify as the fourth branch of government.[144] Moreover, the very existence of such institutions (e.g., central banks, independent electoral committees, bodies for supervision of the audio-visual regulation, and audit courts) and the independence of the appointees within them are today considered a pre-requisite for the absence of state capture.

1.8.3 Corruption, human rights, and the international courts

The post-World War II development of human rights did not have an explicit connection to corruption or its prevention. They were a part of the gradual shift toward decolonization and democratization, as well as the expansion of individual freedom of liberties, and were, as such, advocated for and contested in most of the world.[145] However, as a part of this struggle, the human rights documents developed under the auspices of the United Nations and regional organizations contained many important provisions regarding the exercise of unchecked power. In this regard, the entrenchment of the first generation of human rights and subsequent expansion of second and third generations of human rights represented important milestones that would lead to the curbing of the absolutist power in many countries as well as the creation of more accountable and democratic regimes following the fall of these governments.[146]

One of the new approaches that developed at the end of the 20th century was a theoretical and activist approach from scholars wanting to prevent the impunity for embezzlement of public funds of undeveloped states by adding corruption to the list of international crimes. The inspiration for this move came from an observation that human rights violations and corrupt practices often go hand in hand,[147] and that impunity from human rights violations has the same effect as impunity for mass looting of state funds. This proposal had two elements: the first was the idea for the creation of an international court,[148] while the second was the stretching of the very concept of human rights to acknowledge that corruption often leads to human rights violations and vice versa.[149] Undoubtedly, the authors advocating this view were strongly influenced by strides made in the global advancement and relevance of human rights in the 1990s as well as the proliferation of international tribunals and human rights bodies in this period. The idea failed to garner much support to be implemented.[150] However, the added value of this advocacy was the expanded relevance of the topic, allowing important changes in practices to be made. For example, anti-corruption compliance in the supply chains became an important part of the prevention of corruption.[151] Another example is that of international sanctions, in which the United States and the European Union have begun sanctioning and limiting access to individuals who are involved in corrupt dealings.[152]

We also observe an opposite trend: human rights protection became a check on the investigations and criminal processes against individuals accused of grand corruption and/or organized crime. In particular, this was the case in those criminal processes involving asset seizures and asset recovery. Namely, starting from the 1970s in the US and the end of 20th century in continental Europe, many criminal investigations of individuals accused of organized crime and corruption began involving asset confiscation and limitation on disposal and usage of property both before and after the ending of a criminal trial. This resulted in a significant number of cases where those from whom the assets were forfeited (seized) argued about their human rights violations, in particular the right to peaceful enjoyment of property.[153]

1.8.4 Corruption and criminal law

While other social sciences such as economics, political science, sociology, and anthropology have defined the field of corruption studies and its implications for the state, ethics, public morality, and politics, lawyers primarily created legislation and worked in its implementation. The crime of personal abuse of private office may be traced back to ancient Greece and Rome, both of which featured trials for acts that we would consider to be acts of bribery today.[154] Roman law clearly distinguished between private and public crimes, delineating different procedures and punishments between the two and considering bribery one of the latter's crimes. In the codifications of 19th-century Europe, we observe the presence of bribery and misuse of public office as two separate criminal acts in France, Germany, Austria, and Turkey.[155]

Traditionally, corruption was understood as a victimless crime, one in which both sides enter aware of its illegality and, as such, are unwilling to report it but may be equally motivated to conceal it.[156] This, however, did not mean that the legal good (*Rechtsgut*) understood to be protected by criminal law was considered unimportant. In describing the legal goods pertinent to corrupt criminal acts, the Italian legislator peculiarly differentiated between the impartiality of public administration, its prestige and the fidelity and fairness to the public administration.[157] In modern codifications, criminal acts, such as "misuse of public office," "embezzlement," and "corruption in public office," are regulated by law in some form or another as crimes against public administration.[158] This meant that those involved in the crime, as the recipients of bribe, must be government agents—that is, public officials.

The two understandings concerning corrupt criminal acts evolved over time for different reasons. Pairing corruption with other examples of victimless crimes, such as gambling or prostitution, became unacceptable as the growing relevance of its importance influenced legislators and scholars alike.[159] The definition of perpetrators of the crime as public officials (or, as those to whom a public function is entrusted) was abandoned upon realization of the relevance of private corruption.

The gradual expansion of the definitions and classifications of corrupt acts occurred in most jurisdictions via international law, as the states, during the 1990s and onwards, began to comply with the different anti-corruption conventions.[160] Further, the theoretical reconsiderations of the problem of corruption owing to the experiences of the Mani Pulite campaign in Italy led to a recognition that what the law enforcement and judicial bodies are fighting are not criminal groups that, acting together or independently, commit corrupt criminal acts but rather a system of corrupt exchanges.[161] Traditionally, legislation recognized that the corrupt transaction involved the active, supply side (the one that pays the bribes) and a demand, the receiving side. Consequentially, laws in many countries recognize a difference between passive bribery, a crime in which the public official extorts money from a victim, and active bribery, in which the actor seeks to bribe the public official or another person or entity in exchange for a certain act or omission. In some jurisdictions, such as Italy, what is defined as a criminal act of *concussione* represents the active, supply side of the corrupt exchange, while the act of corruzione defines the passive side.[162] The victim of extortion in the act of *concussione* is relieved of responsibility, as they operated under coercion, thus lacking the subjective element of criminal responsibility (*mens rea*). With regard to the distinction between passive and active bribery in the global context, the influence that the OECD Convention made in the diffusion of the norm of the criminalization of the act of bribery of foreign officials resulted in a tremendous difference in fighting global corruption.[163] This convention impacted transnational practices of bribery by obliging the OECD states to outlaw bribery of foreign officials. To this end, the Convention narrowed the operating space for the transnational corrupt exchanges to take place. The UNCAC aimed much more ambitiously at expanding the field of criminalization to influence trading and private bribery but as non-mandatory provisions.[164] In this period, criminal responsibility that was traditionally reserved for individuals was now expanded to legal entities, primarily corporations. This was an attempt to counter not just the extortive side of the bribery, which was primarily from public officials (the demand side), but also those offering the bribe and to cover a phenomenon where a bribe or trading of influence may occur with regard to a behavior within one or more private entities (the supply side).[165] In some jurisdictions, such as Italy, these rules were involved not in the Criminal (penal) but in the Civil Code, in keeping with the tradition that the criminal responsibility *stricto sensu* should be reserved for individuals and not business entities.[166]

The growing relevance of corruption in public law is also illustrated by an ever expansive regulation of matters in order to prevent corruption, that is the regulation of lobbying, political parties, and their financing, auditing of state institutions, whistleblowing, freedom of access to information, and corruption proofing of legislative procedures.

1.9 Literature gap and the research question

This work aims to join the debate, whose main outlines I have presented in Section F, about the role that the principal–agent and collective action approaches to corruption have in the design of measures intended to fight corruption. I focus on prosecutions of political corruption as legal and judicial anti-corruption measures. This focus encompasses the work that law enforcement agencies and the judiciary have undertaken concerning the prosecution of political corruption in Brazil, Italy, and Romania. More specifically, I focus on major anti-corruption campaigns: the Mani Pulite investigations in Italy in the 1990s, the Lava Jato investigations in Brazil in the 2010s, and the investigations of Romanian National Anti-Corruption Directorate (DNA) in the prosecution of political corruption in Romania between 2008 and 2018. The investigations in each of these countries were related to the wrongdoings and alleged wrongdoings of hundreds of elected and appointed officials and political figures, and their impact on the political and legal lives of the societies in which they occurred was substantial. The sheer scale of these investigations, which encompassed hundreds of appointed and elected officials, the media attention,[167] as well as the attention they received in academic studies of corruption, convinces me that it is more appropriate to refer to them as judicial anti-corruption campaigns rather than investigations.

Given that these events, in which the judiciary, or at least parts of the judicial system of the country with significant support from the media, took a stand against corrupt actions of a greater part of the political class over a relatively short period (not more than one decade), I believe it is appropriate to classify the campaigns as both big-bang (collective action) measures and typical principal–agent measures.[168] Namely, the campaigns were both an attempt to prosecute a large number of high-ranking political office holders (an action that would undoubtedly endanger their political projects) and an attempt to mobilize the population in the fight against corruption. They aimed for more than just ending impunity for corruption; a moral rejuvenation and an attempt to create a new political class were, as I will demonstrate, present as elements of the campaigns. By analyzing them as both principal–agent and big-bang events, I aim to contribute to understanding the functionality of anti-corruption strategies, their design, and the factors that make them work. The campaigns have occurred in countries that belong to the civil law tradition; however, one of them, Italy, played a significant role in the development of this tradition.[169] However, some of the legal institutes crucial to their success, such as the use of plea bargaining, were legal translations introduced from common law countries and adversarial criminal law systems.[170] The campaigns were carried out by special anti-corruption bodies with rather liberal use of prosecutorial tactics based on plea bargaining, pre-trial detentions, and special investigative measures, such as wiretapping. The campaigns happened within countries that underwent democratic transition relatively recently, as in the case of Brazil and Romania, or in which the political system was long consolidated but externally constrained by the Cold War, as in the case of Italy. Importantly, in all three campaigns, the ambition of the judicial branch was greater than the mere application of legal measures against alleged perpetrators of political corruption criminal offenses. Taken together, these features make the three campaigns comparable, as they are critical legal events that have also had important consequences on the political, legal, and economic lives of the countries.

In this book, I seek to respond to three main research questions: 1) Which factors have led to the emergence of the campaign? 2) How have rule of law challenges impacted the separation of powers within the state? and 3) What were the main impacts of the campaigns? To make them more precise, I will explain their focus.

The first question aims to explain the drivers of the campaigns. Ideally, as I have observed herein, this question would be answered with a comparative study of two states similar in their corruption levels and judicial systems, one in which the campaign happened and the other in which it did not.[171] However, problems related to the collection of information make such a study unlikely to collect the data based on which the comparison could be made, as campaigns are much easier to study when they happen instead of trying to reveal why they did not happen. Therefore, I will attempt to "unpack" the campaigns by applying the concept of judicial reputation to their emergence and challenging this explanation with existing explanations based on legal culture and path development approaches. The second question addresses the two major challenges to the rule of law in the three countries. The first such challenge is the principle of separation of powers in the sense that the balance of powers swung toward the judicial branch of the government, or, more specifically, the judges and prosecutors leading the investigations. The second challenge is that of fair trial standards that were difficult to maintain, given the specific power of the accused and the often-delicate nature of the evidence. In assessing these challenges, I rely on the data gathered in the archives, legal and political expert analyses, indictments, judgments, orders, and other legal documents produced during the campaigns. By processing these data through the methodological lens of the criminal process integrity theory, I assess whether the judges and prosecutors managed to escape the trap of the misuse of public power. I engage with some of the arguments brought forth in these narratives, but I do not intend to "put the trials on trial." I explore the alleged partisanship and overreach of competencies in investigating crimes against fair trial and rule of law standards.

The third question is what impact these campaigns have had on the levels of corruption within societies and their political, legal, and economic systems. To assess this, I will examine the impacts of the campaigns by comparing data gathered from the changes in the indices of corruption, corruption perception, and quality of government. Considering the important limitations of the measurements of corruption through indices of corruption perception and corruption control, I conducted semi-structured interviews in Romania and Brazil to control for the changes that the indices failed to capture.

My research makes important new contributions to knowledge in the field. It positions the campaigns as anti-corruption interventions within the wider theoretical framework of corruption studies. It attributes a key role to judicial reputation as the driver of the campaigns and examines the role of the rule of law and human rights violations within the campaigns and their impact on the legitimacy of the campaigns. Judicial independence, judicial reputation, and the integrity of the judicial process, as some of the key themes that I explore, have been constant topics of examination both in legal science and political science literature, particularly in those dealing with the countries of the common law legal system. However, the actual interplay between these factors within campaigns has scarcely been addressed. I believe that the focus on judicial reputation and the rule of law breaches is a much more adequate way of dealing with the campaigns, as it explains the underlying internal dynamic of judicial and prosecutorial actors during the campaign. As I will explain in Chapter 2, a mere focus on the institutional or cultural developments that assert judicial independence fails to explain why similar institutional arrangements in different countries fail to produce similar outcomes. Additionally, judicial reputation is important within the context of the rule of law breaches, as it may shape the response of the courts toward the campaigns, as I will demonstrate in Chapter 3, particularly regarding the events in Brazil.

1.10 Conclusion

The multi-faceted nature of corruption demands a complex classification, measurement techniques, and policies against its proliferation. The two main approaches to its understanding, the principal–agent and collective action theories, can best be studied through an analysis of complex endeavors that apply the main postulates on which they are based. In this book, the three major judicial anti-corruption campaigns will have introduced the topic of corruption, its varieties, measurements, causes, theoretical explanations within corruption studies and legal studies, and the questions on which this book focuses. The book will proceed to examine the events that have taken place in the three countries and theoretically situate them, as described in Chapter 2. The book will analyze the challenges to the rule of law, such as fair trial standards and separation of powers, in Chapter 3. This is followed by an analysis of the impact of the campaigns on the political, legal, and economic systems of the three countries and the perception of corruption among their citizens in Chapter 4. I conclude by comparing the identified effects and consequences, discussing them, and emphasizing the different approaches to anti-corruption strategies introduced in this chapter.

Notes

1 Bo Rothstein, Anti-corruption: A big-bang theory, (2009), at https://papers.ssrn.com/sol3/papers.cfm?abstract_id=1338614.
2 Bo Rothstein, Anti-corruption: A big-bang theory, (2009) At https://papers.ssrn.com/sol3/papers.cfm?abstract_id=1338614.
3 Brandon L. Garrett, Globalized corporate prosecutions, *Virginia Law Review*, 97, (2011), 1775.
4 Aisha Varraich, Corruption: An umbrella concept, (2014) at https://gupea.ub.gu.se/bitstream/2077/38896/1/gupea_2077_38896_1.pdf.
5 Adam Graycar, Corruption: Classification and analysis, *Policy and Society*, 34(2), (2015), 87–96.
6 See Laura S. Underkuffler, Captured by evil: The idea of corruption in law (observing the difference between corruption and thievery), (2013).
7 The varieties of approaches toward the criminalization of such behavior can be observed in Frank Zimmerman. Criminal Liability of Political Decision-Makers (2017). For a US perspective see Terence A. Parker, Prosecuting Corruption after McDonnell v. United States, *Notre Dame Law Review*, 94(959), (2018).

8 Ugo Mattei, Three patterns of law: Taxonomy and change in the world's legal systems, *The American Journal of Comparative Law*, 45(1), (2007), 5–44.
9 Certain practices that are lawful in the United States, for example, campaign financing and lobbying, would undoubtedly be regulated as corrupt in many other jurisdictions. See Lawrence Lessig, Republic, lost: How money corrupts congress and a plan to stop it.
10 For example, see United Nations Development Programme, Attitudes towards politics in Latin America: A review of regional perception data, 2020. At https://www.latinamerica.undp.org/content/rblac/en/home/library/democratic_governance/attitudes-towards-politics-in-latin-america--a-review-of-regiona.html.
11 Luigi Manzetti & Carole J. Wilson, Why do corrupt governments maintain public support? *Comparative Political Studies*, 40(8), (2007), 949–970.
12 Daniel Treisman, What have we learned about the causes of corruption from ten years of cross-national empirical research? *Annual Review of Political Science*, 10, (2007), 211–244.
13 Susan Rose-Ackerman, Corruption: Greed, culture and the state, (2010) At https://digitalcommons.law.yale.edu/cgi/viewcontent.cgi?article=6368&context=fss_papers.
14 Nancy R. Buchan, Rachel T.A. Croson & Robyn M. Dawes, Swift neighbors and persistent strangers: A cross-cultural investigation of trust and reciprocity in social exchange, *American Journal of Sociology*, 108(1), (2002), 168–206.
15 Abel Polese, 'If I receive it, it is a gift; if I demand it, then it is a bribe': On the local meaning of economic transactions in Post-Soviet Ukraine, *Anthropology in Action*, 15(3), (2008), 47–60.
16 Johann G. Lambsdorff & Björn Frank, Bribing versus gift-giving: An experiment, *Journal of Economic Psychology*, 31(3), (2010), 347–357.
17 Generally, see John T. Noonan, Bribes (1987).
18 Carlo A. Brioschi, Corruption: A short history. (2017); Bruce Buchan & Lisa Hill, An intellectual history of political corruption; Ronald Kroeze & Guy Geltner, (eds.), Anticorruption in history from antiquity to modern era (2014); Eric M. Uslaner, The historical roots of corruption: Mass education, economic inequality, and state capacity (2017); James Heinzen, The Art of the Bribe: Corruption Under Stalin 1943–1953.
19 Marcus Felson. Corruption in the broad sweep of history in Adam Graycar & Russel G. Smith, (eds.) *Handbook of Global Research and Practice in Corruption*, (2011).
20 Alina Mungiu-Pippidi, Deconstructing Balkan particularism: The ambiguous social capital of Southeastern Europe. *Southeast European and Black Sea Studies*, 5(1), (2011), 49–68.
21 For empirical research on the effects of particularism on corruption in societies, see Valentina Rotondi & Luca Stanca, The effect of particularism on corruption: Theory and empirical evidence, *Journal of Economic Psychology*, 51, (2015), 219–235. For a further discussion of this approach see Jan Teorell & Bo Rothstein, Causes of corruption in Paul Heywood (ed.) *Routledge Handbook of Political Corruption*, 137–150.
22 Vito Tanzi, Corruption around the world: Causes, consequences, scope, and cures. *Staff papers*, 45(4), (1998), 559–594.
23 Jana Kunicova & Rose-Ackerman, Electoral rules and constitutional structures as constraints on corruption. *British Journal of Political Science*, 35(4), (2005), 573–606.
24 Teorell and Rothstein, Causes of corruption in Paul Heywood, 85–86.
25 Treisman, What have we learned about the causes of corruption from ten years of cross-national empirical research? at 216.
26 Paolo Mauro, Corruption and growth, *The Quarterly Journal of Economics*, 110(3), (1995), 681–712.

27 Vito Tanzi & Hamid Davoodi, Corruption, public investment, and growth, The Welfare State, Public Investment, and Growth: Selected Papers from the 53rd Congress of the International Institute of Public Finance, (1998), 41–60.
28 Eric C.C. Chang, A comparative analysis of how corruption erodes institutional trust, *Taiwan Journal of Democracy*, 9(1), (2013), 73–92; Edgardo J. Campos, Donald Lien & Sanjay Pradhan, The impact of corruption on investment: Predictability matters, *World Development*, 27(6), (1999), 1059–1067.
29 Jie Bai, et al. Firm growth and corruption: Empirical evidence from Vietnam, *The Economic Journal*, 129(618), (2017), 651–677.
30 Michael T. Rock & Heidi Bonnett, The comparative politics of corruption: Accounting for the East Asian paradox in empirical studies of corruption, growth and investment, *World Development*, 32(6), (2004), 999–1017.
31 Susan Rose-Ackerman, Political corruption and democracy, *Connecticut Journal of International Law Association*, 14, (1999), 363.
32 Licia Cianetti, James Dawson & Seán Hanley, Rethinking "democratic backsliding" in Central and Eastern Europe–looking beyond Hungary and Poland." In Licia Cianetti, James Dawson & Sean Hanley (eds.) *Rethinking 'Democratic Backsliding' in Central and Eastern Europe*, (2020), 1–14.
33 Kamran Abbasi, Covid-19: Politicisation, "corruption," and suppression of science, *British Medical Journal*, 371, (2020), m4425.
34 Laura Policardo & Edgar J. Sanchez Carrera, Corruption causes inequality, or is it the other way around? An empirical investigation for a panel of countries, *Economic Analysis and Policy*, 59(2018), 92–102.
35 Eric M. Uslaner, Trust and corruption revisited: How and why trust and corruption shape each other, *Quality & Quantity*, 47(6), (2013), 3603–3608.
36 Jerg Gutmann & Stephen Voigt, Judicial Independence in the EU: A Puzzle, *European Journal of Law and Economics*, 49, (2020), 83–100.
37 Rasma Karklins, The system made me do it: Corruption in post-communist societies: Corruption in post-communist societies, (2016).
38 For example, see Nita Luci, The making of citizenship against corruption in Kosovo: protest, lies, and the public good. In Davide Torsello (ed.) *Corruption in Public Administration*, (2016); Lejla Farjani, Corruption in a culture of Štela: Understanding informal: Transactions in Bosnia and Hercegovina, (2016); *Rivkin-Fish M. Bribes, Gifts and Unofficial Payments: Rethinking Corruption in Post-Soviet Russian Health Care*, in Haller D., Shore C. (eds.), 2005. Corruption anthropological perspectives, 47–65.
39 Matthew C. Stephenson, Corruption as a self-reinforcing trap: implications for reform strategy, *The World Bank Research Observer*, 35(2), (2020), 192–226.
40 Sophie Lemaitre, Illicit financial flows within the extractive industries sector: A glance at how legal requirements can be manipulated and diverted, *Crime, Law and Social Change*, 71, (2019), 107–128.
41 *Corruption costs the global economy $3.6 trillion dollars every year*. World Economic Forum Dec 13, 2018, at https://www.weforum.org/agenda/2018/12/the-global-economy-loses-3-6-trillion-to-corruption-each-year-says-u-n.
42 See the discussion by Matthew Stephenson on the Global Anticorruption Blog at https://globalanticorruptionblog.com/2016/01/05/its-time-to-abandon-the-2-6-trillion5-of-global-gdp-corruption-cost-estimate/.
43 Lucio Picci & Alberto Vannucci, Lo Zen e l'arte della lotta alla corruzione, 46–48.
44 This index is available at https://www.transparency.org/research/cpi/overview.
45 Worldwide Governance Index is available at https://info.worldbank.org/governance/wgi/.
46 The World Justice Project's Rule of Law Index is available at https://worldjusticeproject.org/our-work/wjp-rule-law-index.

47 Fernando Casal Bértoa, et al. The world upside down: Delegitimising political finance regulation, *International Political Science Review*, 35(3), (2014), 355–375.
48 Mitchell A. Seligson, The measurement and impact of corruption victimization: Survey evidence from latin america, *World Development*, 34(2), (2006), 381–404.
49 Donatella Della Porta & Alberto Vannucci, The 'perverse effects' of political corruption, *Political Studies*, 45(3), (1997), 516–538.
50 Mihaly Fazekas & István János Tóth, From corruption to state capture: A new analytical framework with empirical applications from Hungary, *Political Research Quarterly*, 69(2), (2016), 320–334.
51 Kevin E. Davis, Benedict Kingsbury & Sally E. Merry, Introduction: Global governance by indicators. In Governance by Indicators: Global power through quantification and rankings, 1–15 (2012).
52 Paul Heywood, Measuring corruption, perspectives, critiques and limits, In Heywood (ed.), see note 21, 137–150.
53 Alexander Cooley, How international rankings constitute and limit our understanding of global governance challenges: The case of corruption in Debora Valentina Malito, Gaby Umbach, Nehal Bhuta. (eds.), *The Palgrave Handbook of Indicators in Global Governance*, (2018), 49–68.
54 See Picci and Vannucci, Lo Zen e l'arte della lotta alla corruzione at 67–68.
55 Cecily Rose, International anti-corruption norms: Their creation and influence on domestic legal systems, (2015).
56 Wayne Sandholtz & Mark M.Gray, International integration and national corruption, *International Organization*, 57(4), (2003), 761–800.
57 This move was essentially a consolidation of an epistemic community that promoted the views regarding the importance of corruption in Sarah O'Byrne, "There is nothing more important than corruption": The rise and implementation of a new development idea, Unpublished doctoral dissertation (2012).
58 Samuel Huntington, Democracy's third wave. *Journal of Democracy*, 2(2), (1991), 12–34.
59 Alison D.von Rosenvinge, Global anti-corruption regimes: Why law schools may want to take a multi-jurisdictional approach. *German Law Journal*, 10(6–7), (2009), 785–802.
60 See Daron Acemoglu & James A. Robinson, Why nations fail: The origins of power, prosperity, and poverty. (2012); William M. Dugger, Douglass C. North's New Institutionalism, *Journal of Economic Issues*, 29(2), (1995), 453–458.
61 Johann G. Lambsdorff, Making corrupt deals: Contracting in the shadow of the law. *Journal of Economic Behavior & Organization*, 48(3), (2002), 221–241.
62 Mike Koehler, The story of the foreign corrupt practices act. *Ohio State Law Journal*, 7(2012), 3, 929.
63 Kenneth W. Abbott & Duncan Snidal, Values and interests: International legalization in the fight against corruption. *The Journal of Legal Studies*, 31(S1), (2002), S141–S177.
64 Rachel Brewster, Enforcing the FCPA: International resonance and domestic strategy, *Virginia Law Review*, (2017), 1611–1682.
65 Karen E. Woody, No smoke and no fire: the rise of internal controls absent anti-bribery violations in FCPA enforcement. *Cardozo Law Review*, 38, (2016), 1727.
66 Samuel Huntington, Political order in changing societies, (1968), 59–63.
67 Joseph S. Nye, Corruption and political development: A cost-benefit analysis, *American Political Science Review*, 61(2), (1967), 417–427.
68 Huntington, Political order in changing societies at 63.
69 For an overview of the features of this system that have emerged in the last three decades on a national level, see, for example, Leonardo Borlini, The emergence of the international anti-corruption framework and its domestic implementation: The Case of Italy. Bocconi Legal Studies Research Paper 3010753 (2017).

70 See Jeeyang Rhee Baum, Reining in the bureaucrats: Democratic transition and administrative procedural reform in Korea, *Governance*, 20(2), (2007), 233–254, for the effects that passing such a law has had in Korea.
71 Louis De Sousa, Barry Hindess & Peter Larmour, (eds.) Governments, NGOs and Anti-Corruption: The new integrity warriors, (2012). However, see Steven Sampson, The anti-corruption industry: from movement to institution. *Global Crime*, 11(2), (2010), 261–278.
72 *Panama Papers helps recover more than $1.2 billion around the world. International Consortium of Investigative Journalists*, Apr 3 2019 at https://www.icij.org/investigations/panama-papers/panama-papers-helps-recover-more-than-1-2-billion-around-the-world/.
73 Bo Rothstein, The Chinese paradox of high growth and low quality of government: The cadre organization meets Max Weber, *Governance*, 28(4), (2015), 533–548.
74 For example, much of Donald Trump's 2016 election campaign was dedicated to the theme of fight against political corruption which he dubbed "draining the swamp." See Trump calls to 'drain the swamp' of Washington USA Today Oct 18, 2016 at https://www.usatoday.com/story/news/politics/elections/2016/2016/10/18/donald-trump-rally-colorado-springs-ethics-lobbying-limitations/92377656/; *Slovakia elects anti-corruption party after outrage over murdered journalist*, CNN Mar 1, 2020 at https://www.cnn.com/2020/03/01/europe/slovakia-election-olano-win-intl/index.html.
75 Sarah Engler, Corruption and electoral support for new political parties in Central and Eastern Europe, *West European Politics*, 39(2), (2016), 278–304.
76 *Corruption is both a principal-agent and a collective action problem*, Global Anti-corruption blog April 9 2015 at https://globalanticorruptionblog.com/2015/04/09/corruption-is-both-a-principal-agent-problem-and-a-collective-action-problem/.
77 Nico Groenendijk, A principal-agent model of corruption, *Crime, Law and Social Change*, 27(3–4), (1997), 207–229.
78 See Groenendijk, A principal-agent model of corruption at 14.
79 See the division within the field of neo-institutional economics summarized by Groenendijk, note 77.
80 Dietmar Braun & David H. Guston, Principal-agent theory and research policy: an introduction, *Science and Public Policy*, 30(5), (2003), 302–308. But, see Rudolf Richter, The new institutional economics: Its start, its meaning, its prospects, *European Business Organization Law Review*, 6(2), (2005), 161–200. (arguing that the new institutional economics approach viewed rationality as central, but not as absolute offering bounded rationality instead of a pure rational model of neoclassicist economic theory.).
81 Luca Di Donato, A behavioral principal-agent theory to study corruption and tax evasion. Working Paper 34, LUISS School of Government, (2016), 3–5.
82 The word "institutions" used in the context of principal-agent theory represents not only institutions in the strictly legal sense of the word (i.e., public administration institutions) but also rules (i.e., contracts), private institutions (stock market) and marriage.
83 Alberto Vannucci, Three paradigms for the analysis of corruption, *Labour & Law Issues*, 1(2), (2015), 7–8.
84 Daniel Naurin, Transparency, publicity, accountability-The missing links, *Swiss Political Science Review*, 12(3), (2006), 90.
85 Johannes Andenaes, The general preventive effects of punishment, *University of Pennsylvania Law Review*, 114(7), (1966), 949.
86 Robert Klitgaard, Controlling corruption, (1988), 73–75.
87 Bo Rothstein & Jan Teorell Getting to Sweden, Part II: Breaking with Corruption in the Nineteenth Century. *Scandinavian Political Studies*, 38(3), (2015), 238–254.
88 See Uslaner, The historical roots of corruption.

89 For example, this is something that has plagued the fight against corruption in Brazil. However, although this book deals with Brazil as one of its case studies, due to the comparative nature of the study I do not focus on the structural inequality as a variable and I do not explore its connection to the judicial anti-corruption campaigns.
90 Heather Marquette & Caryn Peiffer, Corruption and collective action, DLP Research Paper. This echoes an earlier argument made by Huntington, Political order in changing societies.
91 Rothstein, Anti-corruption.
92 Marquette and Peiffer, Corruption and collective action.
93 Alina Mungiu-Pippidi, Contextual choices in fighting corruption: Lessons learned. Norwegian Agency for Development Cooperation (2011) at https://research.birmingham.ac.uk/portal/files/19752251/CorruptionandCollectiveAction.pdf.
94 Davide Torsello & Bertrand Venard, The anthropology of corruption, *Journal of Management Inquiry*, 17, (2005).
95 The transformation of civil service in Sweden and Denmark is an example of a top-down approach. See Rothstein, note 1 and Mette F. Jensen, Getting to Denmark – The process of state building, establishing rule of law and fighting corruption in Denmark 1660–1900. (2014) QoG Working Paper series.
96 Generally, see Uslaner, The historical roots of corruption.
97 Aruna Roy's movement in the Indian province of Rajasthan is an example of such a movement, Aruna Roy & Nikhil Dey, The right to information: Facilitating people's participation and state accountability. In Asia-Pacific Workshop (2001). Available at https://cccindia.org.in/cs54b.pdf.
98 These mixed approaches, where government officials' actions were combined with a popular mobilization mechanism, can be used to describe the advances made in many Eastern European countries that were part of the big-bang enlargement of 2004. See, for example, Geoffrey Pridham, Unfinished business? Eastern enlargement and democratic conditionality, (2007) https://esiweb.org/pdf/romania_Pridham-Eastern%20Enlargement%20and%20dem%20conditionality-2007.pdf.
99 In this sense, see Stephenson, Corruption as a self-reinforcing trap, Alena Ledeneva, Roxana Bratu, & Phillip Köker, (2017). Corruption studies for the twenty-first century: Paradigm shifts and innovative approaches. *Slavonic and East European Review*, 95(1), 1–20. Anne Persson, Bo Rothstein, & Jan Teorell, (2010). The failure of anti-corruption policies: a theoretical mischaracterization of the problem; Mariano-Florentino Cuellar & Matthew Stephenson, Taming systemic corruption: The American experience and its implications for contemporary debates, *World Development*, 155, (2022), 105755 (2020); Matthew M. Taylor, Getting to accountability: A framework for planning & implementing anticorruption strategies, *Daedalus*, 147(3), (2018), 63–82; Mette F. Jensen & James Kennedy. (eds.) (2013). *Fighting Corruption in Modernity: A Literature Review*, 14–15. In the field of writing dedicated to international development aid and the reforms based on these approaches, we find a similar stance. See Monica Prasad, Mariana B. Martins da Silva & Andre Nickow, Approaches to corruption: A synthesis of the scholarship. *Studies in Comparative International Development*, 54(1), (2019), 96–132; Anders Sundell, Nepotism and meritocracy. *QoG Working Paper Series*, 16(1), (2014), 23. Others distinguish between big-bang and big-push reforms, with the former being a wide set of structural reforms that may also include legislative and societal changes, while the latter represents a large single isolated effort focused on one area. In this sense, see Kevin E. Davis, Anti-corruption law, and systemic corruption: The role of direct responses, *Revista Direito GV*, 17, (2021). Toke S. Aidt, Economic analysis of corruption: A survey, *The Economic Journal*, 113(491), (2003), F632–F652 and Antonio Acconcia & Claudia Cantabene, A big push to deter corruption: Evidence from Italy, *Giornale degli Economisti e Annali di Economia*, (2008), 75–102.

100 Ray Fisman & Miriam A. Golden, Corruption: What everyone needs to know, (2017), 243–244.
101 Stephenson, Corruption as a self-reinforcing trap at 36–38.
102 Martin Rhodes, Financing party politics in Italy: A case of systemic corruption, *West European Politics*, 20(1), (1997), 54–80.
103 Simplice A. Asongu & Jacinta C. Nwachukwu, The incremental effect of education on corruption: Evidence of synergy from lifelong learning, *Economics Bulletin*, 35(4), (2015), 2288–2308.
104 See Janine R. Wedel, Rethinking corruption in an age of ambiguity. *Annual Review of Law and Social Science*, 8, (2012), 453–498 for a description of this evolution.
105 Anne Persson, Bo Rothstein, & Jan Teorell, Why anticorruption reforms fail—systemic corruption as a collective action problem, *Governance*, 26(3), (2013), 449–471. For an understanding of corruption limited to the practice of countries that are aid recipients see Wedel, Rethinking corruption in an age of ambiguity at 477.
106 Cf. United Nations Convention Against Corruption, Chapter II (Articles 5 to 14) and Chapter III (Articles 15 to 23).
107 Tina Søreide, *Corruption and Criminal Justice: Bridging Economic and Legal Perspectives*, (2016); Matthew Stephenson "When the devil turns…": The political foundations of independent judicial review, *The Journal of Legal Studies*, 32(1), (2003), 59–89; Anne Van Aaken, Lars P. Feld, & Stephen Voigt, Do independent prosecutors deter political corruption? An empirical evaluation across seventy-eight countries, *American Law and Economics Review*, 12(1), (2010), 204–244.
108 As Tamanaha observes, we must be terminologically precise here: law and development is not the same as legal development. Law and development is an approach that aims to use the legal solutions as a tool for development, while legal developments are developments in the legal practice that may occur wherever a functional legal system exists. See Brian Z. Tamanaha, Distinguishing law and development from legal development, *Northwestern Law Review Colloquy*, 104(191), (2009–2010).
109 John H. Merryman, Comparative law and social change: On the origins, style, decline & revival of the law and development movement, *The American Journal of Comparative Law*, (1977), 457–491.
110 David M. Trubek & Alvaro Santos, The third moment in law and development theory and the emergence of a new critical practice, (2006).
111 David Kennedy, The international anti-corruption campaign, *Connecticut Journal of International Law*, 14, (1999), 455.
112 Sampson, The anti-corruption industry; Wedel, Rethinking corruption in an age of ambiguity.
113 Generally, see Kennedy, The international anti-corruption campaign.
114 Soreide, Corruption and criminal justice.
115 Paulina Polak & David Nelken, Polish prosecutors, political corruption, and legal culture. In *Central and Eastern Europe After Transition*, (2016), 231–266.
116 John Bell, Judicial cultures and judicial independence, *Cambridge Yearbook of European Legal Studies*, 4, (2001), 47–60.
117 David Nelken, Contesting global indicators in Sally Engle Merry, Kevin E. Davis & Benedict Kingsbury, (eds.) *The Quiet Power of Indicators: Measuring Governance, Corruption, and Rule of Law*, (2015), 317–338.
118 David Nelken, Using legal culture: Purposes and problems, *Journal of Competition Law & Economics*, 5, (2015), 1.
119 David Kennedy, New approaches to comparative law: Comparativism and international governance, *The Utah Law Review*, 545, (1997).
120 Diego Gambetta, Why is Italy disproportionately corrupt: A conjecture, In Kaushik Basu, Tito Cordella (eds.) *Institutions, Governance and the Control of Corruption*, (2014).

121 Gianluigi Palombella, The rule of law and its core. In Gianluigi Palombella, Neil Walker, (eds.) *Relocating the Rule of Law*, (2009).
122 Bojan Bugaric, The rule of law derailed: Lessons from the post-communist world, *The Hague Journal on the Rule of Law*, 7, (2015), 175–197.
123 Alexander Hamilton, James Madison & John Jay, *The Federalist Papers*, (2008), 303.
124 Felson, Corruption in the broad sweep of history at 15.
125 See Rothstein, The Chinese paradox of high growth and low quality of government.
126 David Sebudubudu, Lina Khatib & Alessandro Bozzzini, The atypical achievers: Botswana, Qatar and Rwanda, in Alina Mungiu-Pippidi & Michael Johnston, (eds.) *Transitions to Good Governance: Creating Virtuous Circles of Anti-Corruption*, (2017), 39–45.
127 See Jensen, Getting to Denmark.
128 William Chester Jordan, Anti-corruption campaigns in XIII Century Europe, *Journal of Medieval History*, 35(2), (2009), 204–219.
129 This is also partially due to the fact that many classic as well as contemporary authors refer to moral and ethical corruption and "degeneration" as a cause for the fall of the Roman empire. Such a view obfuscates the understanding of the corruption as "misuse of public office."
130 Buchan and Hill (eds.), An intellectual history of political corruption at 26.
131 Certainly, Montesquieu's ideas about law may be understood much more widely. The very title of the book "the spirit of the laws" points us to his ideas that the law is something that stems out of different cultures in which it exists.
132 Maxwell Cameron, Strong constitutions social cognitive origins of separation of powers, (2013), 18–32 arguing that the separation of powers represents the grammar of the political system.
133 James Madison Federalist Papers No.10 (1787).
134 Buchan and Hill, An intellectual history of political corruption at 159–161.
135 Kroeze, Vitoria, and Geltner, Anticorruption in history from antiquity to modern era at 176.
136 Kroeze, Vitoria, and Geltner, Anticorruption in history from antiquity to modern era at 169.
137 Kroeze, Vitoria, and Geltner, Anticorruption in history from antiquity to modern era at 177.
138 We infer this observation from a (albeit imperfect and incomplete) survey of the literature on rule of law promotion of the 1990s and 2000s, which often relies on both Fuller and Raz. See, generally. Daniel B. Rodriguez, Matthew D. McCubbins & Barry R. Weingast, The rule of law unplugged, *Emory Law Journal*, 59, (2009), 1455; Savend – Erik Skaaning, Measuring the rule of law, *Political Research Quarterly*, 63(2), (2010), 449–460.
139 Palombella, The rule of law and its core at 35.
140 Lon Fuller, The morality of law, (1969).
141 See the comparison of the two checklists in Jorgen Moller, The advantages of thin view in Adam Winchester & Christopher May (eds.) *The Handbook on the Rule of Law*, 28. For a risk in the application of the two approaches, see Palombella, The rule of law and its core, 36–40.
142 Moller, The advantages of thin view at 30.
143 See the discussion in this chapter above, at 12–13.
144 Bruce Ackerman, Good-bye, Montesquieu. In Susan Rose-Ackerman & Peter Lindseth, (eds.) *Comparative Administrative Law*, (2010).
145 See generally, Samuel Moyn, The last utopia human rights in history, (2010).
146 As we will see in Chapter 2, this would have an important effect on the creation post-authoritarian judiciary in Brazil, which would, subsequently, allow for the execution of the anti-corruption campaign. For the transitional justice in Brazil, see, generally, Elin Skaar, Jemima García-Godos & Cath Collins, (eds.) *Transitional*

Justice in Latin America: The Uneven Road from Impunity Towards Accountability, (2016). For the authoritarian character of the Brazilian regime between 1964 and 1978 see Phillipe C. Schmitter, Interest conflict and political change in Brazil, (1971).

147 Anne Peters, Corruption as a violation of international human rights, *European Journal of International Law*, 29(4), (2018), 1251–1287.

148 See Mark L. Wolf, The world needs an international anti-corruption court. *Daedalus*, 147(3), (2018), 144–156.

149 Franco Peirone, Corruption as a violation of international human rights: a reply to Anne Peters, *European Journal of International Law*, 29(4), (2018), 1297–1302.

150 In that sense, the permanent opposition from the United States has been important. See Brett D. Schaefer, Steven Groves & James M. Roberts, Why the US should oppose the creation of an International Anti-Corruption Court, *Backgrounder*, 2958, (2014).

151 Rachel Chambers & Jena Martin, Reimagining corporate accountability: Moving beyond human rights due diligence, *New York University Journal of Law & Business*, 18, (Summer 2022), 773.

152 For a specific effect this has had on the corrupt dealings concerning the extractive industry in Congo, see Donald Trump has shown a surprising enthusiasm for sanctions, *The Economist*, November 28, 2019.

153 Generally, see Michele Simonato, Confiscation and fundamental rights across criminal and non-criminal domains, *Era Forum*, 18(3), (2017), 365–379.

154 Buchan & Hill (eds.), An intellectual history of political corruption at 26; Elizabeth McKnight, Offences against the Res Publica: The role of public interest arguments in Cicero's forensic speeches, *Hague Journal of Rule of Law*, 9, (2017), 237–263.

155 Additionally, we observe that embezzlement was, at that time, considered to be a misuse of personal property that was entrusted to someone, which is different from its meaning today, when it is considered as unlawful disposal of public funds. See Henry Shelton Sanford, The different systems of penal codes in Europe, 1–75, (1854). What is missing from the literature on criminal law and corruption is a more developed understanding of the period between the codifications of criminal law in Europe of the 19th century and the increased relevance of corruption in the 1990s. We fail to learn how the anti-corruption provisions were implemented in practice and how the evolution of the understanding of the corrupt acts impacted the legislators and the judges.

156 Franklin E. Zimring & David T. Johnson, On the comparative study of corruption, *British Journal of Criminology*, 45(793), (2005), 799.

157 Francesco Antolisei, Manuale di Diritto Penale. Parte speciale II, 405, (2016). Cf. Kevin J. Heller & Marcus Dubber (eds.), *The Handbook of Comparative Criminal Law*, (2011), 588.

158 In this sense, see 18 USC 201–218, Criminal Code of Italy articles 314–360, *Criminal Code of Germany Section*, 331–339.

159 However, as the consolidation of text in criminal codes is still performed by the traditional typology of crimes, which involved victimless crimes as one such type in some jurisdictions, we find the classification present, although the understanding of corruption has been changed. In others, such as India, certain types of fraud are still regarded as victimless crimes. See Heller and Dubber, *The Handbook of Comparative Criminal Law* at 312.

160 Brewster, Enforcing the FCPA.

161 Donatella della Porta & Alberto Vannucci, Corrupt exchanges: actors, resources, and mechanisms of political corruption. This idea is similar to that of corruption equilibrium put forward by Stephenson, Corruption as a self-reinforcing trap.

162 Article 317. of the Italian Criminal Code.

163 See Rose, International anti-corruption norms at 59–94.

164 Rose, International anti-corruption norms at 108.

165 See Jeffrey R. Boles, The two faces of bribery: International corruption pathways meet conflicting legislative regimes, *Michigan Journal of International Law*, 35, (2014), 687–691. For a criticism of the approach focusing solely on the supply side in the cases of transnational bribery see Lindsay B. Arrieta, Attacking bribery at its core: Shifting focus to the demand side of the bribery equation, *The Public Contract Law Journal*, 45(587), (2016), arguing that more focus should be put not on the transnational companies but on domestic extorters in countries where the extortion takes place.

166 As per the Legislative Decree 231/2001.

167 Both Mani Pulite and Lava Jato have been featured not only in newspaper articles but in successful TV series such as "The Mechanism" and "1992." The problem of corruption in Romania has been thematized in the 2019 award-winning movie *Collective*.

168 Cf. Rothstein, Anti-corruption.

169 Generally, see John Henry Merryman & Rogello Pérez-Perdomo, The civil law tradition: an introduction to the legal systems of Europe and Latin America, (2018).

170 Maximo Langer, From legal transplants to legal translations: The globalization of plea bargaining and the Americanization thesis in criminal procedure, *Harvard International Law Journal*, 45(1), (2004).

171 For example, one such study tried to explain why no judicial campaign comparable to Mani pulite has happened in France. It found that the existence of more prosecutorial discretion in Italy was a key variable. Carlo Guarnieri, Prosecution in Two Civil Law Countries in David Nelken, Comparing legal cultures, (1997), 183–198.

2 Emergence and the drivers of judicial anti-corruption campaigns

2.1 Introduction

Judicial anti-corruption campaigns happen in highly corrupt contexts and are not preceded by a political revolution. Rather, to the observer, it appears as if the judiciary is independently taking on the corrupt political class. This heroic appearance of the independent judges paving their way through a web of intrigues and scandals that they uncover has made the campaigns retain a prominent spot in the entertainment industry, which has covered them in movies and TV series.[1] Likewise, this paradox of a strong, direct anti-corruption measure led by defiant and charismatic individuals that creates political mayhem flying in the face of danger made it an interesting study for those who are committed to the academic study of political corruption. However, in spite of an interdisciplinary approach needed for their study, prior to the emergence of the Lava Jato campaigns, they were rarely studied in legal science. Rather, they were an object of much attention by investigative journalists and political scientists. The Italian campaign, Mani Pulite (Clean Hands), which happened in the 1990s, is the most analyzed, followed by the Brazilian campaign, with a rapidly growing body of research on the topic. The Romanian campaign still lags despite a plethora of writing on anti-corruption in the country. It has been recognized that the Italian campaign has served as an inspiration for Brazilian legal professionals,[2] while the impacts of the Romanian and Italian campaigns have also been compared.[3] In legal science, the campaigns have been examined partially as evidence of a particular institutional setup of the Italian judiciary,[4] the particular Italian legal culture,[5] evidence of (in-)effectiveness of the European Union's conditionality toward Romania,[6] instances of prosecutorial overreach by Brazilian prosecutors, and abuse of power.[7] More holistic treatments of campaigns combining insights from legal and political science have been attempted in the cases of Italy[8] and Brazil.[9] Authors who were themselves involved in the campaigns in Italy and Brazil have offered their personal views, which, while subjective, have provided valuable insights into how the campaigns operated.[10] Scholars have suggested that judicial independence makes prosecutions more likely[11] and that judicial reputation may have contributed to the Italian campaign.[12] However, the evidence for this

DOI: 10.4324/9781003334811-2

suggestion has been limited to exploring the role of Italian judicial associations and unions.[13] It has been recognized that violations of the rule of law and human rights may have delegitimized parts of the campaigns,[14] and this has been attributed primarily to the partisanship of the judicial actors,[15] their disregard for procedural rules, or successful countermobilizations against the campaigns.[16] Indeed, some of the existing literature characterizes the campaigns as judicial revolutions or consequential extensions of the independence that judicial institutions possess.[17] However, this does not explain the absence of such campaigns in other countries where similar circumstances exist, both in terms of the presence of corruption and judicial independence. It also does not explain how judicial independence is shaped in these legal systems during and after campaigns. Because the simultaneous policy reforms on many fronts or mass-scale prosecutions that would qualify as big-bang events have been sporadic and largely instituted in state-building, post-communist settings, we have little comparative legal research investigating them as anti-corruption big-bang events. It would only be after the Lava Jato campaign, as its unintended consequences became evident, that the comparative legal studies of corruption flourished.[18] Instead, the law focused on national or international approaches to corruption. However, even in this field, much of the research is descriptive, with little theoretical contribution, focusing instead on particular aspects of the campaigns.[19]

Political science studies have explained many of the consequences that the political and, to a lesser extent, the legal systems of these countries have endured as a result of these issues.[20] They also established that the grand-scale prosecution of political corruption was presented as politicization by those who were conducting countermobilization against the campaigns.[21] Others, trying to challenge the mainstream narrative of these campaigns, have gone even further, portraying the prosecutors as people with a political agenda who aimed to favor domestic or external political actors, or in the case of Romania, as agents of the intelligence agencies.[22] They have also focused on the societal reception of the problem of corruption and the media reporting of these stories as tools for raising awareness.[23] In this chapter, I offer a middle road–an analysis based on a theory grounded in both law and political science. I also contrast how this approach compares itself to others. The analysis, however, starts with the introductory section explaining the main events and developments that have shaped the campaigns.

2.2 The judicial anti-corruption campaigns

2.2.1 Mani Pulite

Due to its high perception of corruption, Italy stood (and still stands) as an outlier to the other developed democracies of the West.[24] This phenomenon has intrigued researchers, who have proposed different explanations, including cultural,[25] criminal,[26] economic,[27] and political.[28] However, there is a consensus that the existence of a "market of corrupt exchanges" was one of the defining features of the Italian political and economic system of the late 1980s.[29] The main characteristics of a system of political corruption were a focus on securing votes through connections with organized crime networks,[30] mass evasion of the implementation of the political party financing law, and its misuse in connection with awards in public procurement.[31]

The Mani Pulite campaign, also known as Tangentopoli (Bribesville or Kickback City), began in April of 1992 with the arrest of the Italian Socialist Party mid-level manager who, after realizing that his own party would not protect him, gave away important details about the public procurement schemes used to extort money from entrepreneurs in the city of Milan.[32] These revelations and subsequent arrests gave prosecutors outside of Milan the courage to continue with the investigations. Two years after the launch of the investigations, one-third of the lower house of the Italian parliament and one-quarter of the upper house, along with more than two thousand former and current holders of official positions, were under investigation.[33] Some of them, like Bettino Craxi, leader of the Italian Socialists, fled Italy to escape prison time, and others left politics for good.[34]

The investigations into political party financing had existed in Italy before; in 1974, the magistrates in Genoa uncovered a corruption scheme that allowed domestic and international oil companies to pay bribes to Italian political parties in exchange for favorable regulation.[35] The revelations led to more stringent but inefficient regulation of party financing; the regulation's design and implementation incited illicit financing.[36] These investigations, however, gave support to the rise of the phenomenon of "attack judges," who believed that they carried out their tasks not to protect the powerful but to affirm new societal values[37] and who were freed from the scrutiny of their supervisors by a process of institutional flattening that gave operational freedom to lower-level magistrates.[38] Interpreting their constitutional duties as carrying out the distribution of justice as a public good, the Italian magistrates of the 1970s focused on far-reaching investigations in the fields of political terrorism and organized crime, with many of them losing their lives as a result of terrorist activities or attacks by organized crime groups.[39]

The campaign contributed to the process of dissolution of the major Italian parties that ruled the country for over 45 years and the emergence of new parties, such as the Lega Nord and Forza Italia, that became new populist political projects that would last well into the next century.[40] The politicians were not the only target for the campaign, as many successful entrepreneurs found themselves investigated for corruption, with many of them willfully collaborating with the Allegations that the campaign was inspired or orchestrated by external actors who wanted to exact revenge upon Craxi or subdue Italy through the destruction of its political class were made but with little evidence produced. However, it is beyond doubt that the prosecutors, perhaps fearful of foreign involvement that was present in Italy throughout its post-World War II history, have established rapport with the U.S. diplomats during the first few years of the campaign.[41] The prosecutors, many of whom harbored an experience from earlier, often failed anti-corruption prosecutions of the 1970s and the 1980s, were aware of the particular position that the prosecutors and the judiciary as a whole enjoyed in the Italian legal system.[42] Unlike other continental legal systems, the judiciary in Italy was perceived as equal to the two other branches of government.[43] More than equal, the judiciary was specific as it was characterized by a particular work style of some of its more prominent members. Known as attack judges, or *pretori d'assalto*, these judges were aware of the inherently political nature of the judicial function and were willing to bravely investigate diverse societal issues such as organized crime, terrorism, labor relations, tax evasion, and corruption, often paying a heavy price for such a pronounced societal role.[44]

This is not to say that the judiciary was completely insulated from the pervasive corruption and distrust that characterized the Italian political system of the 1980s. Investigations into the dealings of the secret Masonic Lodge P2 at the beginning of the 1980s uncovered seventeen magistrates among its members.[45] Four referendums held between 1987 and 1999 on the position of judges signaled the citizens' significant distrust of the role of judges in society.[46] However, their overall standing was superior to that of the other two branches, and their past collective actions confirmed the good reputation that they enjoyed, strengthening the credibility of their actions. The judges seemed ready to exploit this popularity, helping to make the campaigns a public relations event of the first order and dominating the news and publications on the Italian political scene of the 1990s. The media strategy, which undoubtedly involved leaks of materials to the press[47] coupled with a rather liberal use of preventive detention, contributed to a wave of suicides that accompanied the campaigns, with forty-one individuals taking their lives before the judgments in their cases were reached and, in some cases, even before the investigations were ended. This led to criticisms over the use of pre-trial detention for extorting charges and the use of the media campaign against the persons investigated.[48]

The Milanese pool judges had much greater ambitions than just prosecuting the individuals responsible for political corruption and changing the corruption-related legislative framework; they viewed their task as bringing about a moral rejuvenation of society and a change of its political class.[49] Such ambitions were sure to provoke backlash which would begin already in 1994 with the investigations against Silvio Berlusconi. At first supportive of the campaigns, the entrepreneur-turned-politician would soon become a sworn enemy of the campaign and the judges in red togas whom he often blamed for prosecuting him due to their alleged left leanings. Investigations against di Pietro and his own conviction that he should enter politics led to his abandoning of the judicial position in 1996 but the other prosecutors continued the investigations. As Berlusconi lost the 1996 elections, the ruling left-wing coalition showed no desire to follow up on the changes to the law proposed by the prosecutors who demanded changes that would make the collection of evidence easier. Instead, most of the legislative efforts, such as the changes in the statute of limitations, focused on making their work more difficult. The 2001 victory of Berlusconi and the judgment of the High Court of Cassation in the Fininvest trial in which Berlusconi was cleared of all charges would mark the end of the campaign and a continuation of the backlash against the prosecutors. Between 2001 and 2006, most of the legislation that enabled the judicial anti-corruption campaign in such a way that would make future prosecutions less likely and more difficult. An attempt by the magistrates to introduce solutions that would make the prosecutions more efficient by combining the two criminal acts of corruption and extortion by a public official were rejected.[50] The inspections by the Justice Ministry into the works of the Milanese pool of judges intensified during this period and were a source of pressure by the new Berlusconi government against the judges.[51] Beginning in 1995, the backlash took a more personal note. Prosecutions against di Pietro and Davigo for an alleged attempt at a coup d'état started and ended in the late 1990s, with both magistrates cleared of charges. These elections marked the beginning of the end of the campaign, which happened due to several factors. The first was the effect of the statute of limitations, which led to the expiration of the time within which legal actions could have been brought against a person, resulting in acquittals.[52] The second was the perception of the magistrates themselves that they needed legislative and logistical support—which was lacking—and that their actions were supported only when directed against the political establishment. However, in the view of the magistrates, the overall societal perception of their actions shifted from support to a perception that they wanted to change the way of life of the country, and this belief led to a decrease in interest and support for their actions.[53] After the 2001 elections and the victory of Silvio Berlusconi—one of those investigated over the course of Mani Pulite, both for bribery and for the activities of his media empire, Fininvest—the attacks against the judges intensified, and the media became polarized regarding their efficiency.[54]

2.2.2 Lava Jato

Following its transformation from a military dictatorship that lasted from 1964 to 1985 to a democracy—which was formally established with the passing of a new Constitution in 1988—the democratic development of Brazil followed a slow but gradual path of entrenchment of democratic institutions.[55] The Brazilian judiciary was a part of this process. As we described earlier, its judicial council, established in 1979, was dissolved in 1988, as it was perceived as untrustworthy. Its refoundation in 2004 was to be a guarantee of a more independent and freer judiciary and may be seen in a wider context as an attempt to consolidate a judicial branch of government that would be more accountable and limit the misuses of public power that often appeared in the forms of corruption, with which all governments of Brazil had struggled since the return to democracy in 1985.[56] The corruption scandals, which involved public companies, members of the National Congress and government, and political clientelism in the form of vote buying, were pervasive.[57] Much of this was a result of a complex federal system that, coupled with the absence of a strong democratic tradition, led many legislators to switch their allegiances from one party to the other, relying on their own clientelist networks among the voters to support them.[58] The operation of these networks was facilitated by the Brazilian presidential system, in which the presidents, while strongly positioned in the constitution, in practice rarely enjoyed the parliamentary majority needed to govern. This, in turn, facilitated the creation of numerous political parties, a higher number than in most democratic countries in the world.[59]

The Brazilian judiciary acted to prosecute some of the perpetrators of illegal political financing; in 2006, more than fifteen legislators were tried and convicted for trading their votes in support of government initiatives as a part of the Mensalão scandal.[60] This scandal helped kickstart a mini citizen-led anti-corruption campaign, which helped the adoption of legislation preventing electoral participation for individuals with a criminal record and the passage of the freedom of information law.[61] More importantly, as we will see in Chapter 3, the Mensalao trials led to the adoption of doctrinal stances that would inspire the trials in the Lava Jato campaign.

The inspiration for what was to become the Brazilian judicial anti-corruption campaign came from Italy. In 2004, Judge Sergio Moro, one of the leading figures of the Lava Jato trials, wrote an article in which he openly advocated for a similar campaign to happen in Brazil.[62] Moro presented a rather romanticized perspective of Mani Pulite, highlighting the crucial influence of the Italian judicial council, the CSM, in shaping the so-called "attack judges." These judges saw themselves not as mere state functionaries, but as champions of societal interests. Moro's admiration extended beyond the personnel involved; he was particularly impressed by what he considered the cornerstone of the strategy's success—the implementation of pre-trial detention. In his view, this tactic played a pivotal role in eliciting confessions from suspects.[63] He understood their use as a demonstration of the famous logic of the prisoner's dilemma—"If I do not confess, others will confess"—in practice.[64] Indeed, the use of pre-trial detention and plea bargaining in the Lava Jato campaign was one of the fundamental features of the prosecutorial strategy that focused on the gathering of evidence and breaking the "corrupt pact" between the bribers and the bribees and was, as we will see in Chapter 3, inspired by a similar tactic used by the Italian prosecutors. Additional sources of inspiration for the prosecutors were the doctrines borrowed from international criminal law that were focused on the establishment of responsibility of the individual perpetrators who were operating the criminal network.

The Lava Jato campaign started in 2014 when an inquiry into the operations of a carwash in Brasilia uncovered a network of black market currency dealers, one of whom was linked to the executive of the state-owned oil company Petrobras.[65] The site of the carwash inspired the federal police, and subsequently the media, to name the initial investigation Lava Jato (Portuguese for carwash).[66] The investigation of the corrupt Petrobras official led to further revelations of a corrupt network within that company that distributed contracts of inflated value to firms, receiving in return kickbacks that were distributed to political parties. The kickbacks followed a scheme like those uncovered in Italy in the 1990s; the parties in power were allocated a certain percentage from the illicit gains under their share of participation in power at the national level.[67] From Petrobras, the investigations led to Odebrecht, the largest construction company in South America (and a frequent subcontractor of Petrobras), which was found to have a department called the Division of Structured Operations, which had overseen the facilitation of payments of $828 million for domestic and transnational bribery.[68] Having facilitated some of the payments using U.S. dollars, the company fell under the jurisdictional nexus of the FCPA, which allowed the U.S. Department of Justice (DoJ) and the Securities and Exchange Commission (SEC) to bring charges against the company for acts of corruption.[69] The U.S. DoJ law enforcement agencies and courts fined Odebrecht $2.6 billion for the breaches of U.S. law that took place over the course of the company's activity in the first and second decade of this century.[70] The fines against the company in Brazil were made on the basis of so-called leniency agreements that allowed the company to evade bankruptcy and closure in exchange for revelations of all the communication and documents related to corrupt activities.[71] The disclosures of these documents led to a chain of prosecutions that began in the countries of South America.[72]

Spectacular as they were, the events on the international front did not overshadow those in Brazil, where revelations of corruption only exacerbated the crisis of trust in the political leaders. After more than a decade of economic growth and a reduction in poverty and inequality, Brazil faced an economic recession that triggered protests in the country's largest cities.[73] President Dilma Roussef, winner of the 2014 elections, was impeached in 2016, and an unstable political climate brought on by her impeachment and the recession led to the election of President Bolsonaro in 2018.[74] As we will see in Chapter 4, this would have hardly been possible without the 2017 judgment of Lula, the former president and the frontrunner for the 2018 presidential elections. As we will later see, this event triggered the backlash against the campaign.

The actions of judges and prosecutors in Brazil were focused not only on the enforcement of legal norms. They saw Lava Jato as an opportunity to further elevate the status and relevance of anti-corruption through legislative changes and as an opportunity to break with the immoral, corrupt practices of the past. On the legislative front, prosecutors have proposed a wide range of legislation to strengthen the anti-corruption framework and limit the due process rights of accused individuals.[75] The side of moral rejuvenation was seen in the initiative to use the monetary penalties incurred on the companies and individuals recovered by the U.S. DoJ—not as income for the U.S. or Brazilian budget but as a donation to the Lava Jato Foundation for use in wider societal mobilization activities and education against corruption. Eventually, the implementation of this deal was struck down by the Brazilian Supreme Court as illegal under Brazilian law.[76]

Just as the crux of the work in Mani Pulite fell to the Milanese pool of judges, the task force of the Federal Prosecutors' Office in Curitiba carried out most of the investigations related to Lava Jato. This was achieved thanks to a practice that allowed the Prosecutors' Office to self-authorize the initiation of a criminal investigation.[77] As the task force was initially focused on the crimes related to the company Petrobras, whose headquarters were located in Curitiba, the jurisdiction of the 13th Federal Regional Court (of which Judge Moro was a member), located in Curitiba, was established. Extensive media coverage of the campaign and the excellent communication strategy of the prosecutors allowed the leading role in the judicial processes to be given to the trial Judge Moro and the leading prosecutor Deltan Dallagnol. In particular, Dallagnol, who won an international award from the leading international Non-Governmental Organization (NGO), Transparency International, became a national celebrity.[78] He used this position to promote not just the idea of the Lava Jato Foundation, but also an ambitious project of moral rejuvenation of society.[79] In this sense, the Lava Jato prosecutors sought to mobilize public opinion; they succeeded in obtaining the support of many civil society organizations,[80] in particular for the aforementioned legislative changes called Ten Measures against Corruption, most of which were later rejected by the Brazilian National Congress.[81]

The backlash against the campaign was, at first, political and came from the leftist Workers' Party (Partido dos Trabalhadores, PT), as well as from international public opinion. Considered a legendary political figure by the Brazilian and Latin American left, Lula, former President of Brazil and leader of the PT, was nominally charged with corruption for receiving an apartment and donations to his political foundation in exchange for appointments of executive directors of Petrobras.[82] Beyond these nominal charges, the content of the indictment clearly stated the intention of the office of the prosecutor to establish a narrative of a state of political corruption in Brazil and to expose Lula as behind the operations of extortion and embezzlement of public funds.[83] This was the first indictment against Lula but not the first instance in which he was accused of corruption; some of those convicted in the earlier Mensalão scandal claimed that the vote-buying of legislators back in 2006 had happened with his knowledge, but the prosecutors, citing lack of evidence, did not include him in the trial.[84] Lula's supporters, both domestic and international, decried the prosecutions as illegal, mobilizing the support of the international legal community and the United Nations Human Rights Committee in favor of Lula.[85] Books in which lawyers exposed what, in their view, were the illegalities committed in the process[86] were published, and letters of support for his release were signed.[87] What raised the suspicions of the public in particular were the media leaks (made by Judge Moro) of conversations between Lula and then-President Rouseff, in which she allegedly offered a ministerial position in the government to Lula.[88] Had he accepted such a position, which would have offered him temporary immunity from prosecution, the prosecution would have been suspended, at least for a while.

An event that gave wings to these accusations was a 2019 security breach of the mobile phone of Dallagnol that exposed his conversations with Judge Moro, in which Moro seemingly instructed Dallagnol as to which evidence he should suggest for presentation at the trial.[89] Furthermore, the material leaked from the mobile phone included conversations between the members of the prosecution team that revealed their strong political preferences against the political candidates coming from the PT.[90] For many Brazilians, in particular those with leftist tendencies, the trial lost its legitimacy.[91] Following the arrest of the alleged phone hacker, the documentation came to be lawfully possessed by the state to be used in the retrial of Lula, which the Supreme Court in Brazil ordered in March 2021.[92] In April of the same year, the Supreme Court decided that the court of Curitiba would have no jurisdiction over this trial. In December, the Office of the Prosecutor revoked the charges against Lula, for the expiry of the statute of limitations made the crime impossible to prosecute.[93]

However, if it can be said that the prosecution of Lula greatly increased the likelihood of the election of Jair Bolsonaro, it is clear that Bolsonaro did not return the favor to the prosecutors or the judicial branch as a whole. Proposals to introduce a stricter penal responsibility for political corruption, as well as most of the other measures proposed in the Ten Measures against Corruption proposal, were rejected by the President's political allies.[94] Instead, prosecutors' appointments became more politically controlled, as evidenced by Augusto Arras's appointment as Head prosecutor in 2019.[95] Divisions among the members of the judicial branch intensified, with some judicial associations openly supporting Judge Moro and prosecutor Dallagnol against the criticism coming from the political and legal commentators. In contrast, other associations openly criticized Lava Jato and its handling by the prosecutors and judges.[96] While Dallagnol's resignation, which came in September 2020 for private reasons, may be considered the end of the Lava Jato campaign[97]; the formal disbanding of the Lava Jato Task Force came some months later.[98]

2.2.3 The Romanian judicial anti-corruption campaign

Three significant distinctions differentiate the Romanian anti-corruption campaign from Mani Pulite and Lava Jato. First, the Romanian campaign did not have an opening case that prompted the investigations (the role played by the Mario Chiesa case in Italy or the inquiry into the broker exchange office in Brazil), nor did the campaign have a name attached to it by either the judiciary or the media. Second, while both the Lava Jato and Mani Pulite campaigns had certain international elements (more pronounced in the case of Lava Jato due to the involvement of the U.S. DoJ and the Swiss prosecutors[99] in the case), Romania's anti-corruption campaign, while being fully carried out by domestic officials, had a stronger international element to it. The internationality came because the requirement for the fight against corruption was a part of the wider rule of law conditionality that was imposed on the country as a part of its negotiations with the E.U. and the later (2007) accession to the E.U.[100] This specific conditionality was focused on the design of institutions that were to guarantee prosecutions, such as the Directorate National for Anti-Corruption, a specialized prosecutorial body, and those that would guarantee judicial independence, such as the Superior Council of Magistracy (SCM). Thirdly, the companies involved in the corruption scandals in Italy and Brazil were some of the biggest and most successful companies existing in the two countries. In Romania, to the contrary, we can speak about the involvement of the highest political officials in a number of cases that were of smaller value, judged both by the involvement of the companies and the monetary amounts in question.

The *esprit du corps* that Moro advocated for in Brazil was, despite a less than impressive tradition of judicial independence, formed in DNA thanks to the management of its head, Laura Codruta Kovesi. She favored a young cadre, insisting on strong courtroom training, which made her team of prosecutors skilled, ambitious, and eager to tackle corruption.[101] Aided by the material supplied by the Romanian intelligence service, SRI, DNA was in a position to pick up the pace of the prosecutions for political corruption in 2010 and, in the following seven years, produce hundreds of arrests and investigations. The primary target of prosecutors was the PSD cadres, not so much because of their political preference but because this party had spent the longest period in power during Romania's transition from authoritarian communism (during which corruption was often essential for survival) to democracy and E.U. membership. This eighteen-year period from 1989 to 2007 was marked by a high rise in inequality, an informal economy, an antagonistic relationship between the state and the society, and other conditions which made corruption in Romania a widespread phenomenon.[102]

Along with Bulgaria, Romania was the only new E.U. member state subjected to the Co-operation and Verification Mechanism (CVM), a monitoring tool devised by the E.U. to focus the country's efforts on curbing corruption as a key element in entrenching the rule of law.[103] While the rule of law entrenchment was not to be based only on prosecuting corruption, the CVM relied heavily on prosecutions as one of the key metrics of success.[104] Thus, the country's progression toward satisfying rule of law standards was based on the successful evaluation of the prosecutors' work.

These differences do not, however, discount the campaign's significance on the domestic judicial or political actors or the public, as its other elements are like those in Italy or Brazil. The Romanian market of corrupt exchanges had a similar structure to that of Italy and Brazil. The Italian and Brazilian markets were focused on securing the votes of parliamentarians and citizens, the allocation of public procurement, and with it the funds for the political parties whereas the Romanian market was somewhat more focused on personal enrichment and crimes of lower material value.[105]

The Romanian campaign also came after a period of democratic consolidation that followed a split with the past. However, the fall of Ceausescu's regime in 1989 did not bring lustration (vetting)[106] of the old cadres of the dictatorial government. The judges and prosecutors who had supported and operated the system, known as the toughest in Eastern Europe, were largely left unchecked—a policy that only Romania and Bulgaria of all the new E.U. member states implemented.[107] As previously noted, the judicial council was already established in 1991, but with very few checks on who could be a part of it, indicating that it relied on communist judges and prosecutors. In 2005, the council was stripped of one of its competencies, namely the appointment of judges and prosecutors for the creation of the specialized Directorate of National Anti-Corruption (DNA). Instead, this body was created by the appointment of prosecutors by the president and the Ministry of Justice with the judge, Daniel Morar, and prosecutor, Laura Codruta Kövesi, handpicked for the position by both the president and the European Commission.[108] Following the model established in Spain, the DNA was attached to the high court in Bucharest and had fourteen separate offices nationwide.[109] Retaining its independence from both the court and the executive branch, the DNA relied on the recruitment of younger, less experienced cadres, shaped by their experience and their training at the judicial academy.[110] Hence, the year 2006 may mark the start of the anti-corruption campaign that would, however, pick up its pace of prosecutions only in 2010.

Between 2010 and 2017, the Romanian judiciary prosecuted close to 4,500 corruption cases, including eighteen former ministers, several generals, the speaker of the parliament, two head prosecutors, two prime ministers, one president, one prince, prominent members of the legal community, and hundreds of state officials.[111] All of this was done with a 92% conviction rate that was praised by the CVM's E.U. observers while at the same time being criticized as evidence of rigged trials.[112] The high conviction rate and the high number of those prosecuted did not significantly lower the perception of corruption[113] but it may have helped increase the public's trust in the work of the judiciary and other state organs.[114] Thanks to the investments made by foreign donors to strengthen civil society, Romania developed a culture of anti-corruption protests and mobilization that saw the DNA prosecutors as agents of legality. Unlike Brazil and Italy, in which the lead prosecutors deliberately sought a public outreach, Laura Kovesi, as the public face of the campaign, did not seek publicity but was more made into a hero by the foreign press.[115] Romania was one of the few countries at the time that declared corruption a national security threat,[116] allowing for a significant role of its national security agency, the Serviciul Roman de Informatii (SRI), in the investigations.[117]

It was the criticisms of this role of the SRI that would lead to a political and legal backlash against the campaign. Not only did the SRI, using formally legal court authorizations, intercept telecommunications at a rate that exceeded that of the United States, a country that has fifteen times the population of Romania,[118] but it was also suspected of using the informers within the judiciary as agents and effectively operating the investigation teams mixed with those of the prosecutors' offices and the police. Effectively, this could mean that the SRI, acting under the pretext of protection of national interests, decided on who would be prosecuted. The 2016 election victory of the Social Democratic Party (Partidul Social Democrat, PSD), the political force that controlled much of Romania's transition from socialism to capitalism[119] in the post-1990 period and whose leading figures were tried and convicted for corruption, strengthened the backlash.[120] This party saw itself as the main victim of the campaign, and upon its return to power in 2016, it worked to establish a narrative that the real rulers of the country are the hidden centers of power within the intelligence agencies and the judiciary.[121] That narrative was to justify the subsequent measures to establish political control over the judiciary, to loosen the anti-corruption legislative framework, and to go after lead prosecutor Laura Kovesi. In 2016 and 2017, the judgments of the Romanian Constitutional Court ordered the Romanian parliament to limit the scope of certain corrupt criminal acts, such as the abuse of public office.[122] Furthermore, the Constitutional Court declared some of the co-operation protocols between the SRI and Romanian institutions unconstitutional, rendering the use of evidence collected by the SRI inadmissible and thus slowing down the pace of the investigations.[123]

The 2017 attempt to deregulate certain elements of the criminal act of misuse of public office by lowering the financial threshold that would represent the constitutive element of the criminal act led to massive demonstrations against the government. The demonstrations revealed that corruption and the fight against corruption have become one of the key divisive issues in Romanian society that led to the mass mobilization of NGOs and citizens.[124] The divisions did not bypass the Romanian judicial community, with more than one thousand predominantly younger judicial officeholders demonstrating not only against these norms but also against creating a separate judicial inspectorate that would investigate the crimes of judges.[125]

In 2017, the inspections of the work of the DNA by the Ministry of Justice led to requests for Kovesi's removal on charges that she had abused her office and violated the principles of separation of powers. The claim was that by launching an investigation into the alleged procedural violations of the Romanian government in the legislative procedure for the adoption of the said law, Kovesi had violated the constitutional principle of the separation of powers.[126] After a prolonged political battle between Romanian President Iohannis and the PSD government, Kovesi was removed from office in July 2018, after which she took the Romanian state to the European Court of Human Rights, successfully claiming that her right to freedom of speech and due process had been violated.[127] Her removal did little to damage her domestic or international reputation. As one of the leading European corruption fighters, she was appointed to the newly created position of European Public Prosecutor in 2019.[128] This series of events from 2018 to 2019 may be understood to constitute the end of the campaign. Just as in Italy and Brazil, the backlash against the campaigns would leave the judiciary in a more difficult position to launch anti-corruption investigations on a scale similar to that of the 2010–2018 period.

2.3 The theory of judicial reputation

The empirical data concerning the three campaigns, their start, the main events that characterized them, and the whole narrative surrounding them testify to their extraordinary nature. As stated, they are powerful anti-corruption actions taking place in a highly corrupt environment in which judges and prosecutors take the heroic role of crusader-like figures that aim to save the state. Uncharacteristically for judicial professionals coming from civil law jurisdictions, through their actions, they become the face of the campaigns. Antonio di Pietro, Piercamillo Davigo, and Gherardo Colombo, the three leading magistrates of the mani pulite pool of prosecutors became more than faces of the campaign. Di Pietro, in particular, owing to his particular style became almost a popular hero. His name was chanted on the football stadiums, his vernacular became promoted by journalists and citizens wrote written to him. The liveliness of his character, or the bravery of his actions, cannot fully explain his popularity. Judge Moro and prosecutor Dallagnol experienced a similar degree of popularity in Romania and Brazil. The two very different people from the animated Italian prosecutor di Pietro remained in the spotlight of the public through strategic communication, especially in the case of Dallagnol, whose advocacy measures and high public profile attracted followers.[129] In the case of Kovesi, the situation was a bit different. Her profile was raised not so much through strategic communication but through a complex narrative-building fueled by the European integration processes of which citizens expected to end corruption and through strong civil society activism. Taken together, these two factors have elevated the Romanian anti-corruption campaign to a level of metaconstitutional discourse[130] and helped her actions enjoy support that was far greater than the support of any of the Romanian public figures at the time.

For these reasons, it is difficult to establish a satisfying theoretical framework that fully explains the behavior of the judges and prosecutors and the dynamic of the campaigns. After many considerations, I have decided to apply the theory of judicial reputation as developed by Ginsburg and Garoupa. As explained below, this framework against competing explanations best explains judicial behavior because it captures the legal professionals as they become agents of change in society while taking account of the institutional changes enabling such behavior. It accounts for the judges' awareness that their duty and loyalty are toward the law but also toward the audiences to which they speak, and that may be critical or favorable to their behavior. It does not put the judicial actors on a pedestal but looks at them "as actors situated within broader political structures."[131]

2.3.1 *History*

Judicial reputation originated within the U.S. legal system. As the courts relied on precedents to justify their decisions, it was observed that not all sources of precedents were viewed in the same way by the judges: some were cited more often than others. Thus, in 1936, Mott introduced the concept of judicial reputation as a synonym for judicial influence. According to him, judicial reputation correlated to the number of citations of one judge by other judges.[132] In a system in which the promotion of judges was based on their reputations as well as on their political orientations, citations could be understood as legal capital, a source of prestige and privilege to those recognized as leading voices of the judiciary. Furthermore, reputation can also predict the outcome of the decisions of the courts in a specific group of cases[133] and might be based not necessarily only on what the judges decide but also on what they refrain from deciding or considering.

The gradual evolution of transnational courts, such as the International Court of Justice (ICJ) and the European Court of Human Rights (ECtHR), represents an excellent illustration of this. For both courts, a fitting example may be a desire to preserve themselves from what might be perceived as an unnecessary overreach in judicial decision-making. This is what prompted the ECtHR to adopt a margin of appreciation doctrine that limits its own exercise of jurisdiction in matters that are to be left to the national judicial systems of the Council of Europe (CoE) member states to decide.[134] In the case of the ICJ, this reputation may, for example, explain its decisions concerning the jurisdictional immunities of the state where the Court sought to highlight the importance of non-legal options for the resolution of the case.[135] In the U.S. legal system, for example, the reputations of Supreme Court Justices Cardozo and Frankfurter differed greatly: while the first was built on rhetorical strength applied to decision-making, the latter was built on restraint.[136]

Judge Richard Posner explored judicial reputation as one of the key topics of his work, seeking to connect it to the general law and economics that he used in his legal analysis and, in particular, the analysis of judicial behavior. Famously, Posner built on the previous concept of judicial reputation to define judges as rational actors who seek to maximize the utility of the judicial function.[137] However, even for him, fame and reputation were strongly connected, with the latter also being a prominent feature of extraordinary judges.[138]

Judicial reputation originated within the common law system, where judges were appointed at the mid-stages or later stages of their careers based on their merits. When a judge or prosecutor was appointed, his prior work and his leanings toward certain interpretations of the law were the decisive factors that guided the decision of the legislator or other state organ regarding the appointment.[139] In contrast, in civil law jurisdictions, reputation was less important, as the vast majority of the judges were career-based judges who would enter the judiciary at the very beginning of their career, usually on the basis of a rigorous exam that would be administered after they passed their bar exams.[140] These judges would then gradually climb the ladder of the judiciary. The differences between the common law and civil law systems bring about a difference in the consideration and understanding of the concept of reputation. For the merit-based appointments of common law jurisdictions, the practice of issuing separate opinions was and still remains important as "they undercut the idea of a homogenous, uniform, bureaucratic judiciary."[141] Unlike this approach on merit and diversity, for the career-based appointments of the civil law jurisdictions, the individual opinions of the judges mattered less, as the appointments were much less based on the personality of the judges or their political leanings. Further, in civil law countries, the conformity of individual judges with the opinions of the supreme judicial bodies (usually, the supreme courts) mattered much more as a factor in the decisions on the quality of the judicial decision-making by an individual judge or prosecutor.[142]

Garoupa and Ginsburg build on the previous development of the concept of reputation developed by U.S. authors, but their ambitions for the concept go far beyond what was stated previously. For them, judicial reputation is the essential quality of the judiciary. They use judicial reputation "to explain how judges respond to the incentives provided by different audiences and how legal systems design their judicial institutions to calibrate the locally appropriate balance between audiences."[143] First, they want their concept of reputation to expand beyond the borders of common law countries. Second, they have taken judicial reputation as a concept already well developed in U.S. law and academia, turning it into a central concept that explains important features of the functioning of the judicial branches in different countries. For Garoupa and Ginsburg, reputation explains compliance with the decisions of the judiciary, in which case reputation matters, as the judiciary "has no influence over either the sword or the purse,"[144] meaning they lack the prerogatives of operating a budget and mobilizing the police and the army, which the other two branches possess. Compliance with the decisions of the courts is thus derived from reputation.[145] Also, the concept of reputation explains the importance of the perceptions of both judges and candidates for judicial positions regarding the quality of the judicial system itself. Judges, as much as other professionals, need to believe in the qualities of the judicial system of which they are a part. The system itself should be interested in the ideas that the judges have about it, as a system with a bad reputation will attract bad candidates, including those seeking personal enrichment or to indulge their laziness.[146] Channeling legal philosophers Ronald Dworkin, Garoupa, and Ginsburg claim that judicial reputation explains the team production of the judiciary, the understanding that no holder of a judicial office operates alone but is akin to the writer of a serial novel.[147] When they talk about reputation, they do not mean just the reputation of an individual judge or a court but also the reputation of the judiciary as a whole; they distinguish between individual and collective reputation.[148]

For these reasons, judges' and prosecutors' reputations are shaped not only by their behavior and their conformity with institutional and operational independence, but also by the views of their audience. Garoupa and Ginsburg define the "audience" as the judicial councils, the judges of the higher courts, the wider legal community, and the general public.[149] Based on this classification, we differentiate between the legal and political audience, which may be domestic or international.[150] The internationality of the audience became an important factor, as the interaction of legal practitioners and scholars around the world has intensified since 1990, fueled by the rise of globalization. Ginsburg and Garoupa see this development as primarily driven by the rise of citations of foreign judgments in national cases and the emergence of transnational networks of judicial councils and judicial associations.[151] Numerous posts and offices created in transnational and international judiciaries provided career opportunities that motivated judges to build their reputations within national systems so that they might progress more easily to these positions.[152] Meanwhile, consideration of the domestic audience primarily involves domestic public opinion. This means that, when taking action, judges will seek to play to domestic and international audiences to improve their personal reputations. Moreover, these actors will not abide only by the three aforementioned constraints on their work, but they will seek creative ways to conform to the principles by which they are bound when playing to the interests of domestic and international audiences.

Despite judicial reputation expanding to encompass different legal systems and their features, Garoupa and Ginsburg simply define judicial reputation as "the stock of assessments about the actor's past performance."[153] They also acknowledge that judicial reputation is linked to judicial independence. Regardless of the legal culture or legal system in which they operate, judges universally portray themselves as impartial and non-partisan. Yet, judicial reputation does not end with independence. Instead, judicial reputation encompasses behavior that touches upon all the concepts previously mentioned.

However, in applying the theory of judicial reputation to civil law systems, Garoupa and Ginsburg encounter a problem. Namely, from a more formal and traditional point of view, judges and prosecutors in these systems depend primarily on three things: i) the disciplinary framework guiding their work, ii) the application of legal reasoning to the cases they adjudicate or lead and the attitudes that the appellate courts or international and transnational courts will take toward their decisions, and iii) the scope of duties entrusted to them by the constitution and the laws.[154] Granted, the disciplinary framework and legal reasoning are both subject to interpretation that requires specialist knowledge of how the legal systems function. Decisions of the appellate courts, while sometimes relevant for judges' progress in the systems where their promotion depends on the quality of decisions measured as conformity with the judgments of the appellate courts, are not necessarily grounds for disciplinary action—let alone dismissal.[155] Additionally, in the ordinary functioning of the legal system, we rarely see judges removed from positions of power and questioned before the public on their actions, just as we rarely see judges influencing the media and explaining their actions. This is especially true for civil law jurisdictions in which, according to the old French maxim, "the judge is the silent interpreter of the law."[156] All of this creates a problem when applying judicial reputation to civil law systems.

To address this problem of their theory's applicability, Ginsburg and Garoupa first provide evidence that the hybridity of the existing legal systems is becoming a widespread feature of their design and that "clear" systems no longer exist.[157] One piece of evidence for this movement is the emergence of judicial councils in many civil law jurisdictions as the primary bodies protecting judicial self-governance and independence.[158] Ginsburg and Garoupa view these bodies as mediators between judges and society, implementing judicial reputation into the design of legal systems.[159] In a wider context, the establishment of the councils signals that society views judges as agents, a view significantly promoted in U.S. literature on judicial relationships from an economic analysis of law standpoint.[160]

We discussed the principal–agent theory and the law and economics approach to the judiciary briefly in Chapter 1. We observe that when we apply the principal–agent model to existing judicial systems, the judges and prosecutors might be understood as agents entrusted with the task of being, respectively, society's arbiters and prosecutors of crimes. The principal in this case is society, the citizens of the state whose interest in an independent judicial system resolves their disputes and promotes order and fairness, as the judiciary interprets. The tension between judges and prosecutors as agents and society as principals may emerge because of the asymmetry of information, which prevents society from having a clear oversight of their actions, leading to the famous "Who guards the guardians?" dilemma. But, this dilemma–seen in the context of the judicial anti-corruption campaigns–does not appear immediately. Rather, the citizens, as the primary audience of the campaigns, are first preoccupied with the idea that the judges and prosecutors, as their agents, are acting on behalf of a common good to eliminate political corruption and end impunity for corrupt acts.

2.3.2 The judicial councils in Italy, Brazil, and Romania

Generally, all judiciaries tend to view themselves as independent; no judiciary prides itself on being subservient to the legislature, the executive, or public pressure. As judicial independence allows the judiciary to serve society as an independent arbiter and act as a constraint on the power of the executive and legislative branches,[161] it becomes necessary for the judiciary to be organized in such a way to perform these tasks with little or no interference while remaining connected to the citizens in whose name the tasks are carried out. However, unlike legislators, who are usually elected directly, judges and prosecutors, generally, are not appointed by citizens.[162] Instead, judges are usually appointed either by the executive (usually the justice ministry or a president), parliaments, independent judicial councils, or a mix of these.[163] In jurisdictions that are the subject of this work, the role of selection and appointment of judges and prosecutors to their positions has been granted to the judicial and, in the case of Brazil, prosecutorial councils. The role of these councils is not merely constitutional (defense of the independence of judges) and technical (participation in the appointment of judges and preparation of the budget for judicial institutions) but also that of a mediator between the expectations of the society and the judges.[164] In the following section, we will see what that meant for the different institutional setups in the three countries of our case study.

Italy established one of the first judicial council institutions in its 1947 Constitution.[165] The Supreme Council of the Judiciary (Consiglio Superiore della Magistratura, CSM), was set up in 1958 and tasked with securing the independence of judges from political influence.[166] Although the original idea of an independent, self-governing body for the Italian judiciary dates back to the 1920s,[167] the emergence of the model codified in the Italian Constitution of 1947 was inspired by the democratic constitution-making that occurred immediately following the defeat of fascism in World War II and a clear political will presented to define Italy as a democratic country.[168] With its membership derived primarily from the judiciary (two-thirds of the members) and with the remaining members appointed by the parliament (also with the inclusion of the President of the State and the Supreme Court of Cassation since 1975), the body was tasked with securing the self-governance of the judicial branch and breaking the political involvement in the work of the judiciary.[169] As Violante describes, the judges' initial demand in the constitutional drafting phase was that only members of the judiciary sit in this council; this was rejected as it was felt that a lack of participation from any other branch of government would make the judiciary too independent and disconnected from the overall system of power distribution in the country.[170]

It proved difficult to break political involvement in judicial matters. Despite a firm constitutional commitment to democracy, post-World War II Italy was highly polarized between the conservative Christian Democrat party (Democrazia Cristiana, DC) and the Communist Party (Partito Comunista Italiana, PCI). This political polarization had two main contradictory effects on the judiciary. On the one hand, as witnessed in particular during the so-called "years of lead" in the 1970s and early 1980s, which saw many illegal, terrorist, and organized crime activities carried out in Italy, the judiciary was under strong pressure to support government's policies.[171] On the other hand, both main political actors in the country played within the democratic field— counting on the judiciary's independence not because they were committed to the rule of law, but because they counted on the realistic possibility that they could find themselves out of power and that the judiciary, if not independent, could easily be weaponized against them.[172] Thus, the parties were willing to maintain judicial independence because it preserved political competition and prevented the creation of a one-party dictatorship. As such, the intense political competition in Italy did not diminish but, rather, contributed to the independence of the judiciary.

This can be attributed to two specific institutional features. First, the organization of the Italian judges in different judicial associations that have greatly contributed to a move from the restrained formal independence granted by the 1958 establishment of the CSM to real independence.[173] Despite these associations being based on their political leanings, they have been instrumental in making the position of judges stronger and building more trust within the judiciary itself. Belonging to an association meant a chance to stand up for the rights of judges cultivate stronger contacts and work on the expression and strengthening of professional culture.[174] Second, the role of the prosecutors (pubblico ministero) who, being a part of the judiciary, have retained institutional independence over the direction of the criminal investigations that was superior to those of their colleagues in most other democratic European jurisdictions.[175] This reduced their chance of instrumentalization by either the organized crime networks or the security sector, which both operated in the country in sometimes intertwined roles.[176]

From the late 1970s, the Italian judicial councils became blueprints for judicial councils in other parts of the world, such as Spain, Portugal, and Brazil. In the 1990s, the Italian model was accepted in an even wider fashion as part of the efforts of the World Bank, the European Union, and judicial non-governmental organizations to promote democracy and the rule of law.[177] Just as post-World War II Italy did, Brazil and Romania, which have used it as an inspiration,[178] have undergone important transitions: dictatorships that rested on authoritarian and even fascist traditions have fallen.

The establishment of a judicial council in Brazil in the era of military dictatorship that conducted serious and widespread abuses of human rights was a move to legitimize the regime before its international critics.[179] In 1988, after a democratic transition, the council was suspended; it was understood to be of little practical use as it was controlled by many of the cadres loyal to the dictatorship. In 2004, however, the judicial council was reinstated as the country attempted to solidify the judicial independence that took root between the mid-1980s and that time.[180] The prosecutorial council was also created, with the main difference being that the president of the country retained the right to appoint the chief prosecutor, with the proviso that the candidate was nominated by the prosecutors and approved by the Senate.[181] Overall, Brazilian public prosecutors were regulated as a hybrid institution; appointed by the Parliament at the proposition of the executive, they were not part of the judiciary, as their Italian and Romanian colleagues were, yet they retained significant investigative and discretionary powers that considerably expanded beyond the prescriptions of the 1988 Constitution.[182] Specifically, the Brazilian prosecutors were free to create special investigatory teams and have greatly profited from the wide discretion given to them concerning the usage of plea bargain agreements.[183] While the institutional arrangements differ, Brazilian prosecutors enjoy a level of independence and authority comparable to their Italian and Romanian counterparts. The absolute majority needed in Congress in order for the chief prosecutor to be appointed decreased the likelihood of an outsider being appointed to lead the institution.[184] So too, the proliferation of the association of judges and prosecutors allowed these two groups to specialize and advocate for those issues that they considered relevant and related to their political goals.[185]

In Romania, the judicial council was created in 1991 following the adoption of a new constitution that took place upon the fall of the communist dictatorship of Nicolae Ceausescu and, as in Brazil, as an attempt by the new government to consolidate its international standing.[186] Initially following the French judicial council as its institutional model, the council was stripped of most of its powers in 1997, but, following external pressure primarily from the E.U.

member states, reformed and restrengthened in 2003.[187] Just as in Brazil, the judicial council in Romania has conducted no vetting procedure, which has effectively meant that all the judges who were a part of one of the most totalitarian regimes of former Eastern European states have largely remained in their places.[188] In 2003, the role of the prosecutors who were, just as in Italy, a part of the Romanian judicial system was also reformed; some of their authority, such as that to decide on the pre-trial detention of the accused, was removed from them, but their institutional independence, primarily from the Ministry of Justice, was strengthened.[189] Following the strengthening of the judicial councils, numerous judicial and prosecutorial associations formed—not so much on political grounds as on the different views of the judicial system that gradually began to emerge but took little role in the development of policy or legislation. It would only be later when the backlash against the judiciary began, that the judicial associations began to play a prominent role in the protection of judicial independence.[190] Additionally, we see that the emergence of all three judicial councils was tied to the Romanistic legal tradition and democratic transition.[191]

2.3.3 *The elements of judicial reputation facilitating anti-corruption campaigns*

The narrative of the investigations thus far suggests that the agency theory and the judicial reputation theory represent an adequate theoretical framework for explaining anti-corruption campaigns. The actions of all three judicial spearheads of the campaigns enjoyed wide public support, though this support did not have the same level across the three jurisdictions. In Italy, especially during the first two years of the campaign, it was almost plebiscitary, as evidenced by the popularity of the Milanese pool of judges, while in Romania and Brazil, the popularity of those prosecuted dictated the polarization toward the judicial campaigns. Based on the political considerations of the population in Romania and Brazil, the prosecutors were considered a part of a political plot to destroy a certain political option (PT in Brazil and PSD in Romania) or a welcome effort to clean the country of corruption. Internationally, the Romanian campaign had done much to elevate the international standing of the country, earning praise from the E.U. authorities and preventing a freeze in the E.U. structural funds allocation.[192] The Italian campaign, on the other hand, did not elevate the standing of the country but actually worsened the country's reputation for corruption.[193] Regarding Brazil, the reaction of the international audience was mixed, as the initial overwhelming support was replaced by doubts over the (il)legality of the prosecutorial actions[194] and later a thorough dismissal of the effort in the academic and practitioners circles.[195]

The judges and prosecutors, especially in the Italian and Brazilian investigations, operated with a strong presumption that what lies at the core of the corrupt behavior of political actors is a lack of a normative ideal for the establishment of a freer and more just society. Seeing the main institutional actors of that view in the political parties and their leadership, the prosecutors viewed them as criminal organizations that needed to be dismantled or heavily punished for their actions. Thus, they perhaps acted without full awareness of the consequences that their actions would lead to but with full awareness of the inevitability of the political crisis that would emerge or be intensified. The judges and prosecutors did not stop there. Some of the key figures of Lava Jato and Mani Pulite entered politics: Sergio Moro became the Minister of Justice of Brazil, Piercamillo Davigo and Antonio di Pietro refused such positions in government in 1994, and di Pietro started his own political project, the Italy of Values (Italia dei Valori, Idv), in 1998.[196] Laura Kovesi did not officially enter politics, but owing to the political support of European political actors, she became the first European Public Prosecutor.[197] For both di Pietro and Moro, the decision to leave the judiciary was presented as a logical extension of their fight against corruption.[198]

The Lava Jato prosecutors and judges, inspired by the Mani Pulite prosecutors and their handling of the media, deliberately used a media strategy that kept the public informed of their actions and served to shape public opinion toward a desired political outcome.[199] The revelations made following the leaks of Dallagnol's conversations demonstrated their fear that the PT candidate winning the 2018 elections would undo the progress they believed had been made in the fight against corruption. Similarly, the Romanian DNA preferred the political options that were opposed to PSD, as this party was worst hit by the anti-corruption campaign, and the Italian prosecutors (at least, prior to the 1994 elections) viewed Berlusconi as a lesser evil compared to the old or reformed political parties.[200] Just like the domestic audience, their actions also targeted the international audience. In the case of Romania, this internationalization was institutionalized, as the CVM monitored the efficiency of the Romanian prosecutors, leading to the recommendation of Kovesi for the position of the first European Public Prosecutor. In the case of Brazil, Dallagnol was recognized as an emerging figure in the global anti-corruption civil society awarded by Transparency International but also as a negotiator who went well beyond his mandate to obtain data from Switzerland or to hand over data to the American authorities, thereby facilitating the prosecutions against Odebrecht in that jurisdiction.[201] While the Italian campaign played the least to the international audience, informal contacts between di Pietro and U.S. diplomats suggest an awareness on his part that he needed to not be obstructed by external influences on the Italian political scene.[202]

If the judges demonstrated a propensity or an awareness that their actions actively shaped the political landscape, it should also be noted that the political mobilization against them and their actions was also a serious affair. In Italy, di Pietro and Davigo faced investigation for the abuse of office in obstructing investigations and coup attempts.[203] In Brazil, thanks to the expiry of the statute of limitations (and the fact that both Moro and Dallagnol left the judiciary), all disciplinary charges have been dropped, but both of them faced an uncertain political future after having briefly worked in corporate compliance.[204] Dallagnol's mandate in Congress was revoked by the Brazilian court, which found that he shouldn't have been allowed to run in elections as charges against him were pending. Laura Kovesi was removed from office in a procedure that was later disputed by the European Court of Human Rights.

The efforts to impede investigations extended beyond personal vendettas, encompassing legislative maneuvers designed to obstruct and restrict inquiries, particularly in Italy and Romania. In Italy, upon assuming office in 1994, the Berlusconi administration implemented strategic changes to the criminal legal system aimed at prolonging proceedings. This tactic was intended to exploit the statute of limitations, allowing certain criminal charges to expire before trials could conclude. The strategy proved effective, resulting in the acquittal of defendants in several high-profile cases due to time constraints rather than lack of evidence.[205] While President Bolsonaro, who came to power in Brazil following the 2018 presidential elections, promised an anti-corruption campaign, he failed to deliver on this promise, instead limiting the independence of the prosecutors, as we will see in Chapter 4.[206] The Romanian Constitutional Court's decision to declare that the crime of misuse of public office applies to many of the corrupt acts prosecuted by the DNA has also significantly impaired the investigations in Romania, as has the decision on the use of data gathered through surveillance.

I believe that the analysis in this chapter demonstrates that the judges and prosecutors in all three cases were motivated by more than just a desire to see justice done. Both the legal culture and the institutional judicial structures of the countries influenced what they did in these campaigns; they sought to root out the corrupt practices of the institutional actors, communicate with both the international and the domestic audience, and elevate their own standing both within the legal system and outside of its boundaries. Their views of judicial reputation were inclusive enough to include their political views, and yet legal enough to convince them that they remain impartial, inspiring them to mobilize their colleague and the society *en general* using both judicial and extrajudicial means (i.e., the creation of foundations in the case of Brazil and a desire to change the political class in Italy).

Table 2.1 Judicial reputation as an element of anti-corruption campaigns

Elements of anti-corruption campaigns	*Italy*	*Brazil*	*Romania*
Domestic audience	Yes	Yes	No
International audience	No	Yes	Yes
Formal independence of the office of the public prosecutor from the executive	Yes	Yes	Yes
Specialized prosecutorial units	No	Yes	Yes
Pre-existing political crisis of the executive and the legislative branches of government	Yes	Yes	Yes
Political ambitions of the prosecutors	Yes	Yes	Yes
Significant political backlash	Yes	Yes	Yes
Attempts to curb the power of the judiciary and its ability to prosecute corruption	Yes	Yes	Yes

2.4 Legal culture and institutional theories as alternative explanations for the campaigns

The theory of judicial reputation is not the only possible theoretical approach to explain the emergence of campaigns. Researchers exploring campaigns from the standpoint of comparative law have focused on legal culture, path dependency theory, and prosecutorial behavior as explanations for judicial behaviors and the emergence of campaigns. Analysis based on these approaches often contains a description or analysis of institutions that contributed to the emergence of the campaigns, in that sense resembling the approach used by the theory of judicial reputation.

Both legal culture and path dependency are widely used in comparative law insomuch that they represent a trope within the field.[207] Legal culture, in the widest sense, represents "values, opinions, attitudes, and beliefs about the law."[208] As such, it may differ between societies, individuals, and societal groups, but in the context of comparative law, it can be understood in two ways. The first is methodological, as an approach that allows us to identify specific traits that exist within a particular legal system (or a family of legal systems), thus mapping the cultural foundation enshrined in certain legal institutions.[209] The second is more general as a variable that sets the legal system in motion. Given such a wide application of legal culture, why do Garoupa and Ginsburg explicitly state that their theory of judicial reputation is superior to explanations based on legal culture or tradition when much of their work explicitly relies on works based on legal culture[210] and when judicial reputations themselves are heavily based on what was traditionally part of the U.S. legal culture?[211] What they have in mind is that the first approach, in which everything legal is somehow related to culture, fails to distinguish between culture as a whole and culture-based analysis.[212] The latter is something that the theory of judicial reputation itself cannot escape because judicial reputation is related to the judicial culture within a country. However, the theory of judicial reputation retains a unique approach based on the economics of the relations within the judiciary. This is more likely to inform us of the evolutionary path of the judicial culture (i.e., through events such as judicial campaigns) than sharp distinctions based on legal tradition (i.e., that of the career or recognition judiciaries) or long-observed behavioral patterns favored by legal culture.

Path dependency theory posits that the "decisions we make depend on past decisions made and issues that have occurred well before the present day."[213] In its evolutionary form, path dependence is linked to the works of the great German jurist Savigny, founder of the historical school of legal thought, who believed that the gradual evolution of the law that stems from experience, rather than logic, explains the trajectories of the development of the legal system.[214] In its modern form, path dependency explains the persistence of legal rules and their embeddedness within a particular legal system.[215] It seeks to determine how legal history and, in particular, the institutions that were created over its course impact the legal systems of today. In so doing, path development pays particular attention to the concept of critical junctures, developments, and events that crucially shape legal systems.[216] Garoupa and Ginsburg are less averse to this approach than to those based on legal culture, as judicial reputation theory itself has a strong interest in institutional development, for example, judicial councils.

Approaches based on the legal culture or path dependency theory are useful for explaining certain elements of anti-corruption campaigns. For example, some of the legal solutions that served as the building blocks of the campaigns relied heavily on elements borrowed from the common law legal system. These elements are the use of plea bargaining as a way of securing witness involvement[217] (which, in the Brazilian case, led to the highest-profile case of the prosecution of former President Lula) and the introduction of judicial councils as the mechanism of judicial self-governance that strengthened the independence of the judiciary, encouraging their campaigns. The adoption of these two legal transplants—in particular, in the Brazilian and Romanian cases[218]—facilitated a more efficient execution of the campaigns. Furthermore, it may be argued that the path dependency of the three legal systems facilitated a backlash against the campaigns; if the campaigns were indeed the result of the reputation-seeking activity of the judges, then the backlash was a natural response that came not necessarily only from the political activities of those seeking to quell the campaigns and to return the political system to its "normal" state. Finally, the embeddedness of certain institutions within a legal system and the results they create provide evidence of the usefulness of a path-dependent approach. For example, the institutional embeddedness of the CSM in Italy represented a break from the previous model of the executive-controlled judiciary that produced important outcomes for the emergence of anti-corruption campaigns.[219] Similarly, the Romanian judicial council did not prevent the backlash that happened against the judiciary in the country but allowed more space for the judicial organizations that were to mobilize resistance against it.[220]

However, I believe that these approaches to anti-corruption campaigns, while useful to a certain degree, do not provide a holistic approach to the campaigns. First, legal culture theory views the civil law/common law distinction as a given, excluding the growing hybridity of the legal systems analyzed.[221] For example, an approach based on legal culture would limit the individual roles that judges and prosecutors have played in defining the international audiences of the campaigns, the use of media, and the elements of the backlash, viewing them as falling outside their scope or less important. As a result, legal culture would reject the role that the reputation of judges plays in explaining campaigns. Second, path dependency theory, or at least some of its strains, acknowledges that gradual bursts of activity may be instances in which the legal system changes quickly, incorporating some or all of the introduced features into a new paradigm. However, path dependency theory focuses more on introducing institutional rules than on the practices and events that shape the legal system. As such, while the campaigns have led to certain legislative initiatives and changes, their immediate effects were not institutionalized—notwithstanding the aforementioned attempts to establish the Lava Jato Foundation in Brazil.

Let's look at some of the offered explanations for the emergence of anti-corruption campaigns. We observe that while they mostly rely on empirical data collected by scholars researching the campaigns, traces of the legal culture and path dependency approach are present. For example, Della Porta analyzes the vast amount of data on the evolution of the Italian judiciary from the 1960s onwards, finding that it gradually evolved from a judiciary that colluded with the interests of the executive to a more non-partisan judiciary that had political leanings and sympathies while remaining impartial.[222] She highlights the role of the CSM, which acted as an institutional safeguard for the magistrates, and observes that the collusion between judges and politicians that previously existed decreased at the beginning of the 1990s for two reasons: the decrease in the value of the political parties for judges, which occurred as the political parties lost their legitimacy at the beginning of the 1990s, and the civic virtues of the judiciary, which emerged as its values evolved as a result of the fighting role of the judiciary in the 1980s.[223] While I agree with the first conclusion, we must observe that, as Della Porta writes in 1998 (6 years after the beginning of Mani Pulite), at least 200 judges were under investigation for corruption,[224] which is a sign that the presence of the virtues was perhaps not evenly spread throughout the judiciary.

Nelken, who has written significantly on Italian legal culture, limits his explanations, in this regard, to the role that the CSM has played in granting the Italian judiciary its independence and the acknowledgment that the Mani Pulite was not the first anti-corruption inquiry of the Italian judiciary, suggesting the possibility that the Italian judiciary was, in a sense, waiting for the right moment to prosecute those responsible for corruption.[225] He observes that the political leanings of the magistrates were undoubtedly present, but also notes that this feeling was hardly uniform for the judiciary as a whole, given that, traditionally, cases of political corruption in the pre-Mani Pulite days remained unresolved before the court in Rome, which was known as the place where corrupt judges would simply let a case expire via the statute of limitations.[226] A culture-based approach falls short in identifying anti-corruption activities within the judiciary as a defining characteristic of the three legal systems or their judicial actors. Cultural explanations alone are insufficient to elucidate the emergence of anti-corruption campaigns. To comprehensively understand these phenomena, it is necessary to draw upon insights from political science and other social sciences.

Pederzoli and Guarnieri similarly acknowledge the role that the CSM played in the evolution of the Italian judiciary,[227] rightly predicting that introducing judicial councils in other countries that choose to embrace such a model of judicial self-governance will gradually increase the independence of judges. In their view—which turned out to be quite prophetical—this will not lead to a judicial revolution but to internal fragmentation of the judiciary itself along political lines.[228] Indeed, this is what has happened in Romania and Brazil. In both countries, we observe that the activities of the judicial organizations focused on the defense of the independence of the branch and on an effort to criticize prosecutorial overreach. However, Nelken and Guarnieri's argument that the system of mandatory prosecutions[229] in Italy was instrumental to the effects of the campaign does not seem convincing.[230] A system of mandatory prosecutions exists as a counterbalance to the principle of prosecutorial independence, serving as a check on discretionary decision-making to ensure that the investigations are carried out without bias.[231] However, the authors citing it fail to make a convincing case for how this principle was crucial for the emergence of the campaigns, and even its thorough application in practice remains a contested point in the literature.

The path dependence approach, characterized by the attention it pays to the events that bring the legal systems to one legal family or another, would certainly highlight the fact that Romania's entrance into the E.U. has had an important impact on the general trajectory of the legal system. This observation certainly holds: The CVM monitoring mechanism was an important tool for determining the international audience for judicial anti-corruption campaigns. Yet, the same mechanism was set up for Bulgaria, which failed to produce a similar effect in that country.[232] Or, to use the example of Brazil, there is no doubt that the effect of democratic constitution-making that characterized the creation of the 1988 Brazilian constitution set in motion a chain of events that have led to the strengthening of judicial and prosecutorial independence. Yet, comparable democratization events have occurred in Argentina and other Latin American countries, where important trials and other legal events that occurred in the aftermath of these democratizations were perhaps on an even greater scale than in Brazil.[233] However, they have not led to comparable judicial actions inspired by judicial reputation, such as the Lava Jato campaign. Finally, comparative lawyers have noted similarities between the Italian and French systems of organizing prosecutions, finding cultural differences stemming from post-World War II as developments that have led to different standards of exercising discretion among prosecutors.[234] However, this difference does not explain the capacities for dealing with large-scale political corruption—occasional prosecutions of political corruption appeared in France (and in most other European countries) as well, without ever matching the scale of those in Italy.

What is common to the explanations inspired by a legal culture or path dependency approach offered for the campaigns occurring in Romania and Brazil[235] is that they highlight the loss of legitimacy of the legislative and executive branches of power. Unlike judicial reputation theory, which sees the power of the judicial branch as inherent to itself, these explanations see the strength of judges' and prosecutors' actions in the exploitation of the shift in the balance of powers between the branches. In the case of Brazil, judges and prosecutors have counted on public support for their actions, thus acting as representatives of civil society. However, the explanations—at least concerning Italy—downplay the political ambitions of the leading judicial actors, and, in doing so, remain confined to positing that, overall, the judges performed within their constitutional duties. More recent literature, in particular dealing with Brazil, acknowledges the high probability of the existence of a political agenda but remains, in my view, partisan to Lula viewing the politicization of the campaign as a bad thing per se instead of following a more nuanced approach to the political leanings of the judges and prosecutors that the theory of judicial reputation allows us.[236]

The concept of critical junctures in path development theory offers a potential bridge to the idea of judicial reputation. We can enhance our understanding of judicial reputation by recognizing that institutional settings and events, including judicial anti-corruption campaigns, can serve as critical junctures. This enriched perspective could enable legal theorists to examine the evolution of legal culture as a series of pivotal institutional events driven by the reputation-seeking behaviors of actors within the judicial branch. This approach would allow for reevaluating the introduction of judicial councils in legal systems, which path dependency theories consider crucial. Rather than viewing these councils as guarantors of a legal system's readiness to combat corruption, they would be seen in a new light. Specifically, the councils would be recognized for their role in shielding judges and prosecutors from unwarranted disciplinary actions. The explanation of prosecutions as driven by prosecutorial zeal is the closest to the one I offer in this chapter.[237] The phrase *esprit du corps* that I use to describe the collective spirit built through experience and a particular understanding of judicial reputation may also mean the zeal with which one engages in one's work.[238] Both approaches focus on the behavior of prosecutors and judges, seeing them as central to the events that unfolded. The differences, however, exist. As with independence, most prosecutors would never admit that they are driven by commands from others and that they lack the zeal to pursue offenders, even in cases where the perpetrators are highly ranked members of the political class engaged in white-collar crime. Where one should draw the line between zealous and non-zealous prosecutors remains difficult to assess, just as is the case with judicial reputation. However, a merely zealous prosecutor will not necessarily accomplish the prosecutions described in this book. On the other hand, the prosecutors relying on reputation rely on more than just their commitment to prosecutions as they mobilize society and legitimize their behavior through their reputation. To put it more simply, zealousness is a part of reputation, but reputation is much more than zealousness.

2.5 Conclusion

The theory of judicial reputation offers significant advantages as a theoretical framework for the consideration of judicial anti-corruption campaigns. First, this theory convincingly explains why judges and prosecutors go beyond their legally and constitutionally mandated duties in prosecuting and adjudicating corruption. It explains the wide reformist and legislative plans they offered for the rebuilding of their societies and their anticipation that their campaigns might be a turning point for society. Second, it explains why the judges and prosecutors, when provided with an opportunity for political positions, domestic in the case of Italy and Brazil and international in the case of Romania, did not shy away from taking them; they were looking to bolster their individual reputations. Third, the constant leaks of information by prosecutors are more evidence that there were attempts to sway public opinion in their favor through deliberate media campaigns and not mere communication tools. Fourth, the situations preceding the beginnings of the three campaigns were hardly unique for the three countries. For example, strong judicial councils, independent prosecutorial teams, widespread corruption, crises of legitimacy, and the loss of support for the executive and legislative branches of government had existed across Eastern Europe and Latin America in the preceding fifteen years. However, judicial campaigns did not occur in most of these countries. Certainly, the normative ideal of the Italian judiciary forged in the anti-Mafia campaigns of the 1970s and 1980s can, to a certain extent, be the differentia specifica, distinguishing it from many jurisdictions of the world. However, the campaigns also occurred in Brazil and Romania, where such a normative ideal, even if present, is much less pronounced in shaping the normative view of the judicial profession by those within it. In fact, the two campaigns contributed precisely to the development of such a normative ideal.

Finally, it is the concept of the judicial reputation that provides for an adequate positioning and understanding of the role that the judicial councils play; they do not guarantee an independent judiciary, as evidenced by the backsliding that occurred in Romania in the aftermath of the campaigns, but rather a judiciary that is more insulated from political pressures and has more opportunity for individualization. Therefore, the paths taken by both the judiciary and other institutional actors in other jurisdictions with comparable legal reforms, institutional setups, and prevalence of corruption were much less intrusive and focused not so much on the prosecution but on the prevention of corruption. Fifth, if we apply path dependency theory to our cases, none of them has led to a sharp turning point for strengthening the judiciary or to an anti-corruption framework. Instead, the effects were reconsidering the judiciary's role in the distribution of power and a decrease in the scope of authority bestowed upon the judges and prosecutors in the fight against corruption.

Notes

1 For example, the magnificent Italian TV series 1992, the Romanian Oscar-winning film Collective and the Brazilian TV series The Mechanism.

2 Rodrigo Chemim, Mãos Limpas e Lava Jato: A corrupção se olha no espelho, (2019); Sergio F. Moro, Considerações sobre a operação mani pulite. *Revista cej*, 8(26), (2004), 56–62.

3 Alina Mungiu-Pippidi, Explaining Eastern Europe: Romania's Italian-style anti-corruption populism, *Journal of Democracy*, 29(3), (2018), 104–116.

4 Donatella Della Porta, A judges' revolution? Political corruption and the judiciary in Italy, *European Journal of Political Research*, 39(1), (2001), 1–21.

5 David Nelken, The judges and political corruption in Italy, *Journal of Law and Society*, 23(1), (1996), 95–112.
6 Martin Mendelski, 15 years of anti-corruption in Romania: Augmentation, aberration and acceleration, *European Politics and Society*, 22(2), (2021), 237–258.
7 George Meszaros, Caught in an authoritarian trap of its own making? Brazil's 'Lava Jato' anti-corruption investigation and the politics of prosecutorial overreach, *Journal of Law and Society*, 47, (2020), S54–S73; Fabio Kerche & Joao Féres Júnior, Operação Lava Jato e a democracia brasileira (2018). Martin Mendelski, Europeanization and the rule of law: Towards a pathological turn. *Southeastern Europe*, 40(3), (2016), 346–384; Mark Tushnet, Institutions supporting constitutional democracy: Some thoughts about anti-corruption (and other) agencies, *Singapore Journal of Legal Studies*, (2019), 440–455. Emilio Peluso Neder Meyer, Judges and courts destabilizing constitutionalism: The Brazilian judiciary branch's political and authoritarian character, *German Law Journal*, 19 (4), (2018), 727–768.
8 Marco Travaglio, Gianni Barbacetto & Peter Gomez, Mani pulite. La vera storia, (2012).
9 Paul F. Lagunes, & Jan Svejnar, (eds.). *Corruption and the Lava Jato Scandal in Latin America*, (2020).
10 Piercamillo Davino & Grazia Mann Ozzi, La corrasion in Italia: percezione sociale e controllo penale, (2007); Maria Cristina Pinotti, et al. Corrupção: lava jato e mãos limpas, (2019); Deltan Dallagnol, A luta contra a corrupção: A Lava Jato e o futuro de um país marcado pela impunidade, (2017).
11 Anne Van Aaken, Lars P. Feld & Stephen Voigt, Do independent prosecutors deter political corruption? An empirical evaluation across seventy-eight countries, *American Law and Economics Review*, 12(1), (2010), 204–244.
12 Nuno Garoupa & Tom Ginsburg, *Judicial Reputation*, (2015).
13 Lucia Manzi, *The Effective Judicial Prosecution of Systemic Political Corruption: Italy*, (2018).
14 Mendelski, 15 years of anti-corruption in Romania, Meszaros, Caught in an authoritarian trap of its own making?, Stanton H. Burnett & Luca Mantovani, The Italian guillotine: Operation clean hands and the overthrow of Italy's first republic, (1998); Carol Proner et al. (eds.) *Comments on a Notorious Verdict: The Trial of Lula*, (2018). www.jstor.org/stable/j.ctvn96gjp.
15 Fabio De Sá e Silva, From car wash to Bolsonaro: Law and lawyers in Brazil's illiberal turn (2014–2018), *Journal of Law and Society*, 47, (2020), S90–S110.
16 Salvatore Sberna & Alberto Vannucci, "It's the politics, stupid!" The politicization of anti-corruption in Italy, *Crime, Law and Social Change*, 60(5), (2013), 565–593.
17 For example, David Nelken, The judges and political corruption in Italy, *Journal of Law and Society*, 23(1), (1996), 95–112; Donatella Della Porta, A judges revolution? Political corruption and the judiciary in Italy, *European Journal of Political Research*, 39(1), (2001), 1–21; Paul F. Lagunes & Jan Svejnar, (eds.) Corruption and the Lava Jato Scandal in Latin America, (2020). For an exception to this stance, and a project that seeks to establish a more nuanced view of the interplay between judicial reputation, judicial independence, and the anti-corruption campaigns, see Manzi, *The Effective Judicial Prosecution of Systemic Political Corruption: Italy*.
18 David Nelken & Michael Levi, The corruption of politics and the politics of corruption: An overview, *Journal of Law and Society*, 23(1), (1996), 1–17. For an exception to this rule see Zimmerman, note 7 (Chapter 1); Louis De Sousa, Hard responses to corruption: Penal standards and the repression of corruption in Britain. *France and Portugal. Crime, Law and Social Change*, 38(3), (2002), 267–294.
19 Exceptions to this include mostly works of US scholars who have sought to explore the themes of political corruption in the United States, such as Lawrence Lessig What an Originalist Would Understand Corruption to Mean. California Law Review, 102, 1 (2014); Underkuffler, note 6 (Chapter 1).

20 Michael Hein, The fight against government corruption in Romania: Irreversible results or Sisyphean Challenge? *Europe-Asia Studies*, 67(5), (2015), 747–776.
21 Sberna & Vannucci, "It's the politics, stupid!".
22 Burnett & Mantovani, The Italian guillotine; Proner et al., *Comments on a Notorious Verdict: The Trial of Lula*, Mattia Feltri, Novantatré: L'anno del Terrore di Mani Pulite, (2016).
23 Bogdan Iancu, Quick fix solutions-anticorruption as core/peripheral modality of the 'rule of law', *Hague Journal on the Rule of Law*, 16(4), (2024), 1–32.
24 *See generally* Miriam A. Golden & Eric C. C. Chang, Competitive corruption: Factional conflict and political malfeasance in postwar Italian Christian democracy, *World Political*, 53, (2001), 588.
25 Diego Gambetta, Why Is Italy Disproportionately Corrupt? A Conjecture, In *Institutions, Governance and the Control of Corruption* 201 (Basu Kaushik & Tito Cordella, eds., 2011).
26 Alberto Vannucci & Salvatore Sberna. Mafia and Political Corruption in Italy, in Italian Mafias Today: Territory, *Business and Politics*, 92 (Felia Allum et al., eds., 2019).
27 *See generally* Andrea Capussela, *The Political Economy of Italy's Decline.*
28 Silvia Colazingari & Susan Rose-Ackerman, Corruption in a paternalistic democracy: Lessons from Italy for Latin America, *Political Science in English*, 113(447), (1998).
29 *See generally* Donatella Della Porta & Alberto Vannucci, The Hidden Order of Corruption (2012).
30 Edward Luttwak, *Italy's Ancien Régime, Soc'y*, 31(70), (1993).
31 The mass evasion of the political party financing legislation is best evidenced by the speech of then president of PSI, Bettino Craxi, who in 1993 publicly stated that most of the financing of the Italian political parties came from illicit sources. *See* TV Zoom Channel, *Tangentopoli Il discorso di Bettino Craxi in Parlamento nel 1992*, Youtube (February 17, 2012), https://www.youtube.com/watch?v=Jud08s96QfY.
32 Alberto Vannucci, The controversial legacy of 'Mani Pulite': A critical analysis of Italian corruption and anti-corruption policies, *Bulletin of Italian Politics*, 2(1), (2009), 233–264.
33 Donatella Della Porta & Alberto Vannucci, (2007). Mani impunite. Vecchia e nuova corruzione in Italia.
34 Only in exceptional circumstances would those tried during Mani pulite return to participate in political life. See Sandro Busso & Attilio Scaglione, Percorsi politici prima e dopo tangentopoli, In Roccco Schiarrone (ed.), Politica e corruzione: Partiti e reti di affari da Tangentopoli a oggi, (2017).
35 Capussela, *The Political Economy of Italy's Decline*, at 154.
36 Martin Rhodes, Financing party politics in Italy: A case of systemic corruption, *World European Policy*, 20(54), (1997) (arguing that this inadequate legal framework is responsible for much of the illicit activities of Italian political parties).
37 Luciano Violante, *I Magistrati*, (2012) 47.
38 *See generally* Manzi, *The Effective Judicial Prosecution of Systemic Political Corruption: Italy* (arguing that this process of institutional flattening took place as an internal struggle within the judiciary over the control of the judicial council).
39 Violante, *I Magistrati*, at 53–55.
40 Stefano Guzzini, The implosion of clientelistic Italy in the 1990s: A study of'peaceful change in comparative political economy, (1994), EUI Working Paper, 7–11.
41 Generally, see Andrea Spiri, The End. 1992–1994. (2022).
42 Lucia Manzi, Prosecutorial gatekeeping and its effects on criminal accountability: The Roman prosecutor's office and corruption investigations in Italy, 1975–1994, *Justice System Journal*, 43(3), (2022), 445–469.

43 David S. Clark, Italian Styles: criminal Justice and the Rise of an Active Magistracy In Lawrence M. Friedman & Rogelio Perez-Perdomo (Eds.) *Legal Culture in the Age of Globalization Latin America and Latin Europe*, 269–275.
44 William F. McDonald, Politics, criminal prosecution, and the rationalization of justice: Italy and the United States, *International Journal of Comparative and Applied Criminal Justice*, 14(1–2), (1990), 15–24.
45 Violante, *I Magistrati*, at 91.
46 For a pessimistic assessment of the Italian legal system regarding this and other developments, *see* Maria Rosaria Ferrarese, Civil Justice and the Judicial Role in Italy, *Journal of Intelligent & Fuzzy Systems*, 13(168), (1988).
47 Nelken, The judges and political corruption in Italy, at 110 n.21.
48 *See generally* Burnet & Mantovani, The Italian guillotine, (exploring the criticisms and arguments concerning the abuse of power by the Italian magistrates).
49 Luciano Violante, *I Magistrati*, 36–71.
50 Francesco Cingari, *La corruzione pubblica: trasformazioni fenomenologiche ed esigenza di riforma* [*Public Corruption: Phenomenological Transformations and the Need for Reform*], *Diritto Penale Contemporaneo*, 20(33, 34), (2012).
51 David Nelken, *Stopping the Judges, Italian Political*, 194, (1996), 187–104.
52 Vannucci, The controversial legacy of 'Mani Pulite'.
53 Vannucci, The controversial legacy of 'Mani Pulite'.
54 Vannucci, The controversial legacy of 'Mani Pulite'.
55 *See generally* Glenda Mazarobba, Between Reparations, Half-Truths and Impunity: The Difficult Break with the Legacy of the Dictatorship in Brazil, *Sur—International Journal on Human Rights*, 13(7), (2010).
56 Benjamin Fogel, Brazil: Corruption as a Mode of Rule, *NACLA Report on the Americas*, 51(153), (2019) (explaining the history of political corruption in Brazil).
57 *See generally* Simeon Nichter, Vote Buying in Brazil: From Impunity to Prosecution, *The Latin American Research Review*, 56(3), (2021).
58 Scott W. Desposato, Parties for rent? Ambition, ideology, and party switching in Brazil's chamber of deputies, *American Journal of Political Science*, 50(62), (2006).
59 Scott W. Desposato, Parties for rent? Ambition, ideology, and party switching in Brazil's chamber of deputies, *American Journal of Political Science*, 50(62), (2006).
60 Timothy J. Power, & Eric D. Raile, *Coalitional Presidentialism and Side Payments: Explaining the Mensalão Scandal in Brazil*, 4–5 (University of Oxford Brazilian Stud., Programme, Occasional Paper 03–08, 2008) (explaining the coalition governments and bargaining strategies of the political actors as the reasons behind the scandal).
61 Gregory Michener & Carlos Pereira, A great leap forward for democracy and the rule of law? Brazil's Mensalão, *The Journal of Latin American Studies*, 48(477), 483, (2016) (explaining the effects that the prosecution of legislators and mediators in the corrupt activities had on the democratic development of Brazil and the accountability of public officials).
62 Sergio Moro, *Considerações sobre a operação mani pulite* [Considerations on the Mani Pulite Operation], *The Chemical Engineering Journal* 8(56), (2004).
63 Sergio Moro, Considerações sobre a operação mani pulite [Considerations on the Mani Pulite Operation], *The Chemical Engineering Journal* 8(56), (2004) at 58.
64 Sergio Moro, *Considerações sobre a operação mani pulite* [Considerations on the Mani Pulite Operation], *The Chemical Engineering Journal* 8(56), (2004).
65 Lagunes & Svejnar, *Corruption and the Lava Jato Scandal in Latin America*, at 3.
66 Fausto de Assis Ribeiro, *The Accidental Trojan Horse: Plea Bargaining as an Anticorruption Tool in Brazil*, 9 (Int'l Inst. of Soc. Stud., Working Paper No. 627, 2017).
67 Elizangela Valarini & Markus Pohlmann, Organizational crime and corruption in Brazil: A case study of the "Operation Carwash" Court Records, *International Journal of Law, Crime and Justice*, 11(59), (2019).

68 Fergus Shiel & Sasha Chavkin, Bribery division: What is Odebrecht? Who is involved? *International Consortium of Investigative Journalists* (June 25, 2019), https://www.icij.org/investigations/bribery-division/bribery-division-what-is-odebrecht-who-is-involved/.

69 *See* Nicolás Campos et al., The ways of corruption in infrastructure: Lessons from the Odebrecht case, *Journal of Economic Perspectives*, 35, (2021), 171, 172.

70 *See* Nicolás Campos et al., The ways of corruption in infrastructure: Lessons from the Odebrecht case, *Journal of Economic Perspectives*, 35, (2021), 171, 172 at 185.

71 Raquel de Mattos Pimenta & Otavio Venturini, *International Cooperation and Negotiated Settlements for Transnational Bribery: A Study of the Odebrecht Case, Revista Direito GV*, 17(1), 8, (2021) (explaining the functioning of this legal mechanism in Brazil).

72 Shiel & Chavkin, Bribery division.

73 Thomas J. Vicino & Anjuli Fahlberg, The politics of contested urban space: The 2013 protest movement in Brazil, *Journal of Urban Affairs*, 39, 1001, 1001–1003 (2017) (explaining the recession and dissatisfaction with PT rule as triggers for the protests).

74 *See generally* Wendy Hunter & Timothy J. Power, Bolsonaro and Brazil's Illiberal Backlash, *The Journal of Democracy*, 30(68), (2019) (arguing that the combination of these factors brought the decline of PT and the consequential election of Bolsonaro).

75 De Sa e Silva, From car wash to Bolsonaro, at S95–S96.

76 João Victor Freitas, A plan to share FCPA penalties with Brazil has been thwarted… by Brazil: The Supreme Court's invalidation of the Lava Jato foundation, Global Anti-Corruption Blog (May 3, 2019), https://globalanticorruptionblog.com/2019/05/03/a-plan-to-share-fcpa-penalties-with-brazil-has-been-thwarted-by-brazil-the-supreme-courts-invalidation-of-the-lava-jato-foundation/ (explaining the background and the reasoning behind this decision).

77 Marjorie Marona & Fábio Kerche, From the banestado case to operation car wash: Building an anti-corruption institutional framework in Brazil, *Dados: Revista Ciênca Sociais*, 64(3), (2021), at 4–5.

78 Brazil's Carwash Task Force Wins Transparency International Anti-Corruption Award, *Transparency International*. (December 3, 2016), https://www.transparency.org/en/press/brazils-carwash-task-force-wins-transparency-international-anti-corruption.

79 Deltan Dallagnol, *A luta contra a corrupção: A Lava Jato e o futuro de um país marcado pela impunidade*, (2017); De Sa e Silva, From car wash to Bolsonaro.

80 Ana Luiza Aranha, Lava Jato and Brazil's web of accountability institutions: A turning point for corruption control? In *Corruption and the Lava Jato Scandal in Latin America*, 94, 109(27) (*Paul Lagunes, Jan Svejnar* ed., 2020).

81 Paul Lagunes et al., President Bolsonaro's promises and actions on corruption control, *Revista Direito GV*, 17(1), (2021), 24.

82 *See* Office of the Federal Public Prosecutor, Republic of Parana, Task Force Lava Jato (Indictment against Lula) (2016), https://www.conjur.com.br/dl/denuncia-lula-apartamento.pdf (last visited October 24, 2021).

83 *See* Office of the Federal Public Prosecutor, Republic of Parana, Task Force Lava Jato (Indictment against Lula) (2016) at 5–10, 18–21.

84 Michener & Pereira, A great leap forward for democracy and the rule of law?, at 481–82.

85 *Binding Nature of UN Treaty Body Decisions Rejected by Brazil's Electoral Court*, Opinio Juris (September 14, 2018), http://opiniojuris.org/2018/09/14/binding-nature-of-un-treaty-body-decisions-rejected-by-brazils-electoral-court/ (last visited October 24, 2021).

86 Carol Proner et al., Comentários a uma sentença anunciada: O processo Lula [comments on an announced sentenced: The lula process] (2017) is a gathering of the expertise of prominent Brazilian legal experts to criticize the Lula trial.

87 *Juristas estrangeiros se dizem chocados e defendem libertação de Lula* [*Foreign Jurists Say They are Shocked and Defend Lula's Release*], Folha de Sao Paolo (August 11, 2019), https://www1.folha.uol.com.br/poder/2019/08/juristas-estrangeiros-se-dizem-chocados-e-defendem-libertacao-de-lula.shtml.

88 *Release of tapped phone calls between Lula and Rousseff sparks mass protests in Brazil*, The Guardian (March 17, 2016), https://www.theguardian.com/world/2016/mar/17/release-tapped-phone-calls-lula-rousseff-deepens-brazil-chaos.

89 *Exclusive: Leaked chats between Brazilian judge and prosecutor who imprisoned Lula reveal prohibited collaboration and doubts over evidence*, The Intercept (June 9, 2019), https://theintercept.com/2019/06/09/brazil-lula-operation-car-wash-sergio-moro/.

90 *Exclusive: Leaked chats between Brazilian judge and prosecutor who imprisoned Lula reveal prohibited collaboration and doubts over evidence*, The Intercept (June 9, 2019), https://theintercept.com/2019/06/09/brazil-lula-operation-car-wash-sergio-moro/.

91 Ezequiel Gonzales-Ocantos, The criminalization of corruption in Latin America: Causes and consequences of Lava Jato, *Youtube* (October 13, 2020) https://www.youtube.com/watch?v=C0SiWJ1QnDY&ab_channel=DavidRockefellerCenterforLatinAmericanStudies (between the 18- and 35-minute marks). Note, however, that these focus groups were organized prior to the revelations of the collusion between Dallagnol and Moro—it is reasonable to conclude that later surveys would have revealed even more division and skepticism.

92 Brazilian Judge Strikes Down Lula da Silva's Graft Convictions, *Financial Times* (March 8, 2021), https://www.ft.com/content/41f096a3-f091-485f-873b-d107c61d570d.

93 *MPF reconhece prescrição e pede arquivamento de ação contra Lula* [*MPF Recognizes Limitation and Asks for a Filing of Lawsuit Against Lula*], Con Jur Brazil (December 7, 2021), https://www.conjur.com.br/2021-dez-07/mpf-arquivamento-acao-lula-triplex.

94 Lagunes et al., President Bolsonaro's promises and actions on corruption control, at 14.

95 Emilio Peluso Meyer, Constitutional Erosion in Brazil, (2020), 97–98.

96 For support for Dallagnol and Moro, *see Fraudes de Deltan Revelam Seu Interesse Na Pec Do CNMP, Diz Advogado*, Congresso Em Foco (October 19, 2021) https://congressoemfoco.uol.com.br/temas/ministerio-publico/fraudes-de-deltan-revelam-seu-interesse-na-pec-do-cnmp-diz-advogado/ (documenting that the complaints filed against Dallagnol were left unprocessed until the statute of limitations expired); *A saída de Sérgio Moro do governo*, Associação Juízes para a Democracia (April 24, 2020), https://www.ajd.org.br/noticias/2594-nota-publica-a-saida-de-sergio-moro-do-governo (documenting criticism of the left leaning judicial associations against the Lava Jato campaign).

97 *Head of Brazil's "Car Wash" Anti-Graft Task Force Quits with Team's Future in Doubt*, Reuters (September 15, 2020), https://www.reuters.com/article/uk-brazil-corruption-idUSKBN25S614.

98 *Brazil Dismantles Anti-Corruption Task Force behind Lava Jato*, Organized Crime and Corruption Research Project (February 8, 2021), https://www.occrp.org/en/daily/13817-brazil-dismantles-anti-corruption-task-force-behind-lava-jato.

99 *Hacked Chats Expose Questionable Methods Used by Swiss and Brazilian Prosecutors*, Swissinfo.ch (February 8, 2021), https://www.swissinfo.ch/eng/hacked-chats-expose-questionable-cooperation-between-swiss-and-brazilian-prosecutors/46371446.

100 Aneta B. Spendzharova & Milada Anna Vachudova, Catching up? Consolidating Liberal Democracy in Bulgaria and Romania After EU Accession, *World European*

Policy, 35(39), (2012) (explaining the relevance of the rule of law conditionality for entrenchment of liberal-democratic values). For a critic, see Radosveta Vassileva, Threats to the rule of law: The pitfalls of the cooperation and verification mechanism, *European Public Law*, 26(3), (2020).

101 Interview with a Romanian judicial official, June 2021.

102 Generally, see Cristina Nicolescu-Waggonner, No rule of law, no democracy: Conflicts of interest, corruption, and elections as democratic deficits, (2016).

103 Radu Carp, *The Struggle for the Rule of Law in Romania as an EU Member State: The Role of the Cooperation and Verification Mechanism, The Utrecht Law Review*, 10(1), (2014).

104 *See* Martin Mendelski, Europeanization and the Rule of Law: Towards a Pathological Turn, *Southeastern Europe*, 40(346), (2016), 358–359.

105 Fictitious employment is employment, usually within the public administration or state-owned enterprise, in which a person, usually a party loyalist, is employed in a certain post, often without having any qualifications for it or at a post created to fit the qualifications of the person and not the needs of the public office or enterprise. *See Romania's Dragnea Faces New Trial Over Trump Inauguration Lobby*, Balkan Insight (May 17, 2021), https://balkaninsight.com/2021/05/17/romanias-dragnea-faces-new-trial-over-trump-inauguration-lobby/ (detailing charges against the ex-Romanian prime minister made for crimes of lower material value).

106 *See generally* Kieran Williams et al., Explaining lustration in Central Europe: A "Post-Communist Politics" *Approach, Democratization*, 12(22), (2005) (explaining the relevance of the process); Bogdan Iancu, Post-Accession Constitutionalism with a Human Face: Judicial Reform and Lustration in Romania, *The European Constitutional Law Review*, 6(28), (2010) (explaining the relevance of lustration for the Romanian judiciary).

107 Kieran Williams et al., Explaining lustration in Central Europe: A "post-communist politics" *Approach, Democratization*, 12(22), (2005) (explaining the relevance of the process); Bogdan Iancu, Post-Accession Constitutionalism with a Human Face: Judicial Reform and Lustration in Romania, *The European Constitutional Law Review*, 6(28), (2010) (explaining the relevance of lustration for the Romanian judiciary).

108 Mendelski, 15 years of anti-corruption in Romania.

109 Anca Jurma, DNA (National Anti-Corruption Department): A specialized structure for combating high level corruption in Romania, *Journal of Eastern-European Criminal Law*, 9(9), (2014), 10.

110 Ramona Coman & Cristina Dallara, *Judicial Independence in* Transition, 233 Beiträge zum ausländischen öffentlichen Recht und Völkerrecht, (2012), 835–881.

111 Mungiu-Pippidi, Explaining Eastern Europe, at 106.

112 Jurma, DNA (National Anti-Corruption Department), at 16; David Clark, Romania's corruption fight is a smokescreen to weaken its democracy, *The Guardian* (January 20, 2017), https://www.theguardian.com/world/2017/jan/10/romanias-corruption-fight-is-a-smokescreen-to-weaken-its-democracy.

113 *Corruption Perception Index*, *Transparency International*, https://www.transparency.org/en/cpi/2020/index/nzl (last visited December 24, 2021) (detailing that the perception of corruption in the country oscillated between 2012 and 2020 but remained rather high).

114 *World Justice Rule of Law Index 2020*, *World Justice Project*, https://worldjusticeproject.org/rule-of-law-index/pdfs/2020-Romania.pdf (last visited December 12, 2021) (detailing the discrepancy between the relatively high law and order values and the quality of criminal justice system).

115 Radu Andrei Pârvulescu, Decoupled Rationalisation: Judicial Anticorruption and Fragmentation of Parliament and the Magistracy, 1, 15 (2021).

116 As evidenced by the U.S. government's recent designation of corruption as a core national security issue, this designation is becoming more common.
117 Mendelski, 15 years of anti-corruption in Romania, at 14–15.
118 Mungiu-Pippidi, Explaining Eastern Europe, at 110.
119 Florin Abraham, *Romania Since The Second World War: A Political, Social and Economic History*, (2017), 120–122.
120 *See generally* Ionut Chiruta, Challenging the rule of law in Romania: The metamorphosis of political discourse towards populism, *Problems of Post-Communism*, 70(1), (2023), 76–93.
121 *See generally* Ionut Valentin Chiruta, Using the past in populist communicational strategies: How the memory of securitate is instrumentalised in Romanian politics. *Populism*, 3(223), (2020) (explaining the exploitation of fears created in the past in the politics of contemporary Romania).
122 *See generally* Judgments of the Constitutional Court of Romania Decision No. 392 (Rom.) (June 2016); Judgments of the Constitutional Court of Romania Decision No. 405 (Rom.) (June 2016).
123 Judgment of the Constitutional Court of Romania Decision No. 51 (Rom,) (February 2016), https://perma.cc/59W8-ZG8S.
124 Daniel Brett, Romania's protests: A response to a three-pronged assault on anti-corruption measures, *LSE European Politics and Policy (EUROPP) Blog* (2017), https://blogs.lse.ac.uk/europpblog/2018/09/19/why-romanias-protests-have-failed-to-bring-about-real-change/.
125 Dragos Călin, The Romanian judicial system: Current issues and the necessity of avoiding regress, In *Strategies for Strengthening Democracy*, 30 years after the Fall of the Berlin Wall, 15–21 (2019).
126 Constitutional Court of Romania, Judgment 358/2018 (May 30, 2018), https://lege5.ro/Gratuit/gi4dgojyga4q/decizia-nr-358-2018-asupra-cererii-de-solutionare-a-conflictului-juridic-de-natura-constitutionala-dintre-ministrul-justitiei-pe-de-o-parte-si-presedintele-romaniei-pe-de-alta-parte (last visited December 24, 2021).
127 Kövesi v. Romania, 318 *European Court of Human Rights* (2020).
128 *Parliament wins its battle: Kövesi to become first EU Public Prosecutor*, Euractiv (September 25, 2019), https://www.euractiv.com/section/justice-home-affairs/news/parliament-wins-its-battle-kovesi-to-be-the-first-eu-public-prosecutor/.
129 Mario Luis Grangeia & Joris Alberdingk Thijm, In the name of integrity? Anticorruption discourse of Brazilian operation Lava Jato, *Latin American Research Review*, (2024), 1–21.
130 Bogdan Iancu, The evolution and gestalt of the Romanian constitution, In Armin von Bogdandy, Peter M. Huber, and Sabrina Ragone (eds), *The Max Planck Handbooks in European Public Law: Volume II: Constitutional Foundations*, (2023).
131 Garoupa & Ginsburg, *Judicial Reputation*.
132 Rodney L. Mott, Judicial influence, *American Political Science Review*, 30(295), (1936).
133 Gerard S. Gryski, et al., Models of state high court decision making in sex discrimination cases, *Journal of Polymer Research*, 48(143), (1986) (explaining how this mechanism worked concerning sex discrimination cases).
134 Eyal Benvenisti, Margin of appreciation, consensus, and universal standards, *New York University Journal of International Law and Politics (JILP)*, 31(843), (1999) (explaining how the search for a consensus within the ECtHR and the court's rejection to act as a supranational voice of rationality and morality may be harmful in the long run).
135 For a critique of this stance, *see* Gianluigi Palombella, *Theory, Realities and Promises of Inter-Legality*, in Inter-Legality 375 (Jan Klabbers & Gianluigi Palombella, eds., 2019). For an overview of the case, *see* The International Court

of Justice, Jurisdictional Immunities of the State (Germany v. Italy: Greece intervening), https://www.icj-cij.org/en/case/143.

136 Mark B. Rotenberg, Politics, personality and judging: The lessons of brandeis and frankfurter on judicial restraint, *Columbia Law Review*. 83, 1863 (1983) (reviewing bruce allen murphy, the brandeis/frankfurter connection (1982); h.n. hirsch, enigma of felix frankfurter (1981)).

137 Richard A. Posner, What do judges and justices maximize? (The Same Thing Everybody Else Does), *The Supreme Court Economic Review*, 3(14), (1993).

138 Michael H. Cardozo, Judicial reputation evaluated: The Cardozo instance. *Cardozo Law Review*, 12, (1990), 1915, 1917.

139 For the uses of judicial reputation in predicting appointments, *see* Thomas J. Miceli & Metin M. Coşgel, Reputation and judicial decision-making, *Journal of Economic Behavior and Organization*, 23(31), (1994).

140 Garoupa & Ginsburg, *Judicial Reputation*, at 28–35.

141 Garoupa & Ginsburg, *Judicial Reputation*, at 31.

142 Garoupa & Ginsburg, *Judicial Reputation*, at 30–31.

143 Tracey E. George & G. Mitu Gulati, Courts of good and Ill Repute: Garoupa and ginsburg's judicial reputation: A comparative theory. *University of Chicago Law Review*, 83, (2016), 1683, 1684.

144 The Federalist No. 78, at 402 (Alexander Hamilton) (Gideon ed., 2001).

145 Garoupa & Ginsburg, *Judicial Reputation*, at 24–25.

146 Garoupa & Ginsburg, *Judicial Reputation*, at 82.

147 Garoupa & Ginsburg, *Judicial Reputation*, at 24.

148 Garoupa & Ginsburg, *Judicial Reputation*, at 22.

149 Garoupa & Ginsburg, *Judicial Reputation*, at 60 (explaining that judges may want to impose their own visions of justice).

150 Garoupa & Ginsburg, *Judicial Reputation*, at 141–66.

151 Garoupa & Ginsburg, *Judicial Reputation*, at 171.

152 Garoupa & Ginsburg, *Judicial Reputation*, at 15.

153 Garoupa and Ginsburg, *Judicial Reputation* at 15.

154 *Cf*. John O. Haley, The civil, criminal and disciplinary liability of judges, 54 *The American Journal of Comparative Law*, 281, (2006) (presenting a comparative overview of accountability of judges in the United States).

155 *See* Katarzyna Gajda-Roszczynialska & Krystian Markiewicz, Disciplinary proceedings as an instrument for breaking the rule of law in Poland, *Hague Journal on the Rule of Law* [H.J.R.L.], 12(451), (2020) (Neth.) (explaining how the Polish government promoted disciplinary sanctioning of judges that was often based on their views concerning the legitimacy of changes that the government made to the legal system).

156 *See generally* John Henry Merryman & Rogelio Pérez-Perdomo, The civil law tradition: An Introduction to the Legal Systems of Europe and Latin America (4th ed. 2018) (presenting a comparative overview of civil law systems).

157 Garoupa & Ginsburg, *Judicial Reputation*, at 50, 53.

158 *See* Michal Bobek & David Kosař, Global solutions, local damages: A critical study in judicial councils in Central and Eastern Europe, *German Law Journal*, 15, (2014), 1257 (arguing that councils are instrumental in preventing accountability of judges).

159 Garoupa & Ginsburg, *Judicial Reputation*, at 59–60.

160 *See* Pauline T. Kim, Beyond principal-agent theories: Law and the judicial hierarchy, *Northwestern University Law Review* 105, (2011), 535.

161 *See* Federalist Papers, note 144, at 235, 238.

162 Notable exceptions to this rule existed in traditional societies and still exist in some jurisdictions in the United States.

163 *See* Pablo Castillo-Ortiz, The politics of implementation of the judicial council model in Europe, *The European Political Science Review*, 11, (2019), 503 (U.K.) (identifying the different institutional setups of judicial governance in Europe).
164 Garoupa & Ginsburg, *Judicial Reputation*, at 105.
165 While judicial councils exist within common law systems, their role are not equal to judicial councils developed after the Italian model. *See* John J. Parker, The Judicial Office in the United States, *The New York University Law Review*, 23, (1948), 225.
166 *See* Nuno Garoupa & Tom Ginsburg, Guarding the Guardians: Judicial Councils and Judicial Independence, *The American Journal of Comparative Law*, 57, (2009), 103, 106–07.
167 *See* Carlo Guarnieri, Magistratura e Politica: Il Caso Italiano [*The Judicary and Politics: The Italian Case*], *Journal of Political Science Education*, 21(3), (1991), 15.
168 *See generally* Violante, *I Magistrati*, 3–41 (It.) (2009) (explaining the institutional evolution of the Italian judiciary).
169 *See* Patrizia Pederzoli & Carlo Guarnieri, The judicialization of politics, Italian style, *Journal of Modern Italian Studies*, 2(321), (1997), 329 (U.K).
170 Violante, *I Magistrati*, at 26.
171 Romano Canosa & Amedeo Santosuosso, *Il Processo Politico in Italia [Political Process in Italy]*, 23 Critical del Diritto 9 (1982) (explaining the choice of the Italian state to use primarily the judicial means in countering the wave of terrorism that the "years of lead" campaign brought).
172 *See* Matthew Stephenson, When the devil turns… The political foundations of independent judicial review, *The Journal of Legal Studies*, 32(59), (2003) (arguing that political actors do not attempt to capture the judiciary because they count on the balance of power produced by electoral outcomes); *see also*, Violante, *I Magistrati*, at 47 (expressing skepticism of the Italian left toward the judiciary, which they viewed as conservative).
173 *See* Capussela, *The Political Economy of Italy's Decline* at 27 (2018).
174 Manzi, *The Effective Judicial Prosecution of Systemic Political Corruption: Italy*, at 92–95.
175 Guarnieri, note 167, at 142–143.
176 *See generally* Alexander stille, excellent cadavers: The Mafia and the death of the first Italian Republic (1996) (describing the life of magistrate Giovanni Falcone, who spent his career trying to prosecute the Mafia, who then assassinated him for these efforts).
177 Today, more than 60% of countries in the world have some sort of a judicial council that ensures judicial independence. However, in the late 1980s, this percentage was only 10%, and when the council was set up in 1958, there were few large jurisdictions (such as France) outside of the U.S. that had that model. But, compared to France, the Italian judiciary was much more insulated from political control. *See* Garoupa & Ginsburg, *Judicial Reputation*, at 106–107; *see also* Linn A. Hammergren, Do Judicial Councils further judicial reform? *Lessons from Latin America*, 28 (2002) (discussing similar experiences in Latin America).
178 I stress that the full replication of the Italian model was not done in either of the countries; rather, the elements of the Italian model served as a basis for its development by domestic and international legal experts involved in this undertaking. *See* Michal Bobek & David Kosar, Global Solutions, Local Damages: A Critical Study in Judicial Councils in Central and Eastern Europe, *German Law Journal*, 15, (2014),1257, 1268.
179 Garoupa & Ginsburg, *Judicial Reputation*, at 115.
180 Fábio Kerche et al., *The Brazilian Councils of Justice and Public Prosecutor's Office as Instruments of Accountability*, 54 *Revista de Administração Pública* 1334 (2020) (explaining the institutional evolution of the judicial and prosecutorial councils in Brazil).

181 Fábio Kerche, Ministério Público, Lava Jato E Mãos Limpas: Uma Abordagem Institucional [Public Ministry, Lava Jato and Mani Pulite: An Institutional Approach], Lua Nova: Revista de Cultura E Política, 105(6), (2018).
182 Marona & Kerche, From the banestado case to operation car wash, 3.
183 Ezequiel A. Gonzalez-Ocantos, Paula Munoz Chirinos, Nara Pavão, Viviana Baraybar Hidalgo, The Drivers of Prosecutorial Zeal: Institutional Change and Three "Moments" (with Stories from Brazil, Italy, and Beyond). In: *Prosecutors, Voters and the Criminalization of Corruption in Latin America: The Case of Lava Jato*, (2023), 27–73.
184 Fabiano Engelmann, The 'Fight against Corruption' in Brazil from the 2000s: A political crusade through judicial activism, *Journal of Law and Society*, 47, (2020), S75–S78. Also, see Salo Coslovsky, Relational Regulation in the Brazilian Ministério Publico: The Organizational Basis of Regulatory Responsiveness. *Regulation and Governance*, 5(1), 70–89.
185 Marína Urbániková & Katarína Šipulová, Failed expectations: Does the establishment of judicial councils enhance confidence in courts? *German Law Journal*, 19(7), (2018), 2128.
186 Bianca Selejan-Guţan, Romania: Perils of a "Perfect Euro-Model" of judicial council, *German Law Journal*, 19(1708), (2014), 1714.
187 Bianca Selejan-Guţan, Romania: Perils of a "Perfect Euro-Model" of judicial council, *German Law Journal*, 19(1708), (2014), 1714.
188 Bianca Selejan-Guţan, Romania: Perils of a "Perfect Euro-Model" of judicial council, *German Law Journal*, 19(1708), (2014) at 1711.
189 Martin Mendelski, EU-driven judicial reforms in Romania: A success story?, *E. Eur. Pol.*, (28)23, (2012), 32–33.
190 *Cf.* Castillo-Ortiz, The politics of implementation of the judicial council model in Europe, at 513, 515.
191 Radu Andrei Parvulescu, Decoupled rationalisation: Judicial anticorruption and fragmentation of parliament and the magistracy, 14.
192 Edward Luttwak, Italy's Ancien Régime, *Soc'y*, 31(70), (1993) (explaining the international perception of Italy upon revelation of its corrupt scandals in the 1990s).
193 *What did Lava Jato, Brazil's anti-corruption investigation, achieve?*, The Economist (March. 9, 2021), https://www.economist.com/the-economist-explains/2021/03/09/what-did-lava-jato-brazils-anti-corruption-investigation-achieve.
194 For example see Mariana Mota Prado, Fabio Kerche, & Marjorie Marona, Corruption and Separation of Powers: Where do Prosecutors Fit? *Hague Journal on the Rule of Law*, 16, (2024), 643–669.
195 James L. Newell, Magistrates going into politics: Antonio Di Pietro and Italy of Values, In Andrea Mammone, et al. (Eds.), *The Routledge Handbook of Contemporary Italy*, 227–236, (2015).
196 Vercesi, M. The Effects of Personalisation on Party Change in Italy. 10.
197 Meszaros, Caught in an authoritarian trap of its own making?, at S68.
198 Sergip Fernando Moro, Considerações sobre a operação mani pulite. *Revista Centro de Estudos Judiciários*, 8(26), (2004), 58.
199 Nelken, *Stopping the Judges*, *Italian Political*.
200 Brian Mier, et al. Anticorruption and imperialist blind spots: The role of the United States in Brazil's long coup. *Latin American Perspectives*, 50(5), (2023), 29–46.
201 *Mani Pulite, ex console Usa: "di Pietro mi preannunciò l'arresto di Chiesa,"* Il Fatto Quotidiano (August 30, 2012), https://www.ilfattoquotidiano.it/2012/08/30/mani-pulite-ex-console-usa-di-pietro-mi-preannucio-larresto-di-chiesa/338126/ (last visited December 24, 2021).
202 David Nelken, Stopping the judges, *Italian Policy*, 11(187), (1996), 190.

203 *See generally* De Sa e Silva, note 75 (describing the role of former prosecutors in corporate compliance).
204 Vannucci, The controversial legacy of 'Mani Pulite', at 252.
205 Lagunes et al., President Bolsonaro's promises and actions on corruption control, at 17.
206 Tom Ginsburg, *Lawrence Friedman's Comparative Law*, University of Chicago, Public Theory Working Paper (2010).
207 Lawrence M. Friedman, *Toward Comparative Law in the 21st Century: Some Thoughts on the Rule of Law, Legal Culture and Modernity in Comparative Perspective*, 1075–1090 (Kluwer Law International (2002)).
208 Ralf Michaels, *Legal Culture*, (Basedow, Hopt, Zimmermann eds. (2011)).
209 *Compare* Nuno Garoupa & Tom Ginsburg, Hybrid judicial career structures: Reputation versus legal tradition, *Journal of Legal Analysis*, 3(2), (2011), 411, 411–48, *with* Garoupa & Ginsburg, *Judicial Reputation.*
210 Solimine, M. E., Judicial stratification and the reputations of the United States courts of appeals. *Florida State University Law Review*, 32, (2005), 1331, 1331.
211 David Nelken, *Sociology of Legal Culture*, 140–143 (Edward Elgar Publishing, 2020).
212 Jaako Husa, Developing legal system, legal transplants, and path dependence: Reflections on the rule of law, *Chinese Journal of Comparative Law*, 6(130), (2018).
213 Mathias Reimann, The historical school against codification: Savigny, carter, and the defeat of the New York civil code. *American Society of Comparative Law*, 37(95), (1989), 95–119 (explaining the views of Savigny in terms of evolution of law).
214 *See generally* John Bell, Path dependence and legal development, *Tulane Law Review*, 87(787), (2013), 787–810 (describing the relevance of path dependence).
215 Husa, Developing legal system, legal transplants, and path dependence: Reflections on the rule of law.
216 Aranha, Lava Jato and Brazil's web of accountability institutions.
217 Having been established in the Italian legal system by the 1947 Constitution and institutionalized from 1958 onwards, the Italian judicial council cannot be, unlike their Brazilian institutional "siblings," considered a legal transplant, but rather a domestic solution to the question of management of the judicial branch.
218 Manzi, *The Effective Judicial Prosecution of Systemic Political Corruption: Italy*, at 33.
219 *See generally* Dragos Calin, et al., 900 Days of Uninterrupted Siege upon the Romanian Magistracy, A Survival Guide, (2020) (describing efforts of the Romanian judiciary to resist attempts of political control).
220 Michaels, *Legal Culture*, at 6.
221 Della Porta, A judges revolution?, at 11–14.
222 Della Porta, A judges revolution?, at 14.
223 Della Porta, A judges revolution?
224 Nelken, *Sociology of Legal Culture.*
225 Nelken, *Sociology of Legal Culture*, at 103.
226 Pederzoli & Guarnieri, The judicialization of politics, Italian style; *also cf.* Violante, note 37, at 47–66.
227 Pederzoli & Guarnieri, The judicialization of politics, Italian style at 332–334.
228 Marie Manikis & Peter Grbac, Bargaining for justice: The road towards prosecutorial accountability in the plea bargaining process, *Manitoba Law Journal*, 40(85), (2017) (explaining the difference between mandatory and discretionary prosecutions).
229 *See* David Nelken, A legal revolution? The judges and Tangentopoli. In S. Gundle & S. Parker (Eds.), *The New Italian Republic: From the Fall of Communism to the Rise of Berlusconi*, 199–205 (1995).

230 Giuseppe di Federico, *Prosecutorial independence and the democratic requirement of accountability*, *British Journal of Criminology*, 38(3), (1998).
231 Radosveta Vassileva, *Sweet Like Sugar, Bitter Like a Lemon: Bulgaria's CVM Report*, Verfassungsblog (November 16, 2018), https://verfassungsblog.de/sweet-like-sugar-bitter-like-a-lemon-bulgarias-cvm-report/.
232 Gonzalez-Ocantos, Munoz Chirinos, Pavão & Baraybar Hidalgo, note 183, 47–63.
233 David Nelken, *Comparing Legal Cultures*, (1997), 183–98.
234 Mungiu Pippidi, Explaining Eastern Europe; Hein, The fight against government corruption in Romania; Mendelski, 15 years of anti-corruption in Romania; Lagunes & Svejnar, *Corruption and the Lava Jato Scandal in Latin America*; Moro, note 2.
235 See for example, Meszaros, Caught in an authoritarian trap of its own making?; de sa Silva, From car wash to Bolsonaro.
236 Gonzalez-Ocantos, Munoz Chirinos, Pavão & Baraybar Hidalgo, note 183.
237 Luis de Miranda, Ensemblance the transnational genealogy of Esprit de Corps (2020), 1–8.
238 Ezequiel Gonzalez-Ocantos & Viviana Baraybar Hidalgo, *Lava Jato beyond Borders*, *Taiwan Journal of Democracy*, 15(63), (2019) (describing the impact of the operation outside of Brazil).

3 Rule of law challenges in the judicial anti-corruption campaigns

3.1 Introduction

As we have seen in Chapter 2, the judiciary designs leads, and inspires judicial anti-corruption campaigns.[1] The huge number of cases and high-profile individuals accused of corruption offenses make them stand out from ordinary judicial-based fights against corruption. These features of the campaigns and their political ramifications provoke a backlash against the individual prosecutors and create a powerful counternarrative that follows the campaigns. Much of this narrative uses claims based on the interpretations of those targeted by the campaigns or those who oppose their political ramifications.

The opponents of the campaigns have deployed a large spectrum of criticisms focused on the procedural and substantive law and the practices deployed by the police, the prosecutors, and the courts. Frequent use of surprise interrogations, liberal application of pre-trial detention sequences in which plea bargaining witnesses testify (compared to those implicated in their pleas), and liberal interpretation of judicial secrecy were all elements that threatened the impartiality of the courts as they presented the prosecutors with an opportunity to violate the presumption of innocence as a right granted to the defendants.[2] The number of appeals required before a defendant could be incarcerated, the application of specific interpretations of criminal responsibility, and the collusion between the institutionally independent judiciary and other domestic or foreign political actors have also been recognized as key elements that may lead to some rule of law core principles into question.[3] Even worse, the campaigns may become examples of selective justice and, by definition, inefficient in reducing corruption, leading, instead, to its increase. Allowing disproportional power to the judges and prosecutors, which they acquire by prosecuting high-level politicians, represents a critical intervention in the political system, creating or exacerbating a constitutional crisis and challenging the separation of powers.[4] For that reason, the campaigns are sometimes viewed as judicial revolutions or reputation-seeking activities of the judges, motivated by political preferences or the desire to perform democratic guardianship. In the Romanian case, a specific national security policy that, as discussed in Chapter 2, involved the understanding of the high levels of corruption as a national security threat

DOI: 10.4324/9781003334811-3

enabled the involvement of national security agencies in corruption investigations. Some observers go even further, describing the alleged bias of judges and prosecutors as lawfare against political enemies or treatment of corrupt offenses on a similar footing as terrorism.[5] Finally, the campaigns may be understood as foreign interference operations with the ultimate goal of labeling them as violations of sovereignty and the labeling of prosecutors as foreign agents. The collaboration of the prosecutors with foreign investigative or political bodies and the outcomes of the campaigns were framed in a broader narrative that included a particular outlook on world politics. Critical of the campaigns, some authors have used all the aforementioned procedural and legal elements to present the potential of anti-corruption campaigns to become a systematic attack on the rule of law and the economic and political sovereignty of the state.[6]

Those supportive of the campaigns have argued that the complexity of dealing with organized corrupt groups that include highly positioned and powerful political persons, members of the business community, and individuals with ties to organized crime, judicial anti-corruption campaigns justifies the use of diverse legal techniques used to secure evidence, conviction, and the presence of the accused during trial. Pre-trial detention, plea bargaining, admissibility of evidence, and the application of the criminal legal theory to alleged corrupt behavior are all essential elements of the criminal law response to crime and are integral to describing crucial elements of the campaigns.[7] Heightened media scrutiny of high-profile trials exerts significant pressure on all parties involved.[8] Effective communication strategies of the prosecutors that may involve collusion with the media do not necessarily violate the presumption of innocence, particularly in the context of highly polarized and politicized societies.

Such a response does not negate the important legal challenges that go to the core of a nation's political system. Indeed, the campaigns challenge the separation of powers and the system of checks and balances between branches of government.[9] This happens because mass investigations of politically connected individuals charged with corruption by the judiciary may create a shift of powers that would lead it to decide on or influence matters traditionally outside of its direct or indirect competence.[10] In this chapter, by focusing on the legal practices that have shaped the campaigns, we will investigate the claims of their legality and the challenges to the rule of law that they possess.[11]

The main legal tension in judicial anti-corruption campaigns resembles that in other criminal trials and criminal justice policy generally. It is the tension between crime control and fair trial (due process) principles that represents wider dialectics of the criminal process and can be understood to limit one another.[12] Expressed in its essential form, the principle of crime control means that criminal law exists to suppress crime and ensure that the guilty are brought to justice and impunity is bypassed. Such actions prevent crime and strengthen the institutionalized trust in law and order. The primary concern of this model is efficiency, and it resembles an "assembly line." Meanwhile, the due process model favors the accused by granting them procedural rights, which resembles "an obstacle course."[13] The balance between these two principles constitutes a "battle model" of the criminal process in which the process oscillates between two almost mutually exclusive poles.[14] As criminal trials are central to judicial anti-corruption campaigns, this chapter will investigate the rule of law challenges brought against the campaigns, looking at the defendant's position in a criminal trial. This angle emphasizes the fact that, despite all the adverse effects that judicial anti-corruption campaigns may have, the trials remain central to their understanding.[15] In the trials, the principle of equality in arms, essential for the equal position of the prosecution and the defendant, best materializes itself.[16] The trials and their course over the different instances of the judicial organizations provide plenty of opportunities for the courts to rectify the pre-trial behavior of the state.

As in Chapter 2, here in Chapter 3, where we deal with the corruption trials, we perceive a boundary between civil law and common law systems. A boundary that became porous as traditional distinctions between the diverse paths of development of the inquisitorial or the adversarial systems became more unified. Traditionally, the inquisitorial systems to which the three countries in question belonged were less prone to the dichotomy between fair trial and crime control, as the division of roles in the trial was less pronounced. The role of the prosecutors was less of an adversary to the accused; instead—according to the law on the books—served as a representative of the accusations brought forth against the latter. The role of the judge in the trial was that of an active participant who focused on more than just the formal procedural standards and sentencing.[17] The three legal systems considered in this work have undergone significant alterations in the last three decades, making their legal systems more closely resemble adversarial models. In adversarial systems, judges are less interested in the "material truth of the trial," preoccupying themselves more with the procedural aspects of the case.[18] All three have also significantly altered the mode of the career judiciary typical of the civil law systems into a more merit-based model, traditionally typical of common law systems.

3.2 Fair trials, integrity of the criminal trial, and the rule of law

Following the gradual development of human rights-based approaches to the legal systems post-1945, the focus of the analysis of criminal law has shifted toward a more normative theory of the criminal process grounded in fair trial standards.[19] This approach was especially strong in Europe, where the effect of the European Convention on Human Rights has been particularly strong in securing a more uniform approach to criminal procedure.[20] To what extent are the guarantees of fair treatment present in trial systems, what are the prerogatives of the judge to exclude evidence and determine its applicability in the trial, how do the specific acts of the prosecution alter the specific theory of the trial, or how does the implementation of certain institutes such as plea bargaining dispute the elements of truth-seeking as a part of trial[21] are the key questions related to this approach. Fairness requires exercising participatory rights; within the procedural context of a criminal trial."[22]

The examination that focuses on the integrity of the criminal trial builds on this approach to fair trials under a normative theory of criminal trials.[23] The concept explained the judges' ability to protect the integrity of the judicial system and, to a lesser extent, their own offices. This was done mostly through actions focused not only on protecting the rights of the defendant from undue procedural actions but also on protecting public confidence in the legal system. In this sense, the normative validity of the trial rests on the ability of the judiciary to rectify and review the state's pre-trial behavior.[24] The principle of the integrity of criminal trials is essential for ensuring the legitimacy of the trials through ensuring factually accurate adjudicative decisions consistent with other fundamental moral and political values embedded in the legal system."[25] In a broader sense, the integrity of the criminal trials relates to the integrity of the system, where "system" encompasses criminal trials as well as the entire juridical-investigational complex.[26]

Analyzing fair trial standards and the integrity of the judicial system will help assess the rule of law challenges in the campaigns. Many concepts of the rule of law exist, and the leading legal theoreticians have yet to say the final word on the topic. Yet, it is beyond dispute that the rule of law requires judicial independence, and legal certainty. For our analysis, it is essential to note that the fair trial principles and most of the elements comprising the integrity of the judicial systems represent cornerstones of the rule of law as a standard used to judge the system.

Due to difficulties in data gathering, the analysis excludes two important elements of the campaigns: decisions on pre-trial detention and the media's impact on judges and prosecutors. Pre-trial detention is important as the decisions on pre-trial detention may influence the outcome of a particular trial.[27] Indeed, decisions of the courts on pre-trial detention have been widely criticized, and claims were made that their use in corruption prosecutions may have been detrimental to the principle of fairness of the trials. However, a closer look challenges this view. Few, if any, applications to the European Court of Human Rights (ECtHR) have been made by those investigated or prosecuted for corruption challenging pre-trial detention or the abusive behavior of the prosecutors or police investigators in Italy and Romania. It is beyond doubt that the conditions in pre-trial detention in all three jurisdictions, but especially in Italy and Romania, were below the national and international standards to which the two countries adhered.[28] However, the conditions in the pre-trial detention were not used as a weapon to extort confessions from the prisoners; instead, those faced with pre-trial detention in corruption investigations were treated like ordinary criminals, which, while unexpected for many of them, can hardly be called discriminatory.[29] An exception to this is Sergio Moro's decision for Lula to remain in pre-trial detention during the trial. Moro justified this decision on the defendant's accusation of corruption, which may have violated the presumption of innocence and will be reviewed in the section of this chapter dedicated to Brazil. Likewise, there can be no doubt that the media bias and the atypical involvement of prosecutors and magistrates in the media campaigns discussed in Chapter 2, influenced the presumption of innocence[30] by creating a particular atmosphere of legal and political mobilization surrounding the campaigns. Yet, determining which of the judges, in what specific case, and in what way was influenced and what this contributed to is extremely difficult. An analysis of the judicial discourse conducted by the researchers in Brazil has confirmed that the prosecutors gathered in the Lava Jato Task Force have succeeded in spreading their framing of corruption to the justices of the Brazilian Supreme Court.[31] It is reasonable to suggest that this may have impacted the decision to reverse the longstanding practice of the Brazilian Supreme Court to allow the defendants to stay out of prison (or detention) before exhausting all appeals against the judgment. However, the decision to reverse this practice does not prove the bias against the defendants. It does not equate, as we see in comparative practice, with a violation of the presumption of innocence.[32] In a broader sense, it should be noted that the presumption of innocence is extremely difficult to preserve in modern times due to the mass availability of media resources and their polarizing nature. In countries where the public perceives the political class as corrupt, as in Italy in the 1990s, even a limited outreach of the prosecutors to the media turned them into heroes as a desire to end impunity was shared by both the media and the population. In Brazil, where the communication of the prosecutors with the media was massive and a part of an elaborate media strategy, the practice did not prevent a resurgence of a counternarrative among the general population and the legal professionals.[33] In Romania, there is little evidence to suggest that the presumption of innocence affected the extremely high conviction rate. Thus, automatically qualifying such practices as discriminatory or rule of law violations seems inappropriate.

Leaving these two important topics aside due to data limitations and somewhat overhyped importance, this study focuses on three cases in which courts have reviewed the key episodes of the judicial anti-corruption campaigns. These episodes may be considered ley as they involved actors who claimed they were victims of witch hunts and lawfare, such as Silvio Berlusconi and Luiz Ignacio Lula da Silva. In the case of Romania, where no key trial has emerged, we review the CCR as its jurisprudence revealed the key negatively perceived assessment of the campaign, the collaboration between the prosecutors and the SRI. All three cases also allow us to look at the judiciary's role more broadly. Whereas in Chapter 2, we looked at the specific task forces or pools as places where the judicial reputation emerged as a key driver of the campaigns, in this chapter, we look at how the judiciary as a whole defended or failed to defend the integrity of the criminal process and the fairness of criminal trials. In Italy's Mani Pulite (1992–2000), the blurred line between corruption and extortion influenced how magistrates investigated entrepreneurs who bribed officials and politicians. This ambiguity allowed business leaders to potentially portray themselves as victims of extortion rather than willing participants in corruption. The Brazilian Lava Jato campaign is explored through a key trial that implicated former (and current) President Lula as the leader of a corrupt network dominating state-owned enterprises and politics. Lastly, the study analyzes Romania's anti-corruption efforts, focusing on the Constitutional Court of Romania's review of crucial elements such as evidence usage, crime classification, and judicial independence. This is followed by a discussion in which we examine how much the gathering of evidence is central to the prosecutions. While this may seem like a legal exercise of dubious worth, it is, in fact, central to our understanding of the judicial anti-corruption campaigns. The quintessential meaning of evidence collection dictates interpretations of substantive law and the procedural actions taken by the judiciary. Also, including both procedural and substantive issues allows us to better grasp and qualify the alleged rule of law violations, as it doesn't limit this concept to only one dimension of criminal law.

3.3 Corruption and extortion in the Italian judicial anti-corruption campaign Mani Pulite

Numerous cases of bribery revealed in Mani pulite showed that citizens and companies normalized corruption as part of the rules of the game and were willing to pay bribes to obtain the benefits allocated as a result.[34] Writing before the beginning of the Mani pulite, Antonio di Pietro, one of the campaign's leading prosecutors, called this setting where corrupt exchanges take place the "environment of extortion."[35] By this, he referred to a climate in which no specific actions were required to extort the bribes from the private individuals and companies—the public officials expected payments, and the private individuals expected that they should pay.

Indeed, the Italian Penal Code recognized extortion as one of the two leading corrupt criminal offenses, alongside corruption. The distinction between the two is rooted in the 19th-century codification of criminal law in the central Italian region of Tuscany. Extortion is not a specialized form of corruption but a special form of coercion wherein the public official uses fear of public power to obtain illegal profits by violence, deception, or exploitation of the error of others.[36] The origin of the term comes from the Latin *concusse*, meaning the shaking of the tree in order to collect the fruit. Historically, the legal roots of the criminal offense may be traced to the recognition of extortion conducted by the magistrates and other public officials of ancient Rome.[37] Its similarity with the crime of corruption is that the public agent collects a benefit from a private individual. However, the crime itself belonged to a family of crimes against property, which further distinguished it from corruption, considered either an element of fraud or a crime against public administration.[38] The gradual codification of modern Italian criminal law blurred the original distinction between the extortion of a citizen and the instigation to corrupt someone. The crimes reflected in the understanding that extortion may be committed through coercion and inducement were lost, making coercion the ultimate mode for committing the act.[39] However, understanding what constitutes coercion and the relationship between the individual wills of the public official and that of the extortee became crucial for the campaigns.[40]

The line between the two crimes was more evident in theory than in practice.[41] Both criminal offenses were, at least in 1992 at the onset of the Mani pulite campaign, divided into two sub-elements. Corruption was divided into proper, where the bribe is given to obtain an act of a public official contrary to the duties of office, and improper, where the bribe is taken to omit delay or to commit an act contrary to the official duty.[42] Meanwhile, extortion was divided into two elements: induced, where the will of the extortee was manipulated using his wrong perceptions or errors in perception and judgment, and real, which refers to situations in which the will of the extortee was constrained through threat. This division resulted in two main problems. The first problem was that the fine line distinguishing induced extortion and instigation of corruption was very narrow. That narrowness enabled the prosecutors to start the investigations with extortion charges, later requalifying the criminal offense as corruption or instigation of corruption.[43] This led to criticisms that the entire concept of the environment of extortion does not help delineate between corruption and extortion and that those willing to testify against allegedly corrupt public officials are themselves "members of a community of evildoers."[44] Such criticism also pointed to the second problem, which concerns the previous behavior of the two sides of the corrupt transaction. Accepting the notion of environmental extortion—meaning, in the absence of a concrete action of the public official by which they impact the will of the private person—potentially meant that there would always be grounds for claiming that the will of a private actor has been constrained.[45] The inability of the legislators to amend the Penal Code and the strong divisions in the academic community created a gap in practice and implementation in which the courts pointed out a way toward a division between extortion and corruption, just as they resolved other interpretative gaps concerning the interpretation of what an official act is.[46]

3.3.1 The courts and the line between corruption and extortion

The jurisprudential stances taken by the High Court of Cassation during the Mani pulite campaign defined the nature of extortion. In one concrete case that dealt with building permits in the city of Monza, in which the courts of first and second instance found both the real estate developer and the local politicians guilty of the crime of corruption, the High Court of Cassation reversed the decisions of the lower courts and found that the entrepreneur moved to pay the bribes after waiting for a year to do so, following his (entrepreneur's) realization that this is the only way to complete the development project. The Court, in this case, followed the dynamics of payments and the constraint of the will of the entrepreneur, ignoring the fact that negotiations that preceded the payment of the bribes bore a closer resemblance to a corrupt pact than a constraint of the will of the entrepreneur.[47] Furthermore, the

Supreme Court of Cassation recognized the environment of extortion as an expressive phrase used to describe parts of the Italian public sector and as a defense in cases where a person was charged with corruption. This environment of extortion resembled a "tacit convention of codified rules" that obscures the exact nature of the relationship between the extorter and the victim.[48]

The existence of extortion as a separate and important form of graft had a very direct consequence for the anti-corruption judicial campaign. It allowed many entrepreneurs engaged in corrupt networks to simply claim that they had been the victims of an extorter—sometimes even if they had been found guilty of corruption in the first-instance judgment.[49] Participants in the criminal system of corruption would voluntarily offer information to the prosecutors before another defendant would be in a position to incriminate them, creating a multitude of witnesses and informants.[50] Jurisprudence seemed to stand on a similar position; it found that the environment of extortion allowed for the exemption of actions of the extortee from punishment even in those situations when the actions taken by the extortee were not a result of a feeling of fear developed by a direct threat but to avoid or prevent further economic harm.[51] This did not necessarily correspond to the truth; on many occasions, the entrepreneurs were more likely to offer bribes than the public administrators were to ask them.[52] At the same time, for prosecutors, this has allowed an easier approach for public officials and politically exposed persons[53] who were often targeted in the campaigns through judgments that would not progress beyond pre-trial as the judges eventually refused the evidence gathered through claims that the extortion was insubstantial.[54]

The existence of the environment of extortion, both as a legal construct and as the *de facto* state of affairs in certain sectors of the Italian public administration could be said to have contributed to a more lenient policy toward entrepreneurs. These can be demonstrated through two examples: the Fininvest trial and the investigations against FIAT, at the time, one of the leading carmakers in Italy and continental Europe. Both FIAT and Fininvest were among the biggest companies in Italy.[55]

In the Fininvest trial, which was one of the leading trials of the Mani pulite campaign, the Fininvest representatives charged with corruption from the very onset of the investigation took the stance that the company was a victim of extortion and that all payments that were made were authorized by Paolo Berlusconi, Silvio's brother who was one of the directors of the company.[56] Such a defensive strategy was aimed at protecting Silvio Berlusconi, the head of the Fininvest group and the prime minister of Italy when the investigation was launched. The courts' assessment of Silvio Berlusconi's case varied throughout the six-year process. The Court of First Instance convicted him, the Court of Appeals reversed this judgment and found him not guilty, and the High Court of Cassation finally acquitted him.[57] The main point of contention was whether Berlusconi, as a *de facto* leader of Fininvest, could have authorized the payments. The court concluded that the mere fact that Berlusconi held a leading role in Fininvest was insufficient to establish his role in the payments made to the financial police and that, in any event, Fininvest was a victim of extortion.[58] Additionally, the court took note of the testimonies of Silvio Berlusconi's brother, Paolo, who claimed that he, not his brother, issued the orders to disburse the payments for the corrupt officials of the financial police, finding that the proven communication between Silvio Berlusconi and one of the persons that were to disburse the payments was not enough to establish his criminal responsibility for the acts.[59] Strictly speaking, it could be said that in assessing the responsibility of the two Berlusconis, the courts did not make much of the environmental extortion, focusing instead on the quality of evidence leading to the person who authorized the bribes. The court implicitly recognized that the environmental extortion of the financial police was on such a scale that it chose to accept as logical the assertion that Paolo Berlusconi, as one of the managers of the company, had full discretion in deciding to pay for requested bribes without even notifying his brother, the leader of the company.[60]

Unlike Fininvest, which defended itself by claiming to be a victim of extortion, FIAT approached the Mani pulite investigation by publicly negating that it ever financed political parties through the payment of bribes.[61] In early 1993, a number of its highly positioned individuals began to collect statements to document instances of the company's extortion by public officials.[62] In April 1993, FIAT's main owner, Giovanni Agnelli, spoke of the need to support the magistrates carrying out the Mani pulite campaign, and one of FIAT's leading executives, Cesare Romiti, submitted a list of instances concerning extortion to the prosecutors. This event was largely perceived as a trade-off between the prosecutors and the company.[63] As the prosecutors investigating FIAT observed themselves, could it not have been possible for the company to punish the managers who committed corruption or use the newspapers in which the company owned shares to publish allegations of corruption of public officials?[64] Still, the prosecutors valued Romiti's deposition of evidence and Agnelli's statements as mobilizing other entrepreneurs to denounce widespread instances of extortion by public officials.

Indeed, many mid-level FIAT managers were tried for corruption, for example, in cases which involved public procurement in the area of city transport and illegal financing of political parties in the regions of Veneto, Lombardia, and Piedmont.[65] In 2000, the High Court of Cassation sentenced Cesare Romiti of FIAT to an eleven-month prison sentence for the crimes of illegal party financing but was absolved of tax fraud due to the fact that the law was liberalized in the meantime.[66] Both this epilogue and that of the Fininvest scandal were unconvincing for many observers who felt that compared to Fininvest, FIAT was let off the hook easily as its owner, Agnelli, and Romiti were not charged for every crime that they possibly controlled due to political reasons and because of their public support for the campaign.[67]

3.3.2 Legislative reform

During and after the Mani pulite, many proposals for the reform of the two criminal offenses were forwarded. Those interested primarily in a stricter response against corruption argued for a reconfiguration of the approach to the legal good protected through criminalizing corrupt offenses. Initially, the value protected by the criminalization of both corruption and extortion by a public official was the prestige of public administration. Gradually, these values began to be understood as related to the functionality of the market and the prevention of "the threat for the rule of law, democracy, and human rights."[68] Proposals launched by the magistrates involved in the Mani pulite campaign and the domestic legal experts strongly advocated for a more efficient penal and evidentiary policy in reforming the two criminal offenses. The proposals envisaged a policy of mild sanctions for the private person who would repent and report the act of corruption within one year from its commission.[69] Recognizing, however, that the testimony of private individuals gives them (and the prosecutors) significant leverage over those investigated in the public sector, it was proposed that extortion be eliminated as a separate criminal offense.[70] The proposal was seen as giving excessive investigatory powers to the judiciary and was rejected, with the country retaining its legislative framework until 2012.[71] It took until 2003 for the jurisprudence of the High Court of Cassation to evolve toward an understanding that the environment of extortion and fear of public power are not the key, or rather not the only factors which judges and prosecutors must focus on in establishing the facts of the case. Following the judgment of the High Court of Cassation in September 2003, the earlier extensive interpretation was somewhat limited, and the judges were now expected to focus on the very act of making a threat to ascertain the victim's psychological state.[72] As this decision was made after the end of the campaign, it had less of an effect on high-profile individuals.

In 2012, acting under pressure from international organizations, Italy moved to reform its anti-corruption legislation. One of the main objections raised by the foreign observers was that extortion through passive bribery may be used as a defense in cases of international and domestic corruption. This stance did not mean that Italy should remove extortion from the list of corrupt offenses or subsume the behavior in question as bribery but to "thoroughly examine the practical application of the offense."[73] Also, the claims of the "environment of extortion" present in the jurisprudence of the High Court of Cassation, although absent from law, led many European observers to push for a reform needed to resolve what they believed was a culture of impunity for many domestic bribers in the private sector.[74] As a result of this external pressure, extortion was transformed from a crime that had two modes of operation (real and inducive) into one with only coercion as a mode of operation. The second mode, that of inducement, became a separate criminal offense. Still, this did not resolve all difficulties in distinguishing between the criminal offenses of extortion and corruption. The criteria by which the delimitation should be made were the fear of public power, whether the acts of a private entity lead to the prevention of damages or enrichment,[75] and whether public officials conducted concrete actions to constrain the will of the private person.[76]

The proposal to unite corruption and extortion into a single crime would be desirable in a situation where the extortion environment exists, as it would make evidence gathering much easier. The absence of legislative initiative in this direction forced the prosecutors to explore the tactics that relied on the ambiguities of the distinction between corruption and extortion. Such a strategy favored private-sector collaborators at the expense of public officials. From the standpoint of the integrity of the criminal trial, it may be observed that this was done by sacrificing the truth-seeking activity of the trial at the expense of securing the evidence.

3.4 The trial(s) of Luiz Ignacio Lula da Silva

In the eyes of the Brazilian public, the press conference of Deltan Dallagnol, the leading prosecutor of the Lava Jato Task Force, in which the indictment against Lula was announced, was one of the defining moments of the campaign. Dallagnol used PowerPoint presentation slides with Lula at the center to claim that most aspects of corrupt behavior in Brazil are linked to the current and, at the time, former President. Recognized for his fight against poverty, Lula entered politics in the 1970s when Brazil was still under military rule as a union activist. The Workers Party, which he joined in the 1980s, became a leading party in the country. In a decade in which it was still believed that neoliberalism was the answer to most of the world's economic problems, Lula represented an outlier: a leftist president who created massive state-run programs of inequality reduction,[77] and successfully elevated the standing of Brazil on the international stage.

Brazil uses the presidential political system, which emphasizes the president's role as a symbol of national unity and as a person effectively in charge of the country, leading it with cabinet members who exercise strong executive authority.[78] Still, the Brazilian Congress remains an important check on presidents' power. For Lula's party PT, this meant that, while remaining the strongest party in the country, it needed to forge strong coalitions that would overcome the party diversity stemming from political differences and the country's federal structure.[79] These coalitions were often maintained through corrupt payments, in which bribes were traded for favorable votes, as the Mensalao scandal revealed. Lula, the president at the time, was not personally involved or charged during the proceedings but was aware of the practices of vote buying.[80] Therefore, suggesting that the corruption and money laundering cases, the crux of the Lava Jato investigations, were done with Lula's knowledge did not seem far-fetched. Dallagnol went so far as to label Lula the informal commander-in-chief of Lava Jato.[81] Yet, the prosecutors had second thoughts about indicting Lula, doubting if the case against him and the evidence they had were strong enough.[82] What led them to produce the indictment[83] in which they argued that Lula had received the triplex villa in a seaside resort in exchange for donations and a lenient stance toward executive appointments in the national oil company?[84]

3.4.1 Claus Roxin and the Brazilian criminal law

Part of the reason lies in Brazilian law and its interpretations based on a theory of criminal responsibility. The *Tatherrschaft* doctrine, also known as the control theory of perpetration,[85] based on the works of the German jurist Welzel, traveled to Latin American countries in the interpretation of the German jurist Klaus Roxin.[86] Together with other influential aspects of Roxin's thought, this theory underpinned the prosecution of highly positioned perpetrators of mass human rights violations carried out by the military governments of Latin America in the 1970s and the 1980s.[87] The theory holds that the perpetrators of the criminal act dominate the commission of the crime in such a way that they might determine whether or not the crime gets committed and enjoy power or hegemony over the act.[88] It differs from co-perpetration because indirect perpetration means that the indirect perpetrator uses another person who is, essentially, replaceable to commit an act. As such, the indirect perpetrator has vertical control over an organization and the crimes committed by its members. The indirect perpetrator does not necessarily have to know the perpetrator.[89] It also differs from instigation, as the instigator merely encourages the direct perpetrator but has no decisive influence on the commission of the crime itself.

Thus, the theory is relevant for establishing the distinction between the principals and accessories in the criminal procedure, in particular when the perpetration of a criminal act is committed through the use of others.[90] The theory was developed in order to respond to the factual situation in which numerous acts of the organized structures of power as a vehicle of indirect perpetration are used. It allows for the identification of the person who is behind the action. In international criminal law, this theory was applied alongside its "common law cousin" joint criminal enterprise (JCE) in order to ascertain the perpetrators of the crime and those involved as aiders and abetters and to ascertain the effect of indirect participation in the commission of crimes before the International Criminal Court (ICC).[91] In German law, where this concept originated, the theory was applied in cases in which the leaders of the former German Democratic Republic (GDR) were tried for the offenses carried out by them as indirect perpetrators (e.g., the commission of the killings of those fleeing the GDR).[92] Later, the theory was, despite the critique of its author, Roxin, applied to cases of economic crime. Roxin criticized this application, believing that, in economic organizations that are functioning within a legal system of the state, the alleged indirect perpetrators preserve enough individual autonomy that would allow them to refuse the perpetration of the crime. Thus, their involvement in the crime would make them merely co-perpetrators or accomplices and not simply the tools of a person to whom they are subordinated. In Brazil, the Brazilian Supreme Court first applied the theory in the Mensalao case, important as it was the first major judicial epilogue of the crackdown on political corruption that the country experienced, in order to construct an argument for the responsibility of Jose Dirceu, a leading PT member who has been accused of knowing and directing the disbursement of the payments.[93] The funds disbursed by the Mensalao scheme were channeled to members of the parliament in order to obtain their political support for the reforms to the Brazilian social security and taxation system.[94] The decision to apply Roxin's doctrine was not received without criticism in academic circles.

The court was accused of understanding Roxin's control theory from a mode of perpetration as a basis for responsibility similar to the command responsibility of the international criminal law and not as a mode of perpetration of a specific criminal act.[95] It was noted that the Court's reliance on Roxin's theory was absolutely unnecessary in the first place and a result of a reputation and prestige-seeking behavior by the justices of the Supreme Court. As Roxin's theory was developed to determine the criminal responsibility of the person acting behind the scenes, its application makes little sense within a criminal system that does not recognize the difference between direct or indirect perpetration. The Brazilian criminal law in which the concept of offender is that of a unitary offender, as opposed to the differentiated system of other countries, namely Germany where the concept originated. As such, the Brazilian legal system[96] does not distinguish between different modes of participation in the commission of the act. Instead of recognizing that the crimes in question may have been committed by their perpetrators by the omission of their duties, the court implied that the very fact that the control of an undertaking exists is by the fact that a certain person in a position of power of an organization was involved in corrupt transactions.

The Court interpreted Roxin's work as a perfection of the previous work of German theorists without regard for the differences in their approach to the theory of the *Tatherrschaft* and without distinguishing the work of Roxin from that of previous German criminal law theorists.[97] Furthermore, some of the judges of the Court focused on what *they* believed that the theory or, to be more precise, its translation into Portuguese meant. It appears that the German expression *Tatherrschaft* (literally: control of an undertaking) is translated into the Portuguese language as *dominio di fatto* (dominion of the fact), whereas the literal translation of the term would be *dominio di atto* (dominion of the act), giving rise to a slight language confusion, which the Brazilian Supreme Court used as an opportunity to merge the interpretation of the criminal theory not only to Welzel's ideas but also to the control of the facts that the Court saw as decisive for the establishment of criminal liability and to use the theory to declare culpability and not modes of perpetration of the criminal act.[98] Roxin's theory has in mind organizations with disposable (replaceable) members; however, in the concrete case, all members of the organization were critical to the accomplishment of the task. For these reasons, there is a broad consensus that the reason why the theory was applied in the first place was for prestige as the Court—we can speculate—believed that a justification of the decision that would be grounded in comparative legal doctrine and not only in the mere application of the Brazilian criminal code would strengthen the credibility of the decision. The reasoning of the Court that the reference to Roxin strengthens the establishment of criminal responsibility served as an inspiration to the indictment against Lula,[99] of whom, although the investigation did not officially charge him, there was a general suspicion present that all the payments were made with his knowledge and consent.

The indictment against Lula focused on the alleged bribery in which Lula was indicted for passive corruption and money laundering. The crux of the case concerned the accusation that Lula had received an apartment in a tourist resort on the Brazilian coast. This apartment was—it is argued for in the indictment—given to him for allowing the construction company OAS to be favored by Lula's appointees in Petrobras—the company to which OAS was one of the main subcontractors.[100] The apartment in question never officially became a part of Lula's property. Instead, it remained in the property of the real estate developer to whom OAS paid for the apartment. For that reason, the judgment in the first instance refers to him not as an owner but as a user and a beneficiary of the apartment.[101]

Sensing that the full quid pro quo typical of corrupt exchanges was in doubt, the prosecution sought to establish that the corrupt network of OAS and Petrobras operated with the full knowledge of Lula.[102] Specifically, OAS overcharged Petrobras for 3% of the value of the works on the reconstruction of the refinery in North-East Brazil. From that sum, OAS paid bribes to the members of the PT and then President Lula himself. As a part of this scheme, Lula was not to be paid directly but through the acquisition of an apartment—the one of which he never officially became an owner. This was allegedly done on two occasions: in 2009, when the apartment in the seaside resort was built, and in 2014, when it was renovated, apparently following the orders of Lula's family members.[103] By itself, this would lead us to the conclusion that the apartment was "parked" for him to be used at a later stage.[104]

Although the typical corrupt transaction involves a quid pro quo relationship, there are many documented cases in which the corrupt transaction does not result in an official act of the public administrator or an omission of their duty to act.[105] Therefore, the prosecution could have based the indictment solely on the acquisition of the apartment for Lula, attributing the criminal responsibility to the executives of Petrobras and Odebrecht and the moral and political responsibility to Lula, leaving him from the indictment altogether. Such a move would probably be constructed to mean a lack of courage on the side of the prosecutors, but, it would make the evidentiary process much more manageable. Or, alternatively, they could have focused solely on the quid pro quo existence of the corrupt network parts of which paid the bribes to him. However, it seems that what was important for the prosecutors was to rely on the indirect perpetration of corrupt acts committed through the network of appointed "replaceable members"[106] of the corrupt organization. In the concrete case, those replaceable members were the directors of Petrobras. Therefore, the prosecutor introduced the notion of the existence of a corrupt network with Lula as its head in the indictment[107] to establish criminal responsibility for Lula's perpetration and to strengthen a narrative of a corrupt ambient of Brazilian politics similar to those in Italy. Whereas in Italy, the environment of extortion materialized itself as an ambiance in which people were giving bribes even without being specifically asked to do so, in Brazil, it materialized through the existence of a single person who is at the head of a criminal enterprise through knowing and approving most if not all corrupt transactions. The indictment highlighted the verticality of Lula's relationship with the Petrobras directors to assert this argument.[108] For the same purpose, both the indictment and the judgment refer to Lula's press interviews, which, in their view, prove his negligent and ignorant stance toward the persons accused in the *Mensalao* case.[109]

3.4.2 Plea bargaining

Plea bargaining, introduced into the Brazilian legal system at the beginning of the century, became more efficient after the awards in sentence reduction became operational in 2013, and, in particular, after the 2015 precedent in which the STF allowed those convicted of prison charges in the first instance to start serving a sentence immediately before exhausting appeals.[110] More than half of all pleading witnesses have spent time in detention before signing the agreement[111] which raised worries that they had been coerced into entering the plea bargain. Such was the case with Leo Pinheiro, whose plea bargain and a change of testimony led him to Lula's nine-and-a-half-year prison sentence in the first instance. Pinheiro's sentence was suspended from ten to two and a half years.

The proof of an informal corrupt agreement between OAS and Lula was secured via a plea bargaining procedure between the prosecutors and several witnesses, among which most important was the testimony of one of OAS's managers, Leo Pinheiro. He confirmed the existence of an informal agreement between the then-president Lula and the corrupt company executives of Petrobras and OAS in which the executives, as political appointees, were allowed to extract money for the needs of themselves, the company, and Lula's political party.[112] More importantly, he also confirmed that the villa in question was left for Lula's use and that the refurbishments made in it were done at the request of Lula's family members. Pinheiro's plea bargain and the judgment's reliance on it drew a lot of criticism from the legal public. The bargain was completed in accordance with Brazilian law, but given their relative novelty as the scope in which they were applied was defined only in 2013, it generated a lot of legal uncertainty, especially among the older legal cadres.[113]

3.4.3 The judgment

The judgment did not explicitly rely on the *Tatherrschaft* theory. It did refer—just as the indictment did—to the previous *Mensalao* scandal citing the behavior of Lula, who failed to sanction the members of PT for corruption, commenting on how this does resemble the responsibility of war criminals.[114]

But it concluded that it is not a deciding matter for the court to establish whether or not Lula was, indeed, the head of a criminal group that was extorting money from the companies for private political and economic benefit and that the prosecutors made this argument to make the indictment more convincing. Instead, the judgment focused on the renovation of the apartment and the link between this and the contracts awarded from Petrobras to OAS and Odebrecht. As we have stated, the link between the alleged gift of the renovated apartment and Lula's behavior toward the Petrobras directors lacked a concrete quid pro quo. Acknowledging this, the judgment in paragraph 865 cites US law precedents to conclude that there does not necessarily have to be an official act based on which the corrupt exchange will take place, and that influence peddling may be expected as a future behavior.[115] This is even though Lula was not charged with influence peddling but with money laundering and passive corruption. On appeal, the Federal Appellate Court confirmed the first-instance judgment.

3.4.4 The partisanship of Sergio Moro

However, the hacking of the phone of the lead prosecutor, Deltan Dallagnol, made available the messages that he, the other prosecutors of the Lava Jato Task Force, and Judge Sergio Moro were exchanging.[116] The messages revealed collusion between Moro and Dallagnol. Specifically, Dallagnol received instructions on altering the order of investigative measures, the prosecution's media appearances, and information on possible measures needed to collect evidence in the form of witness testimonies.[117] Additionally, the messages revealed Dallagnol's doubts that the indictment relied too much on indirect evidence and on the desire to portray Lula as a head of the criminal enterprise with very little concrete evidence linking him to such a position.[118] As such, the messages point to possible breaches of the code of judicial ethics (and, in the case of Dallagnol, prosecutorial ethics) and the principle of impartiality of judges, thus questioning the decision reached by Judge Moro in the first instance and the jurisdiction that the court had to try the cases in the first place.[119]

Demands for the Supreme Court to re-open Lula's case were at first weak as the evidence of Moro-Dallagnol link was not gathered through legal means—it was merely leaked on the website of the news organization The Intercept.[120] However, when the Brazilian police identified the hacker behind the leaks and gathered the entire corpus of transcripts, the claims made by Lula's defense team were empowered. Following the request of Lula's attorneys, in March 2021, the habeas corpus petition to the Supreme Court led to the annulment of the first-instance judgment claiming that the Federal Court of Curitiba had no jurisdiction over the case and that the leaked messages brought overwhelming evidence of the bias and partiality of judge Moro.[121] The decision divided the judges; part of the Supreme Court wanted to annul the jurisdiction of the court and, in that way, preserve the judicial process as the territorial jurisdiction would not necessitate an obligation for the proceedings to be restarted completely. Even this would represent a major victory for the defense, as the jurisdiction of the court in Curitiba was essentially tied to the fact that Lula was, in fact, behind the crimes revealed by the Lava Jato.[122] By finding that the court has no jurisdiction, Lula's behavior would not have been exculpated as legal. Still, it would be sufficient to establish that it is not necessarily tied to the grand corruption scheme within Petrobras, as was proposed by the prosecution and loosely inspired by the misinterpretation of Roxin's thought by the Supreme Court in the Mensalao case.[123] Subsequently, in June 2021, ruling on a habeas corpus petition, the majority of the Supreme Court, also found Moro to have violated the principle of impartiality of the court, nullifying all the procedural actions of the case.[124] In January 2022, applying the special rules on the prescription of the Brazilian Criminal Code, the 12th Federal Court ruled that the statute of limitations for Lula to be tried has expired, making further prosecution in the case of the alleged bribe given regarding the apartment on the coast impossible.[125] That event represented the end of the need to apply the control theory in the case of Lula's alleged corruption. Still, the theory demonstrated the power of its narrative, and the judgment's reference to both Lula's behavior during Mensalao and the fact that Lula may not have commanded the entire operation of using public money from Petrobras leads to a credible hypothesis that it was a driving force behind the thinking of both the prosecutor and the judge.[126] Regrettably, the judicial procedure ended without clarifying the relationship between the criminal scheme to extort money from Petrobras and the eventual acquisition of real estate from OAS.

The collaboration between trial judge Moro and prosecutor Dallagnol cast a shadow on their personal and professional integrity and the entire Lava Jato campaign. Both Moro and Dallagnol would leave the judiciary and enter politics, Moro as a part of the government of Jair Bolsonaro, the Brazilian president who won the 2018 election thanks to the imprisonment of Lula and Dallagnol as an independent member of the Brazilian Congress.[127] Following Lula's return to power in 2022, the Brazilian judiciary would gradually deconstruct much of the entire Lava Jato campaign. Finding that a significant portion of evidence gathered for the prosecution of Odebrecht executives was gathered outside of the means of classical international cooperation procedures, the Brazil Supreme Court annulled a part of the judgments made against them.[128]

3.5 The Romanian judicial anti-corruption campaign before the CCR

3.5.1 The security context of the Romanian judicial anti-corruption campaign

As the two previous campaigns testify, the question of evidence gathering and its interpretation is central to the legal strategies, and the framing of that issue was also central to the Romanian judicial anti-corruption campaign. The judicial anti-corruption campaigns bring into question some of the critical legal, political, and societal issues that countries struggle with. In the case of Romania, the campaign and the backlash it generated exposed the peculiar nature of the juridical-security nexus in the country. The collective trauma inflicted on society by the coercive network of control exhibited by the former Communist secret police, Securitatea reinforces the perception of existence of such a nexus.[129] The criticism against the anti-corruption campaign claimed that the campaign was merely a continuation of such traditional authoritative coercion of citizens through the removal of popular politicians by a hidden force accountable to no one. The argument was that the informal network of influence between the current and former members of the security services exercised strong oversight over the judiciary by guiding the prosecutors' investigations. The first reason why this narrative was convincing for a part of the population was the overall perception that many of the former Securitatea cadres escaped unpunished for their crimes committed during the Causescu regime and prospered in democratic, post-1990 Romania as entrepreneurs.[130] The second was that, even following the democratic changes in the country, the Romanian intelligence agency, the SRI, had a large, hardly overseen budget that it used with very little oversight as the mechanism of effective parliamentary oversight, which was to provide civilian control over the work of the SRI.[131]

The SRI's influence over the judiciary was purportedly achieved through its mass surveillance program, which the courts authorized. This program, initiated before Romania acceded to the European Union (EU), declared corruption a national security threat, elevating the fight against corruption to a national priority and development goal. The EU's cooperation and verification mechanism (CVM) benchmarks used the number of indictments as a progress indicator, thereby monitoring the country's efforts.[132] While many other countries that joined the EU post-2004 also committed to prosecuting political corruption, Romania took a unique approach, engaging its national security agency in the fight against corruption and expanding the legal framework governing the agency's operation to include corruption.

Moreover, secret protocols between the SRI and the judicial institutions, including the country's prosecution office, were signed to allow for swift usage of the data gathered by the SRI. Publicly, the SRI acknowledged that the anti-corruption campaign represents a tactical field for the agency and that the agency assesses the quality of the judicial decisions taken in the cases dealing with corruption as well as the behavioral profiles of the judges and prosecutors.[133] Such a statement implies a deep connection between the SRI in the fight against corruption and the judicial proceedings. It implies that the judges signing (or refusing to sign) warrants that allow special investigative measures such as wiretapping to be used may be monitored or that the system that assigns the warrants to the judges may have possibly been rigged to secure that the "right" judge decides on the warrant.

Although very few international standards govern the work of national security agencies[134] some principles can be considered as accepted within democratic countries. Typically, they are excluded from law enforcement duties and tasked with national security matters. However, the question of what exactly are and should be national security matters differs in the national context. On the European level, there is a vast difference in the standards concerning the definition of national security matters.[135] Up until 2020, when some convergence over economic security and prevention of foreign interference as common European national security goals was reached, the EU member states enjoyed wide discretion in defining the contexts of their strategic approaches to national security.[136] Generally, national security agencies are involved in providing evidence to law enforcement bodies for the prosecution of terrorism, organized crime, and other grave crimes against the state. This evidence and the techniques of its gathering must be "in accordance with the law," as the European Court of Human Rights (ECtHR) defined this principle of using the evidence in court trials.[137] In practice, this means that the categories of people that are liable to be monitored, the nature of the offenses subject to surveillance, limits on the duration of such monitoring, the procedure for examining, using, and storing the data, precautions to be taken (to communicate the data intact and in their entirety for inspection by the judge and by defense), circumstances in which data is erased or destroyed, and that the judicial control of surveillance measures against the individual must be legally regulated, accessible, sufficiently clear, and foreseeable, and that the human rights-based judicial (or extrajudicial) review must exist.[138] This combines two principles regulated by the European Convention on Human Rights: the right to private life (Article 8) and the right to an effective legal remedy (Article 13).[139]

The involvement of judges or prosecutors in a secret service would raise doubts about their impartiality, especially as the judges approve warrants for special investigative measures such as wiretapping.[140] For that reason, the legislation bans the engagement of judicial staff as employees of the intelligence agencies. This practice in Romania had another important aspect to it, as most of the corruption trials took place before the High Court of Cassation, where the composition of the panels often determined the outcomes of the cases. Eventual collusion between the prosecutors, judges, and intelligence agencies could easily result in selective justice. The approach taken by the CCR was that it did not attempt to refer to an individual case of surveillance. Instead, the court looked at the very structure of the legislative provisions enabling the judicial anti-corruption campaign to take place. In doing so, the CCR went well beyond the requirements of the ECtHR[141] in its protection of fundamental rights and the defense of the separation of powers.

3.5.2 De-securitization of the campaign

The CCR's first activity, dismantling the wiretap system used by the national anti-corruption directorate (DNA), a specialized prosecutor's office attached to the High Court of Cassation and Justice and operated by the SRI, came in 2016, following a request for a constitutional review of the provision of Article 142 of the Romanian Criminal Code.[142] The Article in question regulated special investigative measures, including wiretapping, widely used to collect data on political corruption.[143] The CCR found the wording of the Article

> The prosecutor shall enforce an electronic surveillance measure or may order that this be enforced by the criminal investigation body or trained personnel working in the police, or by other specialized state bodies.

to be imprecise and for two reasons. The first reason was that the electronic surveillance measures are very intrusive and that the defendant should know which agency carries out these measures. Thus, the phrase "other specialized state bodies" may, according to the CCR, point to any specialized state body that might not necessarily even be a criminal investigative body. The CCR found that "no agency other than criminal prosecution bodies, (…) namely: the prosecutor, the criminal investigation bodies of the judicial police and the special criminal investigation bodies, may participate in such activities."[144] As such, this meant that the involvement of the SRI, which, by definition, is not a criminal investigative body in wiretapping, was deemed illegal. The CCR did not strike down the SRI's authorization to wiretap those suspected of illegal activity—the SRI was authorized for such a role by the Romanian Law on National Security—but it prevented the use of the wiretaps in trials. This judgment did not apply to the previously settled cases but only to those pending and future investigations.[145]

The second reason the Judgment found the electronic surveillance operated by the SRI to be unauthorized and contrary to the Romanian Criminal Code was the question of the review of storage of data storage and the effective duration of the measures. Under the Law on National Security, the total duration of the measures was found not to be able to exceed nine months. But neither this Law nor the Criminal Procedure Code said anything about keeping data and extending the measures beyond the authorization that the court gives. While the CCR acknowledged the role of the pre-trial judge in authorizing the warrants, it found that such a role of a judicial body or a criminal investigative body does not exist in the current provisions governing wiretapping. As a result, the provisions are unclear and unforeseeable, and without an "appropriate degree of precision the manner of screening the intelligence obtained through surveillance, or the procedures for preserving its integrity and confidentiality and the procedures for its destruction."[146] For these two reasons, and following a review of the ECtHR's jurisprudence and the provisions of the criminal codes of many European states, the CCR struck down Article 142 as unconstitutional.[147]

The second decision that would interfere with the SRI's participation in the anti-corruption investigations came in 2018, when the CCR struck down Article 3f of the Law on National Security of Romania as unconstitutional.[148]

This Article gave the SRI the authority to operate to prevent threats to the national security defined as

> undermining, sabotage or any other actions that have as purpose to remove by force the democratic institutions of the state or that gravely harm the fundamental rights and freedoms of Romanian citizens, or may damage the defense capacity, or other similar interests of the country, as well as the acts of destruction, degradation or bringing in an unusable state the structures necessary to the good development of social and economic life.[149]

In its interpretation of the article, the CCR focused on the meaning of the phrase "that gravely harm the fundamental rights and freedoms of Romanian citizens" to discern whether it can be attributed to mean that the SRI has the authority to combat corruption. The CCR held that the provision was unconstitutional finding that

> the commission of specific crimes, such as corruption, cannot be classified as a threat to national security, even if the facts seriously affect certain fundamental rights and freedoms of Romanian citizens. This is because, although some offenses are likely to seriously prejudice certain fundamental rights and freedoms by penalizing those acts in the general interest, they do not have the magnitude necessary to classify them as threats to national security.[150]

According to the CCR, such a classification risks a lack of distinction between individual criminal offenses and those that threaten national security.[151] As a result, many of the actions taken may not be defined within a "clear, precise and predictable regulatory framework" thus risking the protection of the principles of legality and privacy as well as the conditions under which the limitations for human rights may be exhibited.[152] In so doing, the CCR has, as the Dissenting opinion noted,[153] The CCR stretched the concept of predictability concerning the deployment of electronic surveillance measures. It ignored the fact that many European jurisdictions have similar legislation that allows national intelligence agencies to participate in activities concerning serious offenses and fraud while at the same time avoiding criminal proceedings or the indiscriminate gathering of evidence.[154] The two decisions have put in doubt the entire campaign. The SRI was the only agency with the technical capacity to conduct wiretapping, forcing the DNA to hire more than 130 staff to carry out the wiretapping of suspects.[155]

The CCR ruled on the protocols for collaboration between the SRI and the DNA that were concluded in 2005 and 2009.[156] The cooperation between the SRI and the offices of the prosecutor was framed around "the activity of capitalizing the information in the field preventing and combating crimes against national security, acts of terrorism, the crimes that correspond to the threats to the national security and other serious crimes, according to the law."[157] Such wording gave the two contracting parties the freedom to run anti-corruption investigations together as the wording "crimes that correspond to the threat of national security" included corruption as per an earlier interpretation. The CCR reasoning was that the conclusion of the protocols between the SRI leads to an expansion of the legislative scope of the criminal procedure law that allows the prosecutors and courts to act ultra vires. By its decision, the Court struck down the two protocols for collaboration deeming them unconstitutional as a violation of the principle of legality and the separation of powers. The Court found the two protocols to be of "heterogeneous nature," which allowed the prosecutor's offices to transfer some of its competencies to the SRI.[158] Consequently, this led the courts to a situation in which, unaware of the protocols, they were not in a position to administer justice effectively.[159] The CCR noted the Parliament's passivity, finding that it could have easily requested the SRI to declassify and allow the parliament's members to review the protocols.[160] Finally, the CCR ordered that in all of the pending trials based on this cooperation, the courts will verify that all of the norms of criminal procedure have been observed.[161]

It remains difficult to assess the illegal element in the collaboration between the courts, the prosecutors, and the SRI in the criminal procedures against individuals charged with corruption. There is no concrete evidence of SRI influence in the outcome of the investigations and trials and the possible misuse of power by the SRI.[162] From the surveillance data gathered by the SRI, we infer that the CCR's decisions had a significant impact, with the total number of surveillances reduced by 80% following the decision's publication.[163] However, the extent to which the judiciary was less influenced by the SRI following these decisions remained contentious within the judiciary itself. The large majority of the judges grouped in the Association Forum of Romanian Judges, understood the two decisions, along with several other decisions taken by the CCR in the 2016–2019 period, as a challenge to the ability of the judicial system as a whole to tackle corruption.[164] They pointed out that the collaboration between the judiciary and the SRI was purely technical and related to electronic surveillance operations.[165] Viewing the CCR's decisions as intrinsically political and as part of a broader effort to crack down on their independence, they referred some of the subsequent decisions of the CCR that have dealt with judicial independence to the Court of Justice of the European Union (CJEU).[166]

The CJEU found that many of the Romanian Constitutional Court's decisions went against the principles of independence of the judiciary as defined in European Union law.[167] However, the CJEU did not review the SRI's exclusion from the anti-corruption investigation as this matter was within the competence of the national legislation of EU member states and not EU law.[168] Without judgments, analyses, or evidence that would expose the use of wiretapping, the prosecutions' overreliance on wiretapping continues to live in the narrative surrounding the judicial anti-corruption campaign, remaining confined to the level of hearsay. Given the exclusion of a whole class of evidence from the prosecutions of political corruption, the CCR's intervention was more thorough than that of the other two courts. It succeeded in creating more legal certainty and predictability but made the whole campaign toothless.

3.5.3 The CCR and the criminal law

Precision, foreseeability, and clarity of the law were topics that the Constitutional Court of Romania explored in another important judgment that dealt with the anti-corruption campaign, this time through the constitutional review of the definition of the criminal act of abuse of office.[169] In two judgments, 405/2016 and 392/2017, the Court significantly lowered the scope of application of criminal law to the instances of abuse of office, finding that these may happen only through the acts or omissions "in breach of law." Thereby, the Court strengthened the standard that the investigative bodies must adhere to when investigating corruption, limiting their investigation to the breaches of law and not policy failures or other failures of the civil servant that may be interpreted by the court to constitute a criminal act.

However, the Court also opened the way for the reform of criminal legislation in that sense, as the Romanian government led by PSD, which was unfavorable to the anti-corruption campaign, adopted emergency ordinances further to limit the scope of the abuse in office. The ordinances brought half a million protestors who had demonstrated against their adoption to the streets.[170] Perhaps emboldened by what it perceived as a show of people's support, the DNA opened an investigation related to preparing this legislative solution. The Ministry of Justice referred this case to the Constitutional Court, citing the conflict between the separate branches of government as grounds for the court's jurisdiction over the matter. In its judgment 611/2017, the court ruled that the investigation violates the principles of separation of powers.[171]

3.6 Courts protecting integrity?

3.6.1 The prosecutors' drive to secure and interpret the evidence as the main challenge to the integrity of the criminal trials

The three cases selected demonstrate that the main driver of the prosecutorial tactics that may violate the integrity of the criminal process is the drive to secure and interpret evidence to be used during trials. In the Italian case, this was achieved by exploiting the law's vagueness that allowed the prosecutors to exclude or include private sector actors from the prosecutions. This violated the truth-seeking element of the trials but allowed the prosecutors, who at the time had no access to either whistleblowing mechanisms or collaborative witnesses, an alternative source to the evidence needed to secure convictions. In the Romanian case, the gathering of evidence was elevated to the largest scale, becoming an activity performed by the intelligence agency by declaring corruption a national security threat. In the Brazilian case, a foreign legal theory (and, as we have seen in the first-instance judgment, a part of foreign legal reasoning) was applied to interpret the evidence. It seems important to note that the plea-bargaining procedures were not fully institutionalized in all three jurisdictions at the time of the proceedings.[172] Thus, the policy-making function of the trial highlighted by Damaska and Langer remains essential as the mechanisms of cooperation between the defendant and the prosecutor remain underdeveloped, prompting the drive of the prosecutors to secure the evidence.[173]

3.6.2 The ability of the courts to correct pre-trial errors

The Romanian Constitutional Court conducted a thorough judicial review of the campaigns. This Court reviewed the main evidence-gathering measures and the factual independence of the judiciary from the SRI. Still, its work did not lead to protecting the integrity of the criminal trial but rather to prevent and limit further criminal prosecution of corruption, thus ending the judicial anti-corruption campaign. Consequentially, the individual's position in the criminal process was never central to the Court's reasoning. The court's judgments excluded a whole class of evidence, namely the wiretaps of the SRI from the future corruption trials. It appears the Court did precisely that, blaming the lower courts and the prosecutor's offices. It took the role of another branch of government, that of the legislator. The real challenge to the SRI would be an effective parliamentary oversight of its activities as a tool legislators use in modern democracies to curb the power of the intelligence services. Instead, the Court removed it from the corruption investigations altogether, an approach that, although supported as a decision within the margin of appreciation of the national judicial body by the CJEU, seems questionable to us from a crime control standpoint. With this, the CCR curbed the judiciary's power as its capacity to collaborate with SRI and influence the other two branches of government became limited. If its decisions contributed to the integrity of the criminal trials, it was in an indirect way and as a side effect and not as a consolidated attempt to preserve fair trial standards and to determine to what extent the selection of the cases that ended up before the courts—the main problem with the SRI involvement to begin with—were justified. To a certain extent, this is justified as the jurisprudence of European courts is generally suspicious of the engagement of national security agencies in regular police and prosecutorial work. Yet the CCR's broad application and interpretation of separation of powers and the rule of law principles has made effective prosecution of corruption extremely difficult. On a positive note, the judgments may have brought more legal certainty and desecuritization of the campaigns.[174]

The monumental first-instance judgment condemning President Lula survived judicial review before the second and third-instance courts, although some of its errors, such as the omission to review if Lula was part of a criminal organization or not, have not been reacted to. Only in the wake of the leaks that disgraced the leading judge and the prosecutor in the cases did the Supreme Court succumb to the habeas corpus application of ex-President Lula demanding access to the leaks. The Court's approach to reviewing the integrity of the criminal trial was cautious. Instead of engaging with the entire construction of Lula's defense and its approach to delegitimizing the trial and the Lava Jato campaign, the Supreme Court first focused on jurisdictional issues. This is surprising as it aims to convince us that the courts of all instances and the Supreme Court have, for years, ignored the fact that one of the key trials in the history of modern Brazil was conducted before a court that had no competence in the first place. Thus, subtly, the Court rejected and disproved the entire prosecutorial construction of the domain of the fact, with Lula in its center. Without engaging the questions of indirect perpetration which would lead it to question both its previous assumptions concerning *Mensalao* trials and the construction that the prosecutor used in the trial of Lula, the court saved the control theory for potential future usage. Once the lack of personal and professional integrity of prosecutor Dallagnol and Judge Moro became evident and proven by evidence obtained by the police, the Supreme Court struck down the entire trial against Lula and, later, trials of some other high corporate executives involved in the corruption schemes. Such a style of intervention where integrity is seen as balancing with the overall notions of judicial reputation ultimately achieved a just outcome but after a long and bitter legal fight with serious political ramifications.

Compared to the other two courts analyzed in this chapter, the jurisprudence of the Italian High Court of Cassation took a stricter approach toward the integrity of the criminal trial. It carefully reviewed the requirements for extortion and corruption, aware of the societal context in which the two criminalized behaviors often intertwined. In so doing, the Court issued essential precedents correcting pre-trial errors, one of the key functions of judicial oversight over the integrity of the criminal process. The presence or absence of the environment of extortion gradually became less important as the concrete acts of the public official—the extorter—gained more importance. Thus, as its own jurisprudence evolved, the High Court of Cassation gradually limited the possibilities for abuse of power by prosecutors. The legislative response came relatively late, suggesting the importance of the court's actions in protecting integrity.

The comparative evidence from the courts' jurisprudence demonstrates that the judiciary exhibits significant opportunities for self-rectification. This opportunity is not always used to protect the rights of the individual within the criminal trial. Instead, the protection of the integrity of the legal system and/or the reputation of the judicial branch of government appear as more likely sources of inspiration for the actions of the courts. That might not make the judicial anti-corruption campaigns a desirable course of action, as prosecuting high political figures will always be controversial. Still, they are far from being impossible to carry out. The backlash against them stems not from the due process issues but from the political mobilizations by indicted individuals motivated to save their careers. A high risk for manipulation of evidence and prosecutorial overreach must be acknowledged. The courts limit the reach of prosecutorial tactics, preserving the integrity of the criminal process, but at a high cost. This high cost of judicial anti-corruption campaigns makes rectifying pre-trial misuses and errors challenging and of little use to the defendant, whose reputation may have been tainted by the criminal procedure.

3.6.3 The rule of law implications

The Romanian Constitutional Court conducted a thorough judicial review of the campaigns. This Court reviewed the main evidence-gathering measures and the factual independence of the judiciary from the SRI. However, its work did not lead to protecting the integrity of the criminal trial. The court's judgments did help to exclude a whole class of evidence, namely the wiretaps of the SRI from the future corruption trials, but it appears as if the Court here did exactly that for what it blamed the lower courts and the offices of the prosecutor and that is taking the role of another branch of government, that of the legislator. The real challenge to the SRI would be an effective parliamentary oversight of its activities, as a tool that is used by legislators in modern democracies to curb the power of the intelligence services. Instead, the Court removed it from the corruption investigations altogether, an approach that, although supported as a decision within the margin of appreciation of the national judicial body by the CJEU, seems questionable to us from a crime control standpoint. With this, the Romanian Constitutional Court achieved the curbing of the power of the judiciary as its capacity to collaborate with SRI and influence the other two branches of government became limited with the independence of the prosecutor's office limited in particular. If its decisions contributed to the integrity of the criminal trials, it was in an indirect way and as a side effect and not as a consolidated attempt to preserve fair trial standards and to determine to what extent the selection of the cases that ended up before the courts—the main problem with the SRI involvement to begin with—were justified. However, the primary problem with its judicial review is not necessarily in the Court itself but also in matters outside of its jurisdiction. Namely, while the ECtHR guidelines are certainly important in securing the standards of judicial oversight over surveillance measures, neither they nor the Romanian Constitutional Court nor the academic literature defines where exactly lies the boundary between organized crime and corruption.

The almost monumental first-instance judgment condemning President Lula survived judicial review before the second and third-instance courts. Only in the wake of the leaks that disgraced the leading judge and the prosecutor in the cases did the Supreme Court succumb to the habeas corpus application of the ex-President Lula reviewing the trial. Initially, the Brazilian Supreme Court took a much more cautious approach to the review of the integrity of the criminal trial. Instead of engaging with the entire construction of Lula's defense and its "lawfare" approach that sought to delegitimize the trial and the Lava Jato campaign, the Supreme Court found the principle of attraction of competencies of the Curitiba court lacking. Thus, in a very subtle way, the Court rejected and disproved the entire prosecutorial construction of the domain of the fact, with Lula in its center, preserving at the same time the reputation of the judicial profession and allowing for a new process to begin. This also helped the Supreme Court not to engage in the questions of indirect perpetrators, which would lead it to question its previous assumptions concerning the *Mensalao* trials and the construction that the prosecutor used in the trial of Lula.

The jurisprudence of the Italian High Court of Cassation took a stricter approach toward the integrity of the criminal trial concerning the distinction between corruption and extortion, reviewing the requirement for each of the two criminal acts with great care. Thus, correcting a pre-trial error and determining whether the establishment has been more pronounced than in the other two campaigns is possible. However, its jurisprudence concerning the ambient of extortion wandered as the Mani pulite campaign gained or lost its power. The presence or absence of the ambient of extortion gradually became less important as the concrete acts of the public official—the extorter—gained more importance. In such a framing, the High Court of Cassation gradually limited the possibilities for abuse of power by prosecutors.

3.7 Conclusion

Traditionally, the rule of law principles governing criminal trials are more related to procedural fairness than to applications of substantive law. Therefore, many prosecutorial and judicial innovations regarding the use and creative interpretation of substantial law interpretations fall outside of the ambit of a rule of law consideration. Some innovations, such as the widespread use of plea bargaining in the Lava Jato operation, have raised concerns common to all systems where this legal institute was introduced. In contrast, others, such as the distinction between extortion and corruption, are highly context-specific.

However, a common thread of problems arising from prosecutorial actions focused on securing evidence can be observed in all three campaigns. These evidentiary problems mainly drive the tensions between due process and crime control principles. Where the securitization of evidence and its abundance was secured, as in the Romanian case, most opportunities for selective justice appeared. The CCR's jurisprudence, however, decreased the opportunities for an effective criminal prosecution, limiting the options for the judiciary to engage in criminal prosecution instead. The intervention of the CCR created more significant rule of law risks than the judicial anti-corruption campaign itself. In the Brazilian case, where irreparable damage to the public trust in the judiciary was done by the collusion between Moro and Dallagnol, the intervention of the Brazilian Supreme Court couldn't have repaired it. What it could have done was to shine more light on the factual basis for the investigation against President Lula. In the Italian case, the prosecutorial tactic that enabled prioritization was eventually deconstructed through legislative action.

The comparative evidence from the courts' jurisprudence demonstrates that despite serious due process and human rights issues, the judiciary exhibits significant opportunities for self-rectification. However, strong interventions in the system governing criminal accountability for corruption may leave it in a worse state than before such interventions. We must accept that, just as backlashes and political mobilizations against the campaigns are a system feature, checks, and reviews that the highest courts perform lead to the significant rule of law problems that do not necessarily resolve eventual misuses that have led to selective justice.

Notes

1 Generally, see Erhard Blankenburg, Judicial anti-corruption initiatives: Latin Europe in a global setting, in *Political Corruption*, 911–924 (Routledge, 2017).
2 Mariana Mota Prado & Machado M.R. (2022). Turning corruption trials into political tools in the name of transparency. In Sandra Botero, Daniel M. Brinks, Ezequiel A. Gonzales Ocantos (eds.) In *The Limits of Judicialization: From Progress to Backlash in Latin America*, (2022), 266–281.
3 Luciano Da Ros & Matthew M. Taylor (2022). *Brazilian Politics on Trial*, 158–159.
4 Luciano Da Ros, & Matthew M. Taylor, Checks and balances: The concept and its implications for corruption, *Revista Direito GV*, 17, (2021).
5 Guenther Jakobs, On the theory of enemy criminal law, *Archiv für Rechts und Sozialphilosophie*, 337, (2008); Carol Proner et al., Comentarios a una sentencia anunciada. El proceso Lula, *Entornos*, 31(1), (2018), 33; Charles J. Dunlap Jr., Lawfare today: A perspective, *The Yale Journal of International Affairs (YJIA)*, 3, (2008), 146.
6 Cristiano Zanin Martins, Valeska Teixeira Zanin Martins, & Rafael Valim, (2021). Lawfare: Waging War Through Law.
7 See Mariana Mota Prado & Marta R. De Assis Machado, Using criminal law to fight corruption: The potential, risks, and limitations of operation car wash (Lava Jato), *The American Journal of Comparative Law (AJCL)*, 69(4), (2021), 834–879 (which attempts to analyze the criminal law toolbox of the Brazilian judicial anti-corruption campaign).
8 João Araújo Monteiro Neto & Nestor Eduardo Araruna Santiago, Weakening constitutional rules through anti-corruption and impunity discourses: Analyzing the impact of the "Operação Lava-jato" (Car Wash Operation) on the presumption of innocence in Brazil, *Oñati Socio-Legal Series*, 14(1), (2024), 56–75.
9 Da Ros & Taylor, *Brazilian Politics on Trial*.
10 For instance, the trials or the opening of investigations may be planned so that they coincide with the election campaigns, or they may be used to target individuals that are likely to compete in elections.
11 Kevin E. Davis, Anti-corruption law and systemic corruption: The role of direct responses, *Revista Direito GV*, 17 (2021); Prado & Machado, note 2; Marjorie Marona & Fabio Kerche, From the Banestado case to operation car wash: Building an anti-corruption institutional framework in Brazil, *Dados*, 64, (2021); Martin Mendelski, 15 years of anti-corruption in Romania: Augmentation, aberration and acceleration, *European Politics and Society*, 22(237), (2021); Ernesto U. Savona, Beyond criminal law in devising anticorruption policies: Lessons from the Italian experience, *The European Journal on Criminal Policy and Research*, 3, (1995), 21.
12 Herbert L. Packer, Two models of the criminal process, *University of Pennsylvania Law Review*, 113(1), (1964), 1–68.
13 Herbert L. Packer, Two models of the criminal process, *University of Pennsylvania Law Review*, 113(1), (1964), 1–68.

14 John Griffiths, Ideology in criminal procedure or a third model of the criminal process. *The Yale Law Journal*, 79, (1969), 359.
15 Jill Hunter et al. (eds.) The integrity of criminal process from theory into practice, (2016).
16 Sabine Gless & John AE Vervaele, Editorial law should govern: Aspiring general principles for transnational criminal justice, *The Utrecht Law Review*, 9(9), (2013), 4.
17 Sarah J. Summers, The enduring legacy of 'Inquisitorial' and 'Accusatorial' procedural forms in the debate on comparative criminal procedure, in fair trials: The European criminal procedural tradition and the European court of human rights, (2007).
18 Ennio Amodio, The accusatorial system lost and regained: Reforming criminal procedure in Italy, *American Journal of Comparative Law*, 52, (2004), 489.
19 Antony Duff, Theories of criminal law, In *Stanford Encyclopedia of Philosophy* (2009). But see Tyrone Kirchengast, Recent reforms to victim's rights and the emerging normative theory of the criminal trial, *The Criminal Law Quarterly*, 56, (2010), 82 (criticizing the normative theory of trial as putting too much focus on the role of the victim).
20 See Summers, The enduring legacy of 'Inquisitorial' and 'Accusatorial' procedural forms in the debate on comparative criminal procedure, in fair trials.
21 Antony Duff, Lindsay Farmer, Sandra Marshall and Victor Tadros (eds.), Introduction: Theorising the criminal trial, in *The Trial on Trial: Towards a Normative Theory of the Criminal Trial*, (2007), 1–14.
22 John D. Jackson & Sarah J. Summers, Seeking across national boundaries: Judicial impartiality, the prosecutorial role and the right to counsel, in obstacles to fairness in criminal, *Proceedings: Individual Rights and Institutional Forms*, 106, (2018).
23 Hunter et al., The integrity of criminal process from theory into practice.
24 Hunter et al., The integrity of criminal process from theory into practice, at 37.
25 Hunter et al., The integrity of criminal process from theory into practice, at 39.
26 Hunter et al., The integrity of criminal process from theory into practice at 45.
27 See Peter J. Kurlemann & Jörg Kinzig, The acquittal (After Pretrial Detention)–a rare but fascinating phenomenon of the criminal justice system, *European Journal of Crime, Criminal Law and Criminal Justice*, 27(4), (2019), 346–362 (explaining that pre-trial detention is a reliable predictor of later conviction).
28 For example, see Ioan Durnescu & Gabriel Oancea, Pre-trial detention in Romanian: improvements and shortcomings, In *European Perspectives on Pre-Trial Detention*, (2023), 165–184 (for the status of pre-trial detention in Romania).
29 Cf. Da Ros & Taylor, *Brazilian Politics on Trial*, at 128.
30 Perry L. Moriearty, Framing justice: Media, bias, and legal decision making, *Maryland Law Review*, 69, (2009), 849 (explaining the media-induced judicial decision making bias).
31 João Araújo Monteiro Neto & Nestor Eduardo Araruna Santiago, Weakening constitutional rules through anti-corruption and impunity discourses: Analyzing the impact of the "Operação Lava-jato"(Car Wash Operation) on the presumption of innocence in Brazil, *Oñati Socio-Legal Series*, 14(1), (2024), 56–75.
32 Generally, see Lonneke Stevens, Pre-trial detention: The presumption of innocence and Article 5 of the European convention on human rights cannot and does not limit its increasing use, *European Journal of Crime, Criminal Law, and Criminal Justice*, 17, (2009), 165.
33 Carol Proner, Gisele Cittadino, Marcio & Wilson Ramos Filho. A resistência ao golpe de 2016, (2016).
34 Alberto Vannucci & Donatella Della Porta, When anticorruption policy fails: The Italian case eighteen years after "Mani Pulite" investigations, In Dirk Tänzler & Konstadinos Maras eds. *The Social Construction of Corruption in Europe*, (2016), 288.

35 Pierro Colaprico, *Da 'Dazione' a 'Zanzata' Il Vocabolario Di Di Pietro*, La Repubblica (1993). The original term in Italian is "dazione ambientale." Literally, it means ambiental giving, a grammatically incorrect way of phrasing in Italian, which nevertheless stuck, and it, in my view, is a fairly accurate description of the attitude of public officials and citizens towards bribery.
36 Mauro Ronco, L'amputazione della concussione e il nuovo delitto di induzione indebita: le aporie di una riforma, *Archivio Penale*, (2013), 35–38.
37 Vincenzo Mongillo, La Corruzione Tra Sfera Interna e Dimensione Internazionale. *Edizioni Scientifiche Italiane*, (2012), 54–55.
38 Ronco, L'amputazione della concussione e il nuovo delitto di induzione indebita, at 37–38 (citing also similar developments in 19th century law in France, Kingdom of two Sicilies, and Prussia).
39 Ronco, L'amputazione della concussione e il nuovo delitto di induzione indebita, at 37–38 (citing also similar developments in 19th century law in France, Kingdom of two Sicilies, and Prussia) at 39–40.
40 Ronco, L'amputazione della concussione e il nuovo delitto di induzione indebita, at 37–38 (citing also similar developments in 19th century law in France, Kingdom of two Sicilies, and Prussia) at 40.
41 Note that in common law systems, the overlap between corruption and extortion also existed. See James Lindgren. The elusive distinction between bribery and extortion: From the common law to the Hobbs Act, *UCLA Law Review*, 35, (1988), 815–821.
42 Such a distinction is present to this day. See the Italian Penal Code Art. 318. and 319, detailing the distinction between corruption in conducting official acts (proper corruption) and in acts contrary or outside of the duty (improper corruption).
43 Carlo Federico Grosso, Nodi controversi in tema di riforma dei delitti di concussione e corruzione, *Cassazione Penale*, 11, (1999), 3277.
44 Tullio Padovani, Il confine conteso. Metamorfosi dei rapporti tra concussione e corruzione ed esigenze 'improcrastinabili'di riforma, *Rivista Italiana di Diritto e Procedura Penale*, 1302, (1999).
45 Tullio Padovani, Il confine conteso. Metamorfosi dei rapporti tra concussione e corruzione ed esigenze 'improcrastinabili'di riforma, *Rivista Italiana di Diritto e Procedura Penale*, 1302, (1999).
46 Grosso, Nodi controversi in tema di riforma dei delitti di concussion e corruzione. The proposed changes in the Italian criminal code aimed to introduce environmental extortion as a separate criminal offense. Dubbed project Pagliaro, this proposal sought to divide extortion into two separate criminal offenses: one in which the extortion is a result of a direct individual action (or a set of actions) aimed at one or a group of private persons or companies taken by a single or a group of public officials, and the second, a crime of environmental extortion in which public officials capture an entire sector or a part of the public service sector.
47 High Court of Cassation of Italy (1998). Judgment 13395/1998 of July 13, 1998.
48 High Court of Cassation of Italy (1996). Judgment of July 26, 1996, C.E.D. 205880.
49 High Court of Cassation of Italy (1996). Judgment of July 26, 1996, C.E.D. 205880 at 292.
50 Lucia Manzi, Judicial populism and corruption prosecutions in the Mani Pulite operation, *Law & Social Inquiry*, (2024), 17.
51 High Court of Cassation of Italy, Judgment of March 17, 2000, 3488/2000.
52 See, for example, Italo Pardo, Where it hurts: An Italian case of Graded and stratified corruption. In Italo Pardo ed., *Between Morality and Law, Corruption, Anthropology and Contemporary Society*, (2004).
53 Piercamillo Davigo, Il Sistema della Corruzione, 47, (2017).
54 Italo Pardo, Corrupt, abusive, and legal: Italian breaches of the democratic contract. *Current Anthropology*, 59(18), (2018), S61–S64.

55 FIAT has long collaborated with successive governments to develop Italian strategic industrial and labor policies. Comparable in terms of size and importance, Fininvest was a financial holding owned by the media magnate and later five-time Prime Minister Berlusconi. See Alan Friedman, The economic elites and the political system. In Stephen Gundle, Simon Parker (eds.). *The New Italian Republic: From the Fall of the Berlin Wall to Berlusconi*, (2002), 263–267.
56 Gianni Barbacetto et al., Mani Pulite, 191 (2012).
57 High Court of Cassation of Italy (2001). Judgment of October 19, 2001 39452/2001.
58 High Court of Cassation of Italy (2001). Judgment of October 19, 2001 39452/2001.
59 High Court of Cassation of Italy (2001). Judgment of October 19, 2001 39452/2001.
60 High Court of Cassation of Italy (2001). Judgment of October 19, 2001 39452/2001.
61 Barbacetto et al., Mani Pulite.
62 Giorgio Garuzzo, *Fiat Secrets of an Epoch*, 248 (2006).
63 Storia del giorno in cui Cesare Romiti fu salvato dal carcere, IL Riformista (August 22, 2020). https://www.ilriformista.it/storia-del-giorno-in-cui-cesare-romiti-fu-salvato-dal-carcere-146467.
64 Barbacetto et al., Mani Pulite, at 200, 205, 259.
65 Garuzzo, *Fiat Secrets of an Epoch*, at 255.
66 *Cassazione, per Romiti confermata la condanna*, La Repubblica (October 20, 2000) https://ricerca.repubblica.it/repubblica/archivio/repubblica/2000/10/20/cassazione-per-romiti-confermata-la-condanna.html.
67 This theory was proposed by Burnett & Mantovani, note 14 (Chapter 2), who saw this as an attempt of the prosecutors to secure the support of certain sectors of the media that would help them promote their own political agenda.
68 Davigo, Il Sistema della Corruzione, 275–277.
69 Chiara Espureo. La Premialita' Quale Strumento Di Contrasto Alla Corruzione, LUISS 88–100 (2015) (unpublished doctoral dissertation).
70 Chiara Espureo. La Premialita' Quale Strumento Di Contrasto Alla Corruzione, LUISS 88–100 (2015) (unpublished doctoral dissertation) at 90.
71 Chiara Espureo. La Premialita' Quale Strumento Di Contrasto Alla Corruzione, LUISS 88–100 (2015) (unpublished doctoral dissertation) at 91–98.
72 Arcibaldo Miller, La concussione dipende da quanto sia "impressionable" la vittima. *Diritto e Giustizia*, 6, (2004), 39–45.
73 Council of Europe, Third Evaluation Round. Evaluation Report on Italy Incriminations (ETS 173 and 191, GPC2) (Theme I), *Strasbourg*, 122, (2012).
74 Luca Carboni. *La Concussione* in le disposizioni penali della legge anticorruzione numero 190 del 2012 EUT Edizioni 23–35 (Paolo Pittaro ed., 2013).
75 Luca Carboni. *La Concussione* in le disposizioni penali della legge anticorruzione numero 190 del 2012 EUT Edizioni 23–35 (Paolo Pittaro ed., 2013), 34.
76 In that sense, see more recent jurisprudence of the High Court of Cassation of Italy for example, Judgment 8041 of December 1, 2020.
77 Anthony W. Pereira. Bolsa família and democracy in Brazil. *Third World Quarterly*, 36 (9), (2015), 1682–1699.
78 Pedro Floriano Ribeiro and Elodie Fabre, Multilevel party organizations in a fragmented presidential system: The case of Brazil. Regional & Federal Studies, 30(4), (2020), 525–555.
79 Timothy Joseph Power and Matthew MacLeod Taylor, (eds.) *Corruption and Democracy in Brazil: The Struggle for Accountability*, (2011), 31–54.
80 Timothy Joseph Power and Matthew MacLeod Taylor, (eds.) *Corruption and Democracy in Brazil: The Struggle for Accountability*, (2011), 31–54.
81 Richard Lapper, *Beef, Bible and Bullets*, 99–112, (2021).
82 Hidden Plot Exclusive: Brazil's Top Prosecutors Who Indicted Lula Schemed in Secret Messages to Prevent His Party From Winning 2018 Election, The Intercept, https://theintercept.com/2019/06/09/brazil-car-wash-prosecutors-workers-party-lula/.

83 Indictment against Lula, available at https://www.conjur.com.br/dl/denuncia-lula-apartamento.pdfpara, 21. Seven other criminal cases followed this indictment, all linked to the misuse of public money, from Petrobras or construction companies such as OAS and Odebrecht or other corrupt acts concerning public procurement.
84 Lapper, *Beef, Bible and Bullets*.
85 Generally, see Neha Jain, The control theory of perpetration in international criminal law, *The Chicago Journal of International Law*, 12(159), (2011), 166.
86 Luis Greco & Adrian teixeira The theory of crime in latin america and the influence of european theoretical tradition. In Kai Ambos Jose Martinez (eds.) *Gottingen Handbook on Latin American criminal Law and Justice*, 383–385.
87 Francisco Muñoz-Conde and Héctor Olásolo, The application of the notion of indirect perpetration through organized structures of power in Latin America and Spain, *Journal of International Criminal Justice*, 9(1), (2011), 113–135.
88 Gerhard Werle & Boris Burghardt. Claus Roxin on crimes as part of organized power structures, *Journal of International Criminal Justice*, (2011), 191–205.
89 Claus Roxin. Strafrecht, Allgemeiner Teil, Bvand II, *Besondere Erscheinungsformen der Straftat*, Verlag C.H. Beck, (2003), 105–107cited as per Vuletic I. (2014). The organized structure of power" and economic crime "Fimi-Media" case and a view from the croatian perspective, *Journal of Law and Criminal Justice*, 2, 134–135.
90 Gregory Michener & Carlos Pereira. A great leap forward for democracy and the rule of law? Brazil's Mensalão trial, *Journal of Latin American Studies*, 48(3), (2016), 477–507.
91 Elies Van Sliedregt. Individual criminal responsibility in international law, (2012), 78–82.
92 Thomas Weigend. Germany. In Kevin Jon Heller & Markus Dubber (eds.), *Comparative Criminal Law*, Stanford University Press, 265–267.
93 Mota Prado & de Assis Machado, Using criminal law to fight corruption.
94 Kai Ambos. Introduction to the special issue on the Brazilian Mensalão case. *Zeitschrift fuer Internazionales Strafrdogmatik*, 6, (2014), 259–260.
95 Luis Greco & Alaor Leite. Die "Rezeption" der Tat- und Organisationsherrschaft im brasilianischen Wirtschaftsstrafrecht Anmerkungen zur Beteiligungsdogmatik im Urteil des brasilianischen Obersten Bundesgerichtsüber den Korruptionsskandal in der Bundesregierung ("Mensalão-Fall", Ação Penal Nr. 470, Supremo Tribunal Federal. Cf. Supreme Federal Court of Brazil (2012)). Ação Penal 470/MG, p. 1255.
96 The Brazilian legal system changed its position on the concepts of perpetratorship in 1940, following the adoption of new criminal code influenced by the solutions from Norway and Italy. See Stewart J.G. (2016). The Strangely Familiar History of the Unitary Theory of Perpetration in Liber Amicorum M. Damaska, Visions of Justice, Duncker & Humblot. As such, the Article 29 of the Brazilian Criminal code simply states that "who is involved in the crime in any way is responsible for the crime to the extent of his guilt and is to be punished within the prescribed range of penalties" without the distinction of the offenders on the basis of whether they were instigators, perpetrators or abbeters and aiders.
97 Supreme Federal Court of Brazil, (2012) Acao Penal 470/MG, 5203.
98 Supreme Federal Court of Brazil (2012(. Acao Penal 470/MG 5156, 5952.
99 Marona & Kerche, From the Banestado case to operation car wash.
100 Indictment against Lula, available at https://www.conjur.com.br/dl/denuncia-lula-apartamento.pdfpara.
101 Proner et al., Comentarios a una sentencia anunciada at 66.
102 4th Federal Regional Court of Brazil (2018) Judgment of January 24, 2018, No. ACR 5046512-94.2016.4.04.7000 PR 5046512-94.2016.4.04.7000.
103 4th Federal Regional Court of Brazil (2018) Judgment of January 24, 2018, No. ACR 5046512-94.2016.4.04.7000 PR 5046512-94.2016.4.04.7000.
104 Indictment against Lula, available at https://www.conjur.com.br/dl/denuncia-lula-apartamento.pdfpara, 30–33.

105 In this sense, the Italian Supreme Court of Cassation has verified the same stance during the Mani pulite campaign.

106 Indictment against Lula, available at https://www.conjur.com.br/dl/denuncia-lula-apartamento.pdfpara, 8.

107 Indictment against Lula, available at https://www.conjur.com.br/dl/denuncia-lula-apartamento.pdfpara, 5–10, 18–21.

108 Indictment against Lula, available at https://www.conjur.com.br/dl/denuncia-lula-apartamento.pdfpara, 30–33.

109 Indictment against Lula, available at https://www.conjur.com.br/dl/denuncia-lula-apartamento.pdfpara, 30–33; 4th Federal Regional Court of Brazil (2018), note 102, 803.

110 Ezequiel A. González-Ocantos, Prosecutors, voters and the criminalization of corruption in Latin America: The case of Lava Jato, (2023), 69. Later, in 2019, the STF would reverse its decision.

111 Kickbacks, Crackdown and Backlash, 252.

112 Judgment of the 13th Brazilian Federal Court, paragraph 646, 935–937.

113 Luciano Da Ros & Matthew C. Ingram, Law, Courts and Judicial Politics, in Barry Ames (ed.) *Routledge Handbook of Brazilian Politics*, 352.

114 Judgment, note 102, paragraph 803.

115 We see the similar doctrine in Italian criminal law whose jurisprudence also states that an act of office might be simply being in office.

116 Exclusive Leaked Chats Between Brazilian Judge and Prosecutor Who Imprisoned Lula Reveal Prohibited Collaboration and Doubts Over Evidence. June 9, 2019, The Intercept https://theintercept.com/2019/06/09/brazil-lula-operation-car-wash-sergio-moro/.

117 Exclusive Leaked Chats Between Brazilian Judge and Prosecutor Who Imprisoned Lula Reveal Prohibited Collaboration and Doubts Over Evidence. June 9, 2019, The Intercept https://theintercept.com/2019/06/09/brazil-lula-operation-car-wash-sergio-moro/.

118 Exclusive Leaked Chats Between Brazilian Judge and Prosecutor Who Imprisoned Lula Reveal Prohibited Collaboration and Doubts Over Evidence. June 9, 2019, The Intercept https://theintercept.com/2019/06/09/brazil-lula-operation-car-wash-sergio-moro/.

119 Another essential fact often highlighted as crucial evidence of Moro's partisanship is the decision to release the wiretaps of the conversations between Lula and Rousseff Namely, the police recorded, through an official surveillance warrant, a conversation between Lula and Rousseff that may be interpreted as an offer of a ministerial position that would, through immunity, shield him from prosecution.

120 A Group of International Jurists and Scholars Condemns the Conviction of Former Brazilian President Lula as Unfair and Politically Motivated. A Group of Brazilian Prosecutors Defend Their Conduct, and the Conviction. Read Their Dueling Open Letters Here! https://globalanticorruptionblog.com/2019/09/12/a-group-of-international-jurists-and-scholars-condemns-the-conviction-of-former-brazilian-president-lula-as-unfair-and-politically-motivated-a-group-of-brazilian-prosecutors-defend-their-conduct-and/, Global AntiCorruption Blog, September 12, 2019.

121 Summarization of Habeas Corpus request of Lula's defense No. 193 276 available at http://portal.stf.jus.br/noticias/verNoticiaDetalhe.asp?idConteudo=464261&ori=1.

122 4th Regional Federal Court of Brazil, note 102, 154–170.

123 In that sense, see the statement of Lula's defense team available at Global AntiCorruption Blog at https://globalanticorruptionblog.com/2019/09/20/lulas-lawyers-respond-to-the-lava-jato-prosecutors-letter/.

124 *Moro é suspeito para julgar Lula, decide Supremo Tribunal Federal por 7 votos a 4, ConJur*, https://www.conjur.com.br/2021-jun-23/moro-suspeito-julgar-lula-decide-stf-votos.

125 Judgment of the 12th Brazilian Federal Court 1070239-94.2021.4.01.3400 of January 28, 2022.
126 Judgment, note 102, 803 ff. Indictment against Lula, available at https://www.conjur.com.br/dl/denuncia-lula-apartamento.pdfpara, 5–8.
127 Emilio Pelus Neder Meyer, (2021). Constitutional Erosion in Brazil, 97–99.
128 Supreme Court of Brazil, Decision on Petition, 12.357 Distrito Federal, 116–117. (May 21, 2024).
129 Generally, see Ionut Valentin Chiruta, Using the past in populist communicational strategies: How the memory of securitate is instrumentalised in romanian politics? *Populism*, 3(2), (2020), 223–256.
130 For some specific issues with regards to the transition from the older cadres involved in the Securitatea to a more modern SRI, see Lavinia Stan & Marian Zulean, Intelligence sector reforms in Romania: A scorecard. *Surveillance & Society*, 16(3), (2018), 302–305.
131 Marian Zulean & Emilia Şercan (2018). Democratic control of Romanian intelligence after three decades: Quis custodiet ipsos custodes? *Defense & Security Analysis*, 34(4), 365–384.
132 Mendelski, 15 years of anti-corruption in Romania.
133 Alina Matei, Dumitru Dumbravă: SRI este unul dintre anticorpii bine dezvoltaţi şi echipaţi pentru însănătoşirea societăţii şi eliminarea corupţiei, Juridice, April 30, 2015 https://www.juridice.ro/373666/dumitru-dumbrava-sri-este-unul-dintre-anticorpii-bine-dezvoltati-si-echipati-pentru-insanatosirea-societatii-si-eliminarea-coruptiei-v1.html.
134 Kim Lane Scheppele, The international standardization of national security law, *Journal of National Security Law & Policy*, 4(2), (2010), 437–454. (Detailing how the national security response to terrorism kept national characteristics depending on the jurisdiction in spite of UN regulation.).
135 Didier Bigo et al., National Security and Secret Evidence in Legislation and before the Courts: Exploring the Challenges, Centre for European Policy Studies, (2015).
136 Generally, see Satish Sule, National security and EU law restraints on intelligence activities, In Jan-Hendrik Dietrich & Satish Sule (eds.) *Intelligence Law and Policies in Europe*, 335–388.
137 Generally, see Satish Sule, National security and EU law restraints on intelligence activities, In Jan-Hendrik Dietrich & Satish Sule (eds.) *Intelligence Law and Policies in Europe*, 335–388.
138 See Gianclaudio Malgieri & Paul De Hert. European human rights, criminal surveillance, and intelligence surveillance: Towards 'Good Enough' oversight, preferably but not necessarily by judges. In D. Gray, S. Hendricksen (eds.) *Cambridge Handbook of Surveillance Law*, (2017), 509–533. (Arguing that the European Court of Human Rights has recognized that a non-judicial body may also conduct a review of the surveillance warrants.).
139 See Gianclaudio Malgieri & Paul De Hert. European human rights, criminal surveillance, and intelligence surveillance: Towards 'Good Enough' oversight, preferably but not necessarily by judges. In D. Gray, S. Hendricksen (eds.) *Cambridge Handbook of Surveillance Law*, (2017), 509–533. (Arguing that the European Court of Human Rights has recognized that a non-judicial body may also conduct a review of the surveillance warrants.).
140 See Gianclaudio Malgieri & Paul De Hert. European human rights, criminal surveillance, and intelligence surveillance: Towards 'Good Enough' oversight, preferably but not necessarily by judges. In D. Gray, S. Hendricksen (eds.) *Cambridge Handbook of Surveillance Law*, (2017), 509–533. (Arguing that the European Court of Human Rights has recognized that a non-judicial body may also conduct a review of the surveillance warrants.).
141 Claims that the panels of judges composed by the High Court of Cassation in Romania were "handpicked" by either the prosecutors or the SRI, were frequently

made by those opposing the campaigns. See, for example, Dragos Calin, Dan Tapalaga & Cristel Coada (2020). 900 Days of Uninterrupted Siege upon the Romanian Magistracy, A Survival Guide, 155. To the best of my knowledge no substantial evidence has been produced to verify these claims or to map the breach of procedural rights of the accused in such cases.

142 Judgment of the Constitutional Court of Romania 51/2016 at https://perma.cc/59W8-ZG8S.

143 Pippidi, note 3 (Chapter 2) argues that the number of wiretapping warrants issued in Romania surpassed that issued in the United States, a country with a population fifteen times that of Romania.

144 The phrase "in such activities" refers to criminal investigatory activities. See Constitutional Court of Romania, note 142, paragraph 34.

145 Constitutional Court of Romania, note 142, paragraph 52.

146 Constitutional Court of Romania, note 142, paragraph 45.

147 Constitutional Court of Romania, note 142, paragraph 36.

148 Constitutional Court of Romania, Judgment 91/18 of April 20, 2018.

149 Law on the National Security of Romania 51/1991 of July 1991.

150 Constitutional Court of Romania, note 148, paragraph 81.

151 Constitutional Court of Romania, note 148, paragraph 84.

152 Constitutional Court of Romania, note 148 Judgment, note 148, 86.

153 Dissenting opinion to the Judgment of the Constitutional Court of Romania, note 147, 12.

154 Dissenting opinion to the Judgment of the Constitutional Court of Romania, note 147.

155 Dragos Calin & Andreas Codreanu, Situation regarding the Romanian Judicial System at the End of 2018, Revista Forumul Judecatorilor (2018), 27.

156 The protocols can be accessed online at the website of the Romanian National Intelligence Agency, the SRI. https://www.sri.ro/assets/img/news/protocol-de-cooperare/Protocol_declasificat.pdf.

157 The protocols can be accessed online at the website of the Romanian National Intelligence Agency, the SRI. https://www.sri.ro/assets/img/news/protocol-de-cooperare/Protocol_declasificat.pdf.

158 Judgment of the Constitutional Court of Romania, 26/2019, 173. available at https://www.ccr.ro/wp-content/uploads/2020/07/Decizie_26_2019.pdf.

159 Judgment of the Constitutional Court of Romania, 26/2019, 173. available at https://www.ccr.ro/wp-content/uploads/2020/07/Decizie_26_2019.pdf, 189.

160 Judgment of the Constitutional Court of Romania, 26/2019, 173. available at https://www.ccr.ro/wp-content/uploads/2020/07/Decizie_26_2019.pdf, 185.

161 Judgment of the Constitutional Court of Romania, 26/2019, 173. available at https://www.ccr.ro/wp-content/uploads/2020/07/Decizie_26_2019.pdf, 214.3.

162 To the best of my knowledge, the literature offers no conclusive evidence of the specific outcome of the cases in which such collaboration occurred.

163 Mendelski, 15 years of anti-corruption in Romania.

164 Dragos Calin, The Constitutional Court of Romania and the Rule of Law Standards in Dan Tăpălagă, Dragos Călin & Cristel Coadă (eds.). 2020. *900 Days of Uninterrupted Siege upon the Romanian Magistracy A Survival Guide*, 211–228.

165 *Romania's* chief antigraft prosecutor: Protocol with intelligence service did not grant additional rights, *Romania Insider*, April 3, 2018. https://www.romania-insider.com/kovesi-declassified-protocol. Academic review of the CCR engagement is largely critical, seeing it as judicial populism or an attempt to tame the judiciary for the benefit of the corrupt political class. Generally, see Alexandra Mercescu (2021). Non sequiturs in constitutional adjudication: Populism or epistemic deficit? In *Populist Challenges to Constitutional Interpretation in Europe and Beyond*, 194–216.

166 These are cases cases C-357/19, Euro Box Promotion and Others; C-547/19, Asociaţia "Forumul Judecătorilor din România"; C-811/19, Ministerul Public; C-840/19, Ministerul Public; C-859/19, Parchetul de pe lângă Înalta Curte de Casaţie şi Justiţie—Direcţia Naţională Anticorupţie; C-926/19, Parchetul de pe lângă Înalta Curte de Casaţie şi Justiţie—Direcţia Naţională Anticorupţie and Others; C-929/19, CD. A smaller part of the judiciary viewed the activities of the SRI as the main impediment to the independence of the judiciary, claiming that the judges, in fact, are being pressured into collaboration with SRI and that, consequentially, the legitimacy of the entire anti-corruption campaign is doubtful, see National Union of Romanian Judges, 2018. Report on the unlawful involvement of the Romanian secret intelligence agencies, through secret protocols in the Romanian judiciary system at https://www.medelnet.eu/images/2018/Romanian_Judges_Union_-_Report_on_the_unlawful_involvement_of_the_Romanian_secret_intelligence_agencies_through_secret_protocols_in_the_Romanian_judiciary_system.pdf.

167 Judgment of the Court of Justice of the European Union in cases 83/19, 127/19, 195/19, 291/19, 355/19 and 397/19 of May 19 2021.

168 Judgment of the Court of Justice of the European Union in cases C-357/19, C-379/19, C-547/19, C-811/19 and C-840/19 December 21, 2021, 70–74, 287–294.

169 Judgments of the Constitutional Court of Romania 405/2016 of 15.06.2016. and 392/2017 of 06.06.2017. at http://legislatie.just.ro/Public/DetaliiDocumentAfis/190691 and http://legislatie.just.ro/Public/DetaliiDocumentAfis/179919.

170 T. Olteanu & S. Beyerle 2017. The Romanian people versus corruption, *Open Journal of Sociopolitical Studies*, 10(3), 797–825.

171 Judgment of the Constitutional Court of Romania 611/2017 of 03.10.2017.

172 In Brazil, plea bargaining was used in the course of the Lava Jato, helping secure some convictions but was, overall, still not fully recognized by the courts. See Mota Prado & De Assis Machado, note 2, 843, 874.

173 Maximo Langer (2014). The long shadow of the adversarial and inquisitorial categories in Markus D. Dubber & Tatjana Hörnle (eds.), *The Oxford Handbook of Criminal Law*, 903–905.

174 Valentin Stoian (2020). A Rawlsian account of de-securitisation: Securitising and de-securitising corruption in Romania, *Critical Studies on Security*, 8(1), 21–23. (Pursuing the argument of desecuritization practices carried out by the CCR.).

4 Impact of the anti-corruption campaigns

4.1 Introduction

The anti-corruption campaigns described in this book have been credited and discredited for their effects on the economic, legal, political, and judicial systems. Given the rather wide scope of effects generally attributed to corruption, in this chapter, we will assess how their outcomes shape the economic, legal, political, and judicial systems of the countries where they took place. Unlike the assessments made in the previous two chapters, this chapter, despite a plethora of available information, faces the challenge of establishing a strong causal relationship between the anti-corruption campaigns and their impact. This is because the campaigns do not occur in isolation; they unfold amidst a dynamic world that continues to evolve. As they unfold, many other significant developments that shape societies in a substantial way occur simultaneously. This complexity makes the disentanglement of the effects and outcomes of multiple simultaneous processes a key factor that hinders a straightforward analysis and a clear attribution of impact. Moreover, the lack of literature and research focused exclusively on the effects of the campaigns, particularly those in Romania and Brazil, leaves few clear pathways to analysis, making the subsequent assessments original and ambitious but bound to remain imperfect in some of their findings. The chapter examines the effects and impacts on the political, legal, and economic systems and the perception and level of corruption. Certainly, due to the overlap between law, politics, and economy, the boundary between the three areas is imprecise and not always easy to draw. Still, the expected impact is high, at least hypothetically, making it easier to observe and measure. The relevance of corruption, as recognized in the past three decades in the theories of economic development, studies focused on the quality of the rule of law and, in a narrower sense, the field of corruption studies.[1] First, the political impact should be significant because, as explained in Chapter 1, the disclosures of corrupt practices should inform the voters, raising accountability and lowering the support for the corrupt actors. Second, the corrupt investigations reveal a) the weaknesses of the law enforcement system and the regulation of corrupt practices, thereby having the potential to make anti-corruption regulation more efficient, and b) the potential strengthening of

DOI: 10.4324/9781003334811-4

the corrupt networks due to a learning process among the perpetrators of corrupt offenses. Third, the impact on national economics should be significant for two reasons: a) The mass nature of the campaigns acts as a disincentive for future corrupt behavior, making the economy more efficient, which leads to economic growth, and b) the revelation of mass corruption networks makes the future creation of similar networks operating in the same economic field less likely. In that sense, the campaigns should contribute to strengthening the economy and law enforcement and establishing a political system less dependent on corruption or, at least, better controlled for corruption. Although research on the impact of the campaigns has analyzed diverse phenomena, such as the formation of political parties and fragmentation of the party system,[2] the economic impacts have been less studied.[3] The work that has been done in this area focuses largely on the measurements of corruption before and after the campaigns and on the salience of the issue of corruption for political actors and voting behavior.[4]

In the introduction, I have briefly addressed the shortcomings of the indexes for corruption measurement. Their popularity and widespread use are primarily driven by their effectiveness in the public sphere, that is, by the desire of the anti-corruption movement to legitimize itself before the global public opinion and by the thirst for ranking that the global public opinion thrives in.[5] Herein, I restate that using these indexes cannot wholly measure the changes happening in a country, particularly within a short period.[6] What they can do, however, is point to the trends in corruption perception, judicial independence, democracy, and the rule of law quality, thus assessing the societal impact of the campaigns. This holds to be true, especially in Italy, where, owing to the longer time since the emergence of the campaign, it is easier to track the impacts or lack of the impacts of the campaign. In this section, I will compare and evaluate the measurements of different indicators of corruption perception, judicial independence, and good governance.[7] I will consider public opinion surveys and in-depth qualitative or quantitative studies conducted during and after the campaigns to trace the evolution of perceptions toward the presence of political corruption and judicial independence in the countries. I summarize the findings and offer a table that overviews the recorded impact.

4.2 Impact on the political system

4.2.1 Italy

Impacts attributed to the Mani pulite campaign range from an insignificant attempt to curb corruption to the responsibility for the downfall of the Italian First Republic.[8] But what exactly was the purpose of Mani pulite? Its lead protagonist, Antonio di Pietro, has given conflicting statements on this. Speaking in 1996, before the investigating judges in Brescia in the process in which he would be acquitted of charges of misuse of power, he stated: “the Mani pulite project in its final phase, should have led to the reconstruction, replacement of the *classe dirigente*, new laws and new political coalitions."[9] The same di Pietro, speaking fifteen years later, presented the campaign in a different light: as a continuation of the work that the magistrates Borsallino and Falcone started in the processes against the mafia that began in the 1980s.[10] This seemingly contradictory statement seems to point to the evolution of the narrative of the campaigns. In the 1990s, when di Pietro hoped that Mani pulite would bring about significant political transformation, the narrative was used to foster that; when it became evident that the political transformation that happened was not so much the result of Mani pulite but of many other forces at play, Mani pulite's interpretation was reframed as an evolution of the fight against organized crime.

If we accept the first version of the narrative, that of a change in the classe dirigente in the country, Mani pulite has had some successes. Alberto Vannucci, one of the leading researchers of the Mani pulite and its aftermath, believes that the ideas and spirit of Mani pulite have been defeated politically.[11] However, many other factors impacted the Italian political system. Its utilization of the proportional system of representation of votes and multi-preference lists that the candidates used to pursue a strategy based on clientelist practices was widely unpopular and changed in the 1991 referendum.[12] The two main political parties, the communists (PCI) and the Christian democrats (DC), were remnants of the Cold War divisions, characteristic of many Western European democracies but particularly highlighted in Italy. Supported by the Soviet Union, the PCI had a vision of communist Italy that would either leave NATO and pursue a non-aligned policy toward the two main blocs or, later in its Eurocommunist phase, stay in NATO and focus on socio-economic reforms within the society.[13] The DC, on the other hand, supported by the Catholic Church and big business, was a traditional center-right party that relied on conservative values while pursuing at the same time a careful social policy that aimed not to alienate the poor.[14] However, the end of the Cold War standstill made both parties redundant to both their domestic and international constituency.[15] Thus, while many of its important members were tried over the course of the Mani pulite,[16] the conclusion that the Mani pulite by itself brought down the First Republic seems unconvincing; the political system of Italy itself was in a deep state of crisis following the geopolitical changes brought forth by the fall of the Berlin Wall, and thus, the main divide between the two parties lost sense when the global struggle between capitalism and communism ended.[17] The historical defeat of communism left the PCI without its main *raison d'etre*, while at the same time exposing the systemic weaknesses of the DC as the main organizer of the market of corrupt exchanges in Italy between 1945 and 1990.[18] Indeed, DC's connections with the Mafia,[19] secret organizations, and clandestine operations were never fully exposed but existed in the minds of the general public that, in the wake of the corruption scandals, gradually withdrew support from the party. In fact, the impact of the campaigns was stronger on the two parties that stood in the center, PSI and the Liberal Party, which have since ceased to exist completely. Giannuli's observation that the Mani pulite did not destroy the parties but rather that the Mani pulite happened because the political system fell apart seems more adequate.[20] All of this led to a high increase in the electoral volatility that was low between 1953 and 1987, indicating a consolidated party system, in 1994 (at the height of the Mani pulite) reached levels which signified a collapse of the party system.[21]

This clearing of the political space did not bring a change in the composition of the *classe dirigente*; rather, it was the creation of the political parties based on the person, such as Berlusconi's Forza Italia, that was the main political development. But, when Berlusconi found himself targeted by the Mani pulite pool, his reaction toward the judicial campaign (and the subsequent investigations that would follow him into the next decade) was to frame it as a plot of the judges who aimed to subvert the freedom of Italians, exposing them to a rule of the judiciary.[22] The very fact that it was Berlusconi and not some of the DC or PSI politicians that was to attacked the judges as those wearing "red togas" testifies that his Forza Italia, as a newcomer to the political scene, was able to successfully shape the political narrative, thus delegitimizing both the campaign and the main alternative political forces in the country. What greatly helped Berlusconi was the poor regulation of conflict of interest in Italy, which allowed him to pursue "mediatization of politics" and to exploit the media monopoly that his own private financial empire had in attacking the campaign.[23] It allowed him to successfully mobilize many voters who had previously supported DC or PLI.[24] The left parties, dedicated to their own problems of facing the past, did not capture the opportunity to present themselves as anti-corruption champions during the 1996–2001 period.[25]

The evolution of *classe dirigente* and the political class happened, but not in the way that di Pietro hoped for. Namely, while during the Mani pulite years many of the MPs and other political figures resigned in cases of judicial procedures or even investigatory actions against them, in the years that followed, the prosecutions of state officials, not only in Italy but also in other countries, rarely led to such an outcome.[26] The suicides that were interpreted by those critical of the campaigns as evidence of the cruelty of the prosecutors and their tactics would not occur in the later corruption prosecutions and the campaigns that happened in Brazil or Romania. This points to the fact that reputation played much less of a role for politicians after the Mani pulite than in the period of its existence. In that sense, we can speak of a normalization of corruption or wider charges of abuse of office against the political figures.[27] Another piece of information that points in that direction is the fact that looking at the period between 2000 and 2015 (meaning after Mani pulite), the percentage of politicians that were involved in corrupt acts that were not politically active before the 1990s was 60% of all those whose cases ended up before the Court of Cassation.[28] Finally, a substantive change is observed in the appropriation of resources, which post-Mani pulite became intended primarily for personal use or vote trading and rarely, or rarely, for the party's use.[29]

Coming to politics from the judiciary, di Pietro sought to maximize the positive capital of campaigns through his own political project but faced little electoral success. His party never obtained more than five percent of the votes, and it was eventually disbanded following the 2013 election.[30] A later attempt at an anti-establishment and anti-corruption political mobilization was the foundation and the 2013 electoral success of the Five-Star Movement, a party that also attempted to position itself as an actor that preserved the legacy of the Mani pulite.[31] While this is far from the hopes for a change of the political system that the Mani pulite brought, it still presents the overtly negative observations as perhaps a bit too pessimistic. Moreover, empirical evidence suggests a tangible impact of the campaign in certain legislative districts. Where the effects of the campaign were strong through the arrests and investigations against members of local and regional governments, the members of parliament who held parliamentary seats would lose seats in that area.[32] Given the high number of political persons prosecuted in the Mani pulite, this piece of information would conclude that the campaign's impact was strong on the electability of the persons but less so on the electability of the parties that sought to undermine the anti-corruption efforts.

4.2.2 Brazil

As elaborated in Chapter 3, the prosecution of Lula and the way it unfolded made the criticism of the anti-corruption campaign because of its partisanship and assistance in the rise of Bolsonaro almost commonplace. There is, though, evidence to suggest that Lula and the PT would have lost the 2018 general elections even if the campaign, or at least its part that specifically targeted Lula, did not occur. Governing through large coalitions, the PT had been in power since 2002 and, by the time of the 2006 elections, was already steadily but surely losing its appeal with middle-class voters.[33] That loss of appeal was fueled by the transformation of the middle and working class itself; the increase in the share of voters that were members of the growing community of evangelical Christians.[34] These voters felt alienated by the gender and identity politics of the PT. Demonstrations that faced the second term of President Dilma Rousseff (2013–2015), the economic growth that stalled in the second decade of the 21st century, and the changed political preferences of the Brazilian population were all factors that, combined, were enough to end the domination of the PT on the Brazilian political scene and put into question Lula's candidacy for the post of the President.[35] Paradoxically, the prosecution of Lula—if it was indeed conducted for political reasons—backfired, making him a leading candidate in the 2022 Brazilian presidential elections[36] that he eventually won. Additionally, the effects of the authoritarian practices of Brazilian president Jair Bolsonaro and his own implication in corruption scandals[37] greatly undermined much of the anti-PT corruption narrative[38] that was created during Lava Jato. All of this created space in the political scene, with many of those in the Brazilian middle class who would be willing to support an anti-corruption agenda or a political project being left without a clear political project to support. In the 2022 elections, Dallagnol and Moro, following the steps of di

Pietro, tried to fill this hole by standing in the elections as anti-corruption candidates. The political fragmentation, which was one of the elements of the Brazilian political system that facilitated the corruption, only intensified as Brazil went from 26 to 30 political parties participating in parliament.[39] Relatively low volatility, which was a characteristic of the Brazilian party system, which consolidated after the restoration of democracy in the late 1980s,[40] evolved into a more volatile system as the PT and its coalition partners lost much of the support they enjoyed between 2003 and 2016. However, the volatility that characterized the aftermath of the Mani Pulite campaign in Italy was less pronounced in Brazil, as none of the country's leading parties disappeared completely. Instead, a phenomenon that already existed, that of "parties for rent" became more widespread as some of the important candidates ran using different parties that may have only a few deputies in the national Congress yet serve as a useful vehicle for candidates who may have strong clientelist connections with the voters.[41] In 2018, this was the case with some of the deputies as it was before, but also with the winning presidential candidate, Bolsonaro.[42]

While the phenomenon of fragmentation also exists in other jurisdictions, its importance for the Brazilian political scene is such that for any major party, it will be extremely difficult to govern without having a coalition partner that will be entrusted with a large sector of the economy without much oversight. In 2014, the leading party (PT) had 14% of the vote, and in 2018 this shrunk to 12%.[43] Thus, the risk of political corruption—at least in the short term—is greatly increased, as the country may enter what Della Porta calls a vicious circle of electoral volatility and corruption.[44] The ideas that the pool of prosecutors grouped in the Lava Jato task force, alongside some parts of the Brazilian justice system, had regarding the country's foundation and the strengthening of anti-corruption have—at least in the current period—failed to take ground.[45]

4.2.3 Romania

PSD, as the party that was in power the longest in post-communist Romania, suffered the most during the anti-corruption campaigns as two of the country's prime ministers coming from their ranks, namely Adrian Nastase and Victor Ponta, were prosecuted.[46] However, despite the major cases launched against the PSD in the campaigns, the party returned to power in 2016, practically in the middle of the anti-corruption campaign.[47] Upon coming to power, part of the populist rhetoric that was particularly used by the PSD was "that they are in power but they do not have the power."[48] That implied that the power is elsewhere, in the interconnections between the SRI and the judiciary that the Romanian Constitutional Court—as we have seen in Chapter 3—sought to eliminate from its roles in the anti-corruption investigations. It is these actors—it was argued—that are in true control of the state.[49] The reason why the PSD managed to sustain this narrative with the public was the fact that the businesspersons that controlled much of the media were either directly tied to them or viewed the anti-corruption campaigns as problematic because of their own involvement in corrupt deals. The overall climate of distrust arising from the historical link between the security services, judiciary, and politicians helped the PSD to present anti-corruption as non-credible. Internally, despite prosecutions that targeted many non-PSD individuals, the PSD elite genuinely believed that the campaign was primarily targeting them.[50]

Electoral volatility in Romania was impacted by the campaigns at an even lower scale than in Italy and Brazil. On the whole, in the period between 2010 and 2019, no parties have disappeared from the political scene as a result of the campaigns—as a matter of fact, the PSD managed to return to power in 2016 at the height of the campaign. New anti-corruption parties such as USR and PLUS have mobilized the protest vote leading to a shift of representation in the urban middle-class vote which they took from the PDL as the party that gathered the liberal vote prior to the campaign. Electoral volatility did increase at the local level signifying increased accountability but not necessarily leading to the defeat of the incumbent candidates under corrupt allegations—visible from the fact that in 2021 PSD still held the largest number of mayors than any other Romanian party.[51] Again, unlike the situation in Italy or Brazil, the electoral turnout in Romania sharply fell in this decade, signifying a loss of interest in political representation by the citizens.

Seeking to capitalize on the anti-corruption agenda, a party that was to mobilize the citizens on this platform emerged in the form of Union Save Romania (USR), that successfully performed in the 2019 European elections, recording as many votes as the PSD. This was helped by the fact that the referendum on amnesty for corruption offenses was held on the same day, allowing them increased electoral support.[52] In the 2020 elections, they came third in the number of votes, gathering support thanks to what the analysts described as populist anti-corruption rhetoric for the middle class.[53] But, their impact once they entered government in 2020 was weak, as their low administrative capacity and the power-sharing agreements prevented them from exercising a stronger influence.[54] Following the Romanian government's decision not to conform with the CJEU judgments concerning the departments for disciplinary investigations of the judges, the USR left the government.[55] Effectively, this meant that those political forces that aimed to "carry the banner" of the anti-corruption campaign were unable to protect judicial independence and build on the positive legacy of the campaign, such as the increased accountability of politicians and public servants.

But even if the campaign becomes "owned" by a political party, it is unclear whether that would contribute to a change in the political climate or the practices of the government. Namely, as in Brazil and Italy, corruption is hardly the only issue dividing the electorate. Although it is ever-present in Romanian political life and culture and although its appearance holds the power of popular mobilization, as evidenced by the protests of 2016, the institutionalization of anti-corruption rhetoric as a protest stance against the elite does not guarantee the effective combatting of corruption.[56]

4.3 Impacts on the legal system

4.3.1 Italy

Before the passage of the anti-corruption package of legislation in 2012, the period from the mid-1990s onwards was marked by a relative lack of major interventions in the legal system—in times when governments of the center-left were in power—and a series of interventions that the commentators called *ad personam* laws. These laws protected Prime Minister Berlusconi from the trials and prosecutions that started during or after the Mani pulite period—when center-right parties governed the country.[57] Focused on the statute of limitations, the adoption of the measures contained in the so-called "legge ex Cirielli," allowed the cessation of some prosecutions against the companies in which Berlusconi had financial interests.[58] Other laws focused on limiting the prosecution's ability to obtain evidence through international rogatory letters and abolished the crime of false accounting.[59] These three measures directly contributed to a drop in the prosecution of corruption in Italy, saving Berlusconi and those close to him from prosecution.[60] Additionally, measures that would limit the opportunity of prosecutors to appeal against an acquittal were introduced,[61] as well as an opportunity for defendants to challenge the political bias of trial judges by expressing legitimate suspicion of their impartiality.[62] Not all attempts to incapacitate the judiciary to conduct anti-corruption investigations and to undermine its independence were successful. For example, a proposal to create a parliamentary committee that would investigate the misuse of power by the use of politics by the judiciary was proposed, receiving little political support.[63] The judges and prosecutors have also found a way to undermine the law ex Cirielli by applying a different dating system to cases against corrupt individuals.[64]

In 2012, owing also to the international pressure after the country's financial and economic crisis and inspired by the thinking that the effects of corruption are primarily detrimental to economic development, the country enacted an ambitious change to its anti-corruption legal framework. In that period, as we have seen in Chapter 3, law Severino changed the definition of the criminal act of extortion, while the introduction of the Italian Anti-Corruption Authority represented a move toward a more *ex ante* focus on prevention rather than *ex post* focus on repression.[65] Burdened by shortened statutory limitation and the fact that the entrepreneurs were no longer willing to collaborate as they had in the Mani pulite period[66] made the anti-corruption investigations arguably more difficult to conduct and to conclude than in the Mani pulite period. Still, the number of corruption-related investigations, remained higher than in most other European countries; however, these investigations do not necessarily result in convictions or even indictments.[67] Party finance legislation in Italy was a hotly debated topic during and after the Mani pulite campaigns, with one of the main proposals being that the public funding of political parties be ended. The 1993 referendum, in which citizens voted on limitations to public funding, and the (failed) 2000 referendum, in which citizens voted to abolish party funding altogether, did not lead to such a legislative outcome. Instead, party funding was to be more precisely tied to party activities such as campaigning and the work of parliamentary groups and to incentivize private financing.[68] The state audit supervised the measures, but parliament retained control of the sanctions. In 2012 and 2014, a series of changes led to further limitations on party funding and the creation of a Transparency Committee that would impose sanctions on violators.[69]

The expansion in measures related to anti-corruption investigations in criminal legislation would come only in 2019. Finding its political expression in the IDV party of Antonio di Pietro and in the later Five-Star Movement (M5S), the legislative proposal for changes to the Italian anti-corruption law was legitimized as a kind of follow-up of the Mani pulite.[70] While its adoption has not been a direct consequence of Mani pulite (coming in 2019, almost 20 years after the campaign and its leading cases ended), the very fact that its adoption was promoted by not only Di Pietro but also some of the leading political figures at the time testifies that the narrative of Mani pulite still resonates with the public.[71]

However, no significant changes to the work of the judicial councils, misuse of the judicial council, or the general weakening of the judiciary's position (such as those witnessed in Romania) happened.[72] Therefore, the weakening of the general position of the judiciary—if it can so be called—came more as a result of the personalization of politics and the entry of new political actors into the political field who have constantly attempted to delegitimize their work than of the aforementioned legislative interventions.[73] The political actors sought to undermine the reputation of the magistrates, not just those personally involved in Mani pulite but the judiciary as a whole. However, the internal competition that existed between the different judicial associations in Italy, coupled with the relatively strong position of the CSM as a regulator of the branch and also as its protector seems to have prevented a general backsliding of the judiciary's position.[74]

4.3.2 Brazil

The Lava Jato campaign and its different interpretations inspired many legislative changes. First was the overhaul of the party finance legislation, which brought a complete ban on donations from legal persons, a standard stricter than many recommended global good practices, for example, the CoE's GRECO recommendations.[75] The wide exposure of corporate corruption and bribery led to a strengthening of the implementation of corporate compliance programs, within which many of the Lava Jato key actors within the justice sector found a home, including Judge Moro himself, who obtained this position after having briefly served as justice minister.[76]

The seemingly central role that Judge Moro played during Lava Jato owed much to the fact that the Brazilian legal system allows the pre-trial judge (who acts in the pre-trial phase, for example, by allowing the warrants for investigative measures to proceed) to also be the trial judge handling the case, seeing in this no contradiction, as opposed to some European jurisdictions.[77] Propositions to limit such a wide discretionary role of the pre-trial judge have been supported in the aftermath of the campaign but were struck down by the Federal Supreme Court.[78] The most complex legislative proposal that the country encountered was the so-called "Abuse of Authority Law" focused on public agents such as judges, investigators, and prosecutors strengthening their responsibility in cases where they violated public power.[79] This strengthening of the disciplinary responsibility of judges, coupled with a shutdown of the Lava Jato Task Force by the General prosecutor of the Brazilian Public Ministry, was done in violation of an electoral promise that transparency and a continuation of the fight against corruption would be priorities for the Bolsonaro government.[80]

During his time as justice minister, Moro proposed various legislative proposals to strengthen the role of law enforcement agencies and prosecutors in fighting crime. Specifically, he proposed a stricter penal policy and an "illicit act exclusion" clause that would allow those accused of violent criminal acts to plead that they were acting under a heightened emotional state.[81] The proposal was initially rejected, together with most of the other measures that Moro proposed during his relatively brief tenure as the justice minister. The anti-crime package that was to follow up on some of the anti-corruption measures proposed by the civil society and the "ten measures against corruption" proposed by the Lava Jato Task Force[82] was adopted in a watered-down version, essentially allowing only an easier confiscation of the assets.[83] A question of the ownership of the full archives of the Lava Jato investigations and their potential abuse for political purposes was not resolved.[84]

The division that occurred between those who believed that the actions of Moro and Dallagnol, as described in the previous chapters, were legal and legitimate and those who thought they were not manifested themselves within the judiciary. Two of the three major judicial associations in Brazil (the Brazilian Magistrates Association, the Association of the Judges in Labor Courts, and the Association of Federal Judges) publicly supported the nomination of Moro for the position of justice minister and criticized Lula's legal team for appealing to the Human Rights Committee.[85] On the other hand, several less numerous judicial associations, such as the left-leaning Judges Against Democracy, strongly criticized the actions of the Lava Jato prosecutors, their legal strategies, and their conduct in the trials of Lula.[86] Several justices of the Supreme Court made public statements both critical and supportive of the operations.[87] Indirectly, this increased participation of the judges and prosecutors in the political discourse gained steam with the political mobilization of the prosecutors and became more important, as evidenced by the creation of the right-wing-oriented association of prosecutors, Pro-Society Public Prosecutor's Office, which began to openly advocate for the authoritarian practices of Bolsonaro's regime.[88] An overwhelmingly negative stance of the legal academic community, which distrusts the openly authoritarian

Bolsonaro government perceived by many to have come into power riding on the anti-corruption wave created by the Lava Jato,[89] coupled with a strong resistance of the Brazilian Supreme Court to bow down to political pressures, has, so far, highlighted a constituency willing to resist challenges to judicial independence.[90]

As such, the polarization within the judiciary was less pronounced than that observed in Romania, but the opposition to the attempts of the political control of the judiciary was strong, preventing, at least for the time being, greater backsliding.

4.3.3 Romania

As we have seen in Chapter 3, the direct legal impact of the campaigns was the loosening of the anti-corruption framework and an all-out attack of both the Romanian Constitutional Court and the government on the DNA of the safeguards of judicial independence. This charge against the judiciary began following the 2016 elections and the return to power of the PSD, the party that was primarily targeted by the campaigns. This culminated in the gradual disentanglement of the SRI from corruption prosecutions, the firing of the lead prosecutor, Laura Kovesi, and a series of cases brought before the CJEU in which the judges sought to challenge the independence of their work.

The cases initiated before the CJEU and the demonstrations against the legislation indicated a desire of the judiciary to staunchly defend its independence. But, just as in Italy and Brazil, the judiciary soon discovered that they did not seem to have a credible political ally. Despite the rise of the Union Save Romania party and the fact that it entered government, none of the laws adopted before 2020 were repealed following the defeat of PSD in the general elections. Instead, control of the politically engaged judicial council was further tightened over the judiciary. Internal divisions between the judiciary revealed a generational gap between the younger and the older judges. The older, more established judges were wary of the significant power of judicial associations, seeking instead to consolidate their power within the judiciary following the established ties with the Supreme Court and Constitutional Court justices and the judicial council members.[91] Unlike their Italian colleagues, who were able to challenge this thanks to the large representation of the lower court judges in the council, the Romanian judges were left underrepresented in the council.[92] Understood as a threat to corrupt government practices, the campaign that happened between 2006 and 2017 seems less likely to happen again until a change of generations occurs within the judiciary.

One effect of the campaign has been a contribution to the lowering of the overall level of corruption, including petty corruption. The civil service is now less willing to follow illegal orders from their superiors and is more prepared to oppose them, blow the whistle, or slow down the perpetration of illegal acts by refusing to participate in their commitment.[93] However, it is unclear to what extent this is the effect of the judicial anti-corruption campaign and to what extent it is the effect of the gradual modernization of the civil service, considerably funded and trained by the EU.

Party financing legislation was made more stringent following the gradual evolution of the standards in this area developed by GRECO and the pressure from civil society.[94] More public funds became available to the parties as it was recognized that the low level of their public financing might be a part of the problem of appropriation of public resources.[95] This, however, did not resolve the problem of spending in electoral campaigns, thanks to the rise of in-kind contributions to the parties in the form of media manipulation strategies exercised by media moguls close to the government.[96]

4.4 Impacts on the economic system

4.4.1 Italy

Following the strengthening and transformation of the European community into the European Union in 1992, significant economic reforms were launched in Italy that were to facilitate further economic integration and bring economic growth. This growth did not occur; already in 2004 it was recognized that Italy was becoming a laggard compared to other major European economies and that its growth was stagnating, with such a trend continuing up until this day.[97]

A robust positive effect of the Mani pulite was a drop in the costs of public investments in infrastructure that fell across the regions, suggesting a rise in the accountability of public officials.[98] In the south of the country, traditionally divided from the north in terms of economic development ever since the Italian unification in the second part of the 19th century, more investigations that resulted in condemning judgments were launched concerning the cases of public infrastructure and transport. But the divisions in development remained, even gaining ground between 1995 and 2005.[99] Empirical evidence suggests that in the 1980–2005 period, more crimes against public administration were committed in the southern regions and that, since 1995, more judgments of the Supreme Court of Cassation for acts of corruption have been issued for acts committed in the south.[100]

While this suggests a strong performance of the Italian judiciary in overcoming the historical trends in law enforcement problems more present in the south of Italy concerning norms and the punishment of perpetrators, the effects on economic growth have remained lackluster. This indicates that it is most likely that no improvement in the allocation of state funds in the south has occurred as a result of the campaigns or that, if it has, such improvement of allocation has been annulled by ineffective government policies. This would favor the line of reasoning advanced by Capusella, who argues that, post-1990s, Italy had lost its social capacity for growth and the anti-corruption campaign, as it was not able to rebuild the trust lost in the 1980s.[101] Surely, this argument is not without value; as we have seen in Chapter 3, parts of the Italian economic system have been described as feudal capitalism. Still, it appears reductionist to reduce the explanation for the lack of advances in economic development to the question of trust and social capital, losing sight of the fact that levels of trust are institutionalized only in Northern Europe and parts of Asia and the United States.[102]

It seems more reasonable to suggest that the Mani pulite exposed the links to corruption, thereby affecting the existing clientelist networks that have had control over red tape bureaucracy, but that the full success of this was never exploited. Namely, successive Italian governments attempting to conform to the Maastricht criteria and the introduction of a single European currency have led the country to make much less public investment[103] compared to other European states. At the same time, the fall in productivity and the reduced demand for the goods manufactured in some of the sectors where Italy traditionally dominated the global industry stalled the growth for the decades to come.[104] The combined effect of these two processes made the restructuralization of some of the leading enterprises slow and inefficient despite widespread knowledge (unearthed during or as a result of Mani pulite) of the corrupt practices in their work. Thus, the state and its governments have failed to capitalize on the opportunity for economic growth that was unleashed as a result of the revelation of corrupt networks due to both external constraints (austerity demands from the then-European Monetary Union) and the internal accumulated problems in the economy. Additional evidence suggesting an increased effectiveness in the provision of social services at the local and regional levels—a result of their outsourcing to the private sector—seems to support this proposal.[105]

4.4.2 Brazil

The mid-term and long-term effects of the campaign on the economic system were difficult to quantify owing to the fact that the ending of the campaign coincided with the outbreak of the COVID-19 pandemic, which hit Brazil particularly hard. Still, due to the major damage that the campaign caused to the two major business establishments, Petrobras, the state-owned petroleum company, and Odebrecht, the leading construction company and one of the biggest Brazilian companies overall, the short-term effects of the campaign were negative. As the effects of the investigation against Odebrecht spread to the entire construction sector, more than a million jobs were lost as the realization of investments in that sector fell, resulting in the loss of several billion dollars in taxes.[106] More robust evidence suggests a loss of confidence in international investors following the revelation of corrupt practices in leading Brazilian companies,[107] with the preliminary evidence suggesting that restructuralization programs and an increase in internal compliance mechanisms that commenced in both companies following the investigations will, undoubtedly, leave a deeper effect on their practices.[108] For example, it has been observed, that those Brazilian companies that are politically connected have, as a result of the Lava Jato, begun to exhibit a more proactive stance toward transparency.[109] The Brazilian economy, which in 2014, as the year when the campaign started, entered a recession with a 3.5% fall in economic growth while in 2019, as the last pre-COVID year, it grew by 1.1%.[110] Thus, it appears that the campaign did not impact the general economic trend that Brazil found itself in post-2014, which was that of the gradual recovery of the country from the recession that it entered in 2014, and that the campaigns did not lead to a policy paralysis that would have a further negative impact on growth.[111] There remained, however, just as in the case of Italy and Romania, a perception that the campaigns were more helpful to the internationalization of the Brazilian economy and the foreign investors than to the Brazilian companies themselves.[112]

4.4.3 Romania

Much more than the other two countries used in this book as a case study, Romania was perceived as a country unable to develop its potential due to corruption. Although the CVM benchmarks that were used to measure the effectiveness of the fight against corruption were primarily focused on the number of investigations launched by the magistrates,[113] another less pronounced goal of Romanian anti-corruption was economic; namely, to create a more stable environment for foreign investment and the use of EU structural and cohesion funds.[114] Judging by the data on rising foreign investment and strong economic growth in Romania in that period, the campaign has helped Romania achieve this goal, as the country quickly recovered from the 2009 to 2011 recession, becoming one of the leaders in economic growth in Europe in the second decade of the 21st century.[115] The campaigns were, however, criticized for effectively opening the doors to foreign investors as the prosecutions disproportionately focused on the activities of domestic entrepreneurs.[116] However, where foreign investors were themselves involved in dubious practices concerning the exploitation of resources, they would be faced with protests that would voice the dissatisfaction of citizens regarding the potentially corrupt practices.[117]

Much data analysis that would link the effects of anti-corruption to specific sectors of the economy has been inconclusive. What research has been done has identified no effect on public procurement at the local level[118] despite a large number of investigations focused on this particular aspect of corruption.[119] The allocation of central government funds to less developed regions historically preferred by the central government decreased and became more efficient and less politically polarized.[120] Still, the rise in foreign investment and an overall strong economic performance point to a gradual modernization and decoupling from past corrupt practices, which were fostered by neoliberal policies that promoted private investment. In that sense, a hypothesis worth exploring is that a large sector of the Romanian economy, which was in the area of the so-called shadow or gray economy, appears to have been formalized in the period of the campaign, either through the increased work of tax collectors or through corruption itself, as the corruptors sought to bribe the officials in order to begin doing business through official channels.[121]

4.5 Campaigns and the perception of corruption

4.5.1 Italy

"The repression of criminals has the same effects as those typically exerted by predators in the process of natural selection. We caught only the slowest prey, leaving free those who ran fastest," observed Piercamillo Davigo, one of the leading prosecutors of the pool, already in 1996.[122] This line of reasoning, presenting the campaign as an action that did not go far enough, seemed to have embodied not all but much of the general perception of those who saw the campaigns as a missed opportunity to make a break with the past and start over.

The indexes and surveys provide us with a mixed picture. The TI's Corruption Perception Index for Italy recorded a swing between 1994 and 1997, indicating that the perception of corruption among Italian businesspeople and foreign investors present in Italy[123] fell considerably.[124] After that period, no strong developments were recorded up until 2011, when the index fell considerably, reaching the 1996 level again only in 2021. The low values of the index in 2011 may be explained by the general uncertainty and lack of trust that the crisis of the last Berlusconi government, the judicial pressure on him, and the heavy financial crisis that befell Italy projected on those that were surveyed.[125] The recovery of the last decade may be attributed to the rise and application of preventive measures in anti-corruption. Worldwide Governance Indicators for the estimate of corruption describe an overall fluctuation in corruption control, with the values peaking in 2000 at the end of Mani pulite and then reaching their lowest value in 2014, with a gradual recovery afterward.[126] The World Justice RoLI within the 2010–2020 period (thus not covering the Mani pulite years) still reveals some interesting data, putting Italy's rule of law quality well above the world average, only slightly behind its Western European peers such as Germany and France. However, there remains a strong discrepancy between the assessed integrity of the judicial branch of government and that of the executive, which scores much lower than the judiciary.[127] In 2010, the Global Integrity Index measured that Italy actually implements most of its anti-corruption legislative framework with only a small implementation gap.[128] The IPI measured a consistent score for Italy in the 2015–2019 period, with an increase in judicial independence in that period. The QoG index measured a gradual decrease in the quality of government in the southern regions of Italy between 2010 and 2021, with the northern regions reporting a better quality than most of its Western European peers.[129]

In a 2004 survey, only a quarter of the Italian population stated that they believed that corruption in Italy was lower than it was before the Mani pulite.[130] In 2012, 43% claimed that their life was affected by corruption; in 2017, it was still one of the leading countries of the EU in terms of belief in institutional and business corruption by citizens.[131] However, in Italy, citizens believe that there are enough successful prosecutions that would deter corruption,[132] suggesting that, while they recognize the important work that the judiciary carries out in this domain, the solution to the problem of corruption for them lies outside of the judiciary. Also, there is a large discrepancy between the perceived and experienced rates of corruption, with the highest rate of experienced corruption in labor relations experienced by 2.5% of those surveyed.[133] Such a particularity may be reinforced by the view that the campaigns or the role that the judicial system ought to have in running the country may have become a cleavage[134] in Italian politics.[135] Still, the remark of Gherardo Colombo, who concluded that Mani Pulite ended "because citizens started to identify themselves with the people involved in the investigations"[136] may be interpreted as a claim that it was a change in the public narrative that effectively stopped the campaign. Contrary to this, strong empirical analysis seems to support the evidence that Italian voters, both during and after Mani pulite reacted to corruption coverage by the media, and as the coverage would drop, so would their readiness to vote the corrupt politicians out of office.[137] But, as stated previously in this chapter, such analysis loses sight of the general dynamics of Italian politics, which, just like any other, do not revolve only around corruption.

4.5.2 Brazil

Whereas the discreditation of the judicial anti-corruption campaigns in Italy and Romania was more a project of those political forces that perceived them as a threat against their rule in government, the Lava Jato campaign was shaken by revelations of collusion between the judge and the prosecutors of the Lava Jato pool released by the investigative journalists. This makes the legacy of the campaign in Brazil and its effects much more difficult to ascertain. On the one hand, the campaign achieved what previous campaigns, such as Mensalao and Sandcastle, failed to achieve—ending impunity for corrupt acts. On the other hand, this was achieved through means that were not always legal and were explicitly political—the prosecutors and the judge made several decisions that were to have political effects. The impact of the subsequent Bolsonaro presidency on the polarization of public opinion meant that, instead of a critical re-examination of what the campaign achieved, the narrative about the campaign depended on the allegiance of the persons one asks for opinion. From comparative experience with government corruption, the decision of the Bolsonaro's appointee, Head Prosecutor Arras, to shut down the task force in February 2021 with the explanation that the corruption within the government has been eradicated[138] seems premature and a sign that the government itself fears possible anti-corruption, but it also raises suspicion over the control of the data gathered by the prosecutors.[139]

This makes the assessments of the campaigns particularly interesting. Between 2012 and 2018, CPI fell as Brazil went from 75th to 94th on the global scale,[140] meaning that the campaigns, unlike those in Italy and Romania, have had less of an impact on the perception of corruption control. The awareness of corruption as the most important problem that the country is facing grew between 2012 and 2016 from 11% to 19%.[141] A quantitative exploration of citizens' perception of Lava Jato through focus groups led by Oxford University researchers revealed a strong partisan divide on the result of the investigations between those in favor and against the PT—however, those that were not PT supporters were convinced that the campaign was a chance for a permanent reduction of the level of political corruption in the country.[142] When Deltan Dallagnol was found to have civil liability for the actions taken against Lula before the Brazilian courts, he was ordered to pay a substantial sum of money, but most of this was paid by his political supporters.[143] This suggests that, as in Italy, the campaign may have become a cleavage that shapes voters' preferences regarding the country's politics. The World Justice ROLI stagnated with not much oscillation, leaving Brazil in 67th position on the global rankings, but with a perceived drop (from 30th to 40th spot) in the categories of improper government influence in criminal investigations and due process of law and the rights of the accused.[144] Worldwide Governance Indicators measured a fall in all categories observed (voice and accountability, political stability, government effectiveness, regulatory quality, rule of law, and control of corruption) for the 2014–2019 period.[145] The level of victimization of citizens by petty corruption from the governmental sectors lowered between 2013 and 2019.[146] While the IPI has measured an increase in the country's overall integrity, owing to the reforms that lowered the administrative burden for the citizens, a significant drop in the judicial independence has also been recorded.[147]

4.5.3 Romania

The following assessment of Romania was offered by its citizens in 2005:

> Romanians agree with the European Union that their nation does not fight corruption effectively. Although a majority of Romanians are satisfied with the mass media's efforts to combat corruption, the work of the police, government, and courts was unacceptable to more than 24% of the respondents. In fact, 17% of those surveyed believe that the government had taken no measures against corruption. This cynicism also extends to the private sector. For example, 50% of those surveyed believe that wealthy Romanians achieved success by violating the law, and another 24% believe that personal relationships produced wealth. Only 8% believe rich Romanians acquired their wealth through hard work or personal merit. But these attitudes do influence individual behavior: the same Romanian ticket taker who criticizes high level corruption, the nation's failure to defeat it, and the lack of personal integrity will admit a friend to a concert without a ticket.[148]

While the passage above reflected a belief among the population that the mentality of Romanians was the source of corruption, the 2007 surveys revealed a lack of trust concerning public institutions, with 38% identifying the government as corrupt and 69% believing that the refusal to pay a bribe would result in a significant problem.[149] In 2019, Romania stood at the 69th spot in the TI's global transparency rankings, reaching the highest spot in 2016 (in the midst of the anti-corruption campaign) while being lowest in 2010, suggesting that businesspersons and analysts have taken note of the anti-corruption efforts. While the country remained one of the most corrupt EU member states, the gains made in the last decade were undeniable. Part of the perception that may not be captured by the indexes was revealed in the interviews I conducted, with all of the interviewees agreeing that the level of petty corruption in Romania was decreasing dramatically, except in the healthcare sector, where the level of petty corruption remained high.[150] Of those surveyed in 2017, 18% have had an experience with a bribe in public administration,[151] a vast improvement compared to the situation in the first decade of this century. This progress was not matched in the sector of public procurement, which remained perceived—both by domestic and international actors—as corrupt as it was.[152] The World Justice ROLI stagnated between 2015 and 2020, leaving Romania relatively high on the index; however, a closer look reveals that the crime control of corruption strengthened in that period while the aspects regarding the procedural quality of justice went down.[153] Romania's performance according to the WGI was somewhat better, recording an improvement in the rule of law and regulatory quality sections but leaving the levels of corruption control where they were in 2006.[154] The Global Integrity Index measured a drop in the implementation of anti-corruption measures between 2006 and 2010 as well as a significant deviation in the implementation of anti-corruption measures.[155] The Index of Public Integrity recorded no strong changes in the position of Romania, with only slightly lower values for its judiciary in the 2015–2019 period.[156] The QoG index recorded a gradual decrease in corruption in all Romanian regions; however, the capital, Bucharest, remains one of the most corrupt EU member states regions.[157]

From this and the successful mass mobilizations of citizens in anti-corruption protests that occurred when the PSD-led Romanian government tried to curb the authorities of the judicial bodies investigating corruption, we conclude that a significant part of the population viewed the campaign positively as an attempt to end the impunity that surrounded the political leaders who considered corruption the most salient issue in the country.[158] This, however, did not stop a phenomenon that many consider to be loosely tied to prevalent corruption: migration. Namely, most Romanian economic migrants place corruption as one of the top reasons for their migration from the country.[159]

4.6 Conclusion

The campaigns have produced both short-term and long-term effects on the political system. They did not so much create a crisis or political fragmentation as they have fastened such processes where they were present, as in Brazil. An immediate, short-term effect may be observed in the case of Italy, where the campaign aided the collapse of the party system that characterized the Italian

First Republic, and Brazil, where the PT remained a key player in Brazilian politics but lost the presidency of the country. To a lesser extent, the same effect can be seen in Romania, where despite a significant number of prosecutions against the PSD, the party remained a key player in Romanian politics. However, in both Brazil and Romania, the political actors that were the major targets of the campaign remained important actors in political life. Electoral volatility was highest in Italy and significantly less pronounced in Brazil and Romania. It seems likely that the main difference in this sense was the additional external factors that contributed to the fall of the Italian political system that were absent in the cases of Brazil and Romania.

The campaigns did not become moments of refoundation in which the governing establishment irreversibly changed. Instead, and as evidenced by the opinions of the citizens and the electoral results in all three countries, the campaigns have become a cleavage in the politics of all three countries. To be for or against the campaign and the role that the judiciary played during the campaigns became almost synonymous with support for a certain political party. Neither the support for anti-corruption activities nor their negation became a guarantee of political success; the stance toward the campaigns and the role of the judiciary in the country did not become a predictor of political success. An example from Romania is telling; the 2016 elections, won by the PSD, were quickly followed by large anti-corruption demonstrations in which many pro-PSD voters also participated. Thus, voters are able to recognize that "their" political party supports corruption but does not necessarily punish corruption at the elections. Anti-corruption campaigns do not necessarily find a political home with a political project, and when they do, as they have in Italy and Romania, this is no guarantee of either the preservation of their legacy or the political success of the parties in question. The case of Italy, on the other hand, demonstrates that the political parties believe that, even 27 years after the beginning of the campaign, some of its messages still resonate with the electorate and testify to the party's stance against corruption, thus alluding to a long-term impact of the campaigns in the collective memory of the population.

Political parties have, particularly in Italy, become much more compliant with the legislative framework governing their financing. The misappropriation of funds by political parties that existed in Italy in the 1980s does not exist in either of the jurisdictions observed. Neither does the nexus between public procurement and party allegiance that di Pietro termed "dazione ambientale."[160] That is why the views of some of the major chroniclers of all three campaigns, who view their politicization and the presence of actors hostile to the judiciary in government (Berlusconi, Bolsonaro, Dragnea) in power as *prima facie* evidence of their failure, should be rejected.

Given the large amount of information that surfaced concerning the (mis) uses of the political, legal, and economic systems of the countries, the campaigns, in particular in Italy and Romania, established themselves as a means of transitional justice, revealing past injustices concerning the very functioning of the states in which they have happened. Revealing complex networks of influence trading and going far beyond investigative journalism, the campaigns presented corruption as a facilitator of governance. To a certain extent, this explains the salience of the topic of corruption in Italy and Romania as opposed to most other European countries.[161]

The effect on the legal system has been no less significant than that on the political system and more in line with our starting premise from the beginning of the chapter. Becoming a reference point for those who wanted to protect or attack the legacy of the campaigns, the campaigns and the actions of the judiciary have become a reference point for reforms that were to strengthen or loosen the anti-corruption legal framework in all three of the countries. In Brazil and Romania, this led to strong divisions among the judiciary and an increased importance of the role of judicial associations and the judicial council. In Italy, where both the judicial council and the judicial associations were already well-entrenched as institutions, the campaigns did not make such a strong impact on the positions of judges and their associations. The strong negative campaign that part of the political forces mobilized against the judiciary during and after Mani pulite failed to destabilize the judiciary, succeeding in making prosecutions harder. That was also the outcome of the legislative reforms carried out in Brazil and Romania. In none of the jurisdictions were the legislative proposals prepared with the input of the prosecutors and the judges adopted, suggesting a failure of the judiciary to shape the national legislative frameworks as it saw fit. The magistrates, however, fared better with the *esprit de corps* of the "attack judges." As we saw in Chapter 2 and the discussion in this chapter, already established in Italy in the 1970s, this esprit was merely reinforced in the 1990s, with its legacy present in the Italian judiciary to this day. The anti-corruption campaigns helped the formation of such a spirit in Romania and Brazil. However, in Romania and Brazil, the groups of magistrates and prosecutors sharing such an esprit are not getting stronger in numbers and still do not control the key judicial institutions such as the judicial councils and the supreme courts. These internal clashes within the judiciary and the subsequent threats to its constitutional position have led to a constitutional crisis in Romania and have exacerbated the existing constitutional crisis triggered by the Bolsonaro government in Brazil.[162] In Romania this has happened, as evidenced in Chapter 3 through the role of the Romanian Constitutional Court that has, acting in the manner of judicial populism, reached a series of decisions that have helped to dismantle the anti-corruption campaign through the so-called legal conflicts of constitutional nature, through rejection to enter into the judicial dialogue with the CJEU, and through subsequent weakening of the independence of the judicial branch of government.[163]

While the effects on the economic system are the hardest to pinpoint, in particular in Italy and Brazil, we may observe that they are beneficial but not very significant. As observed, in Italy, the rates of economic growth fell at the end of the 1990s without recovering to this day. However, the effect of campaigns is either perceived as weak or irrelevant, as it was insufficient to change the economic paradigm of the country, especially in comparison with the economic reforms that took place at the time. The effects in Brazil were mixed: the investigations led to loss of profit and jobs across the construction sector, while the overall compliance with anti-money laundering and compliance regulations improved with the confidence of domestic investors remaining unchanged. The campaigns have made a marginal contribution, in both Italy and Romania, to privatization in some sectors of public service provision. In that sense, the Romanian campaign has been more significant as an important signal to foreign investors that the protection of foreign investors is of importance to the state. However, the comparative experience of similar Eastern European economies signals that a massive investment flow that happened in Romania was also evidenced in Slovakia, a country that prosecuted very few corrupt politicians during and post the EU enlargement period.[164]

The perceptions of the judiciary became more favorable, most notably in the area of crime control, as a result of the campaigns, but the perceptions of the political class remained largely the same. The improvement of good governance in both Italy and Romania in the post-campaign periods may be attributed more to the effect of good governance and corruption prevention programs that the two countries invested in as a part of their international obligations than to the anti-corruption campaigns. Particularly high is the growth in government quality and regulatory capacity in Romania, with all of the indexes verifying this. However, as verified by objective and subjective measurements as well as prosecution statistics, public procurement programs represent strong pockets of resistance at the local and regional levels. That corruption cases still exist in this area and are being regularly prosecuted in both Italy and Romania seems to testify just to what extent corruption in public procurement had been prevalent prior to the campaigns.

Not all of the indexes seem to have captured the change that the campaigns have brought forward. While we would expect such a performance from the mostly subjective and qualitative CPI and WGI (and the public opinion surveys), it is, in fact, the quantitative integrity indexes that have failed to account for a substantial societal change. From a comparative standpoint, it is hard to explain how Brazil has more integrity in 2019 than in 2015 or how Italy has more judicial independence in 2019 than in 2015. Contrary to this, variations in other indexes seem to broadly correlate with the actions regarding crime control and judicial independence, revealing the impact of campaigns on these two variables.

Table 4.1 Impacts of the judicial anti-corruption campaign

	Italy	*Brazil*	*Romania*
Political fragmentation	Yes	Yes	No
Anti-corruption as a political project of the parties created during or after the campaign	Yes	No	Yes
Electoral volatility as a result of the campaigns	High	Medium	Low
Anti-corruption as a political cleavage	Yes	Yes	Yes
Change in perception of the political corruption by citizens	No	No	No

(*Continued*)

Table 4.1 (Continued)

	Italy	*Brazil*	*Romania*
Changes in perception of petty corruption by citizens	Yes	Yes	Yes
Legislative reform shaped by the judiciary successful	No	Partially	No
Strengthening of the legislative framework governing party financing	Yes	Yes	Yes
General economic impact	Low	Medium	Medium
Strengthening of public procurement framework and practices	Yes	N/A	Yes
Strengthening of disciplinary responsibility of judges	Yes	Yes	Yes
Perception of favorability of foreign investors	N/A	Yes	Yes
Constitutional crisis as a result of the campaign	No	No	Yes

Source: Author, on the basis of discussion and sources in Chapter 4.

Notes

1 Generally, see Chapter 1.

2 Liza Lanzone & Dwayne Woods, Riding the populist web: contextualizing the Five Star Movement (M5S) in Italy. Politics and Governance (2015); Wendy Hunter & Timothy J. Power, Bolsonaro and Brazil's illiberal backlash, *Journal of Democracy*, 30(1), (2019), 68–82; Tamas Kiss & István Gergő Székely, Populism on the semi-periphery: Some considerations for understanding the anti-corruption discourse in Romania, *Problems of Post-Communism*, 69(6), (2022), 514–527.

3 Rocco Sciarrone, (ed.) Politica e corruzione: Partiti e reti di affari da Tangentopoli a oggi. (2017). Ana Julia Akaishi & Pedro H.M. (eds.), *Albuquerque, Corrupção governamental no mercado de capitais: Um estudo acerca da operação Lava Jato*, 58 Revista de Administração de Empresas, (2018), 405–417.

4 Eric C. Chang, Miriam A. Golden & Seth J. Hill, Legislative malfeasance and political accountability, *World Politics*, 62(2), (2010), 177–220; Raffaele Asquer, Corruption charges and renomination chances: Evidence from the 1994 Italian parliamentary election. Available at SSRN 2491224 (2014); Rebecca Weitz-Shapiro & Matthew S. Winters, Can citizens discern? Information credibility, political sophistication, and the punishment of corruption in Brazil, *The Journal of Politics*, 79(1), (2017), 60–74; Mads Bjelke Damgaard, Media Leaks & Corruption in Brazil: The Infostorm of Impeachment and the Lava-Jato Scandal (2018).

5 On the uses of the CPI in that sense, see Theresa Thompson & Anwar Shah, Transparency International's Corruption Perception Index: Whose perceptions are they anyway, Discussion Paper (2005), https://citeseerx.ist.psu.edu/viewdoc/download?doi=10.1.1.370.4882&rep=rep1&type=pdf.

6 This is also because some of the indexes have changed their methodology over time which makes their comparison less likely. See Kristyna Chabova, Measuring corruption in Europe: Public opinion surveys and composite indices, *Quality and Quantity*, 51(4), (2017), 1877–1900.

7 Hazel Feigenblatt & Johannes Tonn, Measuring the opposite of corruption: The evolution of governance indicators at global integrity, In Debora Valentina Malito, Gaby Umbach & Nehal Bhuta (eds.) *The Palgrave Handbook of Indicators in Global Governance*, (2018), 277–299. It should be noted that certain elements included in the indexes, such as transparency of government and open budgets, are not necessarily useful for this inquiry as anti-corruption activities might not impact their changes but—in particular in Italy and Romania—fostered by other factors, such as the evolving standards of transparency promoted by the Council of Europe and the European Union.

8 Donald Sassoon, Tangentopoli or the democratization of corruption: Considerations on the end of the Italy's First Republic, *Journal of Modern Italian Studies*, 1(1), (1995), 124–143.
9 Violante, *I Magistrati* at 170.
10 Antonio Di Pietro. Craxi era solo uno dei tanti. Io puntavo ad Andreotti, mi hanno fermato. *L'Espresso*, January 17, 2020 at https://espresso.repubblica.it/plus/articoli/2020/01/17/news/antonio-di-pietro-bettino-craxi-giulio-andreotti-1.343057/.
11 Sberna & Vannucci, "It's the politics, stupid!".
12 Generally, see Rhodes, Chapter 2.
13 Generally, see Alessandro Brogi, Confronting America the Cold War Between the United States and Communists in France and Italy (2011). For the distance between PCI and the Soviet Union, see Joan B. Urban, Moscow and the PCI in the 1970s: Kto kovo? *Studies in Comparative Communism*, 13(2–3), (1980), 99–167.
14 Piero Ignazi & E. Spencer Wellhofer, Votes and votive candles: Modernization, secularization, Vatican II, and the decline of religious voting in Italy: 1953–1992, *Comparative Political Studies*, 46(1), (2013), 31–62.
15 John Agnew, Genius Loci, the geography of Italian politics, In Andrea Mammone, Ercole Parini & Giuseppe A. Veltri (eds.) *The Routledge Handbook of Contemporary Italy*, 162, (2015).
16 The members of the PCI less so because they were not present in the national level governments, as their presence in government was limited to the local and regional level. However, Mani pulite did not consider illicit financing of PCI that came directly from the Soviet Union, as there was a lack of evidence for the prosecution in which some saw a bias toward the PCI. For an elaboration of this, see Burnett & Mantovani, The Italian guillotine. With regards to DC, although many of its leaders were tried for corruption, one of their key figures, the seven times prime minister of Italy Giulio Andreotti, was tried for the connections of the DC to the mafia in the trial that ended with acquittal in 2004. Despite the fact that neither of the two instances described here gave sufficient grounds for a final judicial resolution, the public opinion was, at the time, against the PCI and DC which helped the cause of Mani pulite prosecutors.
17 Sarah Waters, Tangentopoli and the emergence of a new political order in Italy, *West European Politics*, 17(1), (1994), 169–182.
18 Certain authors claim that the lack of importance of the Mani pulite lies precisely in the fact that corruption scandals existed during the whole period of the First Republic (for example, see Leonardo Morlino & Marco Tarchi). The dissatisfied society: The roots of political change in Italy, *European Journal of Political Research*, 30, (1996), 41–63. I disagree with this assessment; mere awareness about the existence of corruption is not the same as its judicial prosecution, especially on such a grand scale as in Italy in the 1990s.
19 Generally, see Stille, Excellent cadavers.
20 Aldo Giannuli, Classe dirigente Mappa del potere in Italia fra la Seconda e la Terza Repubblica, 105, (2017).
21 Sberna & Vannucci, "It's the politics, stupid!".
22 Donatella Della Porta & Alberto Vannucci, Corruption and anti-corruption: The political defeat of 'Clean Hands' in Italy, *West European Politics*, 30(4), (2007), 830–853.
23 Sberna & Vannucci, "It's the politics, stupid!".
24 However, not all votes of the DC went to Berlusconi—much was gained by the then regional party Lega Nord.
25 Violante, *I Magistrati*.
26 Sandro Busso & Attilio Scaglione, Percorsi politici prima e dopo Tangentopoli. In R. Sciarrone (ed.) *Politica e Corruzione Partiti e Reti di affair da Tangentopoli a oggi*, (2017), 215–217. One-quarter of the politicians investigated in Mani Pulite ended

their careers immediately after the operation, while most of the rest got involved in other parties.

27 Travaglio, Gomez & Barbacetto, Mani pulite at 26.

28 Graziana Corica & Rocco Sciarrone, Profili e carriere politiche. Biografie, cariche, partiti. In Sciarone (ed.) see above note 3, 205. From the individuals prosecuted for corruption after Mani pulite, 40% came from the ranks of pre-Mani pulite politically active persons.

29 Sandro Busso & Roccco Sciarrone, Alal ricerca della corruzione politica. In Sciarrone (ed.), see above, note 3, 462.

30 James L. Newell, Magistrates going into politics: Antonio di Pietro and Italy of values. In *The Routledge Handbook of Contemporary Italy*, (2015), 227–236.

31 In that sense, see analysis in Luigi Curini, Corruption, Ideology and Populism, 107–113, (2018).

32 Generally, see Chang et al., note 4.

33 See Cesar Zucco, The president's new constituency: Lula and the pragmatic vote in Brazil's 2006, *Journal of Latin American Studies*, 40, (2008), 29–49. (Describing the emergence of this development already in the 2006 elections.).

34 Richard Lapper, Beef, Bible & Bullets: Brazil in the age of Bolsonaro, (2021), 148–155.

35 See Alfredo S. Filho & Armando Boito, Brazil: The débâcle of the PT and the rise of the "new right", *Socialist Register*, 52, (2016). Additionally, as we have observed in Chapter 2, the partisanship of the media, which focused the coverage of Lava Jato mostly on the crimes of the PT cadres, created a (to a large extent exact) perception of the leading role of that party in the corruption scheme.

36 Lula 2022? Brazil poised for sensational political comeback, *The Guardian*, July 30, 2021, http://theguardian.com/world/2021/jul/30/lula-2022-brazil-poised-for-sensational-political-comeback.

37 Brazil's Bolsonaro faces more corruption allegations, France 24, July 6, 2021, at https://www.france24.com/en/americas/20210706-brazil-s-bolsonaro-faces-more-corruption-allegations.

38 See Filho & Boito, Brazil: The débâcle of the PT and the rise of the "new right".

39 Wendy Hunter & Timothy J. Power, Bolsonaro and Brazil's illiberal backlash, *Journal of Democracy*, 30(1), (2019), 68, 77. The numbers mentioned represent a change from the 2014 general elections to the 2018 general elections.

40 Frances Hagopian. Delegative democracy revisited: Brazil's accountability paradox, *Journal of Democracy*, 27(3), (2016), 119–128.

41 Cesar Zucco Jr. & Power, T. J. (2021). Fragmentation without cleavages? Endogenous fractionalization in the Brazilian party system, *Comparative Politics*, 53(3), 477–500.

42 André Borges, The illusion of electoral stability: From party system erosion to right-wing populism in Brazil, *Journal of Politics in Latin America*, 13(2), (2021), 166–191.

43 David J. Samuels & Cesar Zucco, Partisans, antipartisans, and nonpartisans: voting behavior in Brazil, (2018), 3–4.

44 Donatellla Della Porta, Political parties and corruption: Ten hypotheses on five vicious circles, *Crime, Law and Social Change*, 42(1), (2004), 35, 43–44.

45 Emilio Peluso Neder Meyer, Constitutional Erosion in Brazil, (2021), 99.

46 Daniel Brett, Trouble at the top: Corruption, anti-corruption and the battle for political survival, *South East Europe Blog*, (2015).

47 Clara Volintiru & George Stefan, Social roots: How Romania's Social Democrats won the 2016 election, https://blogs.lse.ac.uk/europpblog/2016/12/21/social-roots-romania-2016-election/ (2016).

48 Interview with a Romanian civil society activist, July 2021.

49 Ionut Valentin Chiruta, Using the past in populist communicational strategies, *Populism*, 3(2), (2020), 223–256.

50 Interview with a Romanian investigative journalist, July 2021.
51 Andreas Bågenholm & Nicholas Charron. Accountable or untouchable? Electoral accountability in Romanian local elections, *Electoral Studies*, 66, (2020), 102183.
52 Mihaela Ivănescu, An electoral outlier or second order business as usual? A decade of European elections in Romania (2009–2019), *Revista de Stiinte Politice*, 70, 153–166.
53 Kiss & Székely, Populism on the semi-periphery.
54 Interview with a former Romanian politician, July 2021.
55 USR PLUS leaves Romanian government, *EURACTIV*, September 7, 2021, https://www.euractiv.com/section/politics/short_news/usr-plus-leaves-romanian-government/ (last accessed 02/02/2022).
56 Kiss & Székely, Populism on the semi-periphery.
57 See Cristina Dallara, Powerful resistance against a long-running personal crusade: The impact of Silvio Berlusconi on the Italian judicial system, *Modern Italy*, 20(1), 59, 64 (2015). Also, see Violante, note 37 (Chapter 2), 122–125 (criticizing the center-left parties for their inability to prevent the discussion not just on specific cases but on the very position of the judiciary and being too focused on themselves).
58 Generally, see carlo Brunetti Le principali novita introdotte dalla legge 251/05 (cd. ex/Cirielli), 3 Rassegna penitenzinare e criminologia, 47 (2006).
59 See Dallara, note 57 at 64.
60 Picci & Vannucci, note 43 (Chapter 1) at 48.
61 Eventually, the Constitutional Court of Italy declared this measure unconstitutional.
62 Alessandro de Giorgi, Liberta, eguaglianza, proprieta e Bentham al tempo di Berlusconi, 88–98 (2006).
63 Violante, note 37 (Chapter 2) at 110.
64 See Dallara, note 57 at 64–65.
65 Vincenzo Mongillo, La Legge "Spazzacorrotti": Ultimo Approdo Del Diritto Penale Emergenziale Nel Cantiere Permanente Dell'anticorruzione, *Diritto Penale Contemporaneo*, 5, (2019), 240.
66 Davigo, note 53 (Chapter 3) at 64.
67 See Carlo Guarnieri, Cristina Dallara & Michele Sapignoli, Political corruption in Italy: Many investigations few convictions, *Civitas—Revista de Ciências Sociais*, 20(3), (2021), 324–334.
68 Pizzimenti E., The evolution of party funding in Italy: A case of inclusive cartelization, *Modern Italy*, 22(1), 71–85.
69 Pizzimenti E., The evolution of party funding in Italy: A case of inclusive cartelization, *Modern Italy*, 22(1), 71–85.
70 See the Uniti contra corruzione, A un anno dall'entrata in vigore della legge #Spazzacorrotti at https://www.youtube.com/watch?v=XoK84NUILWQ&t=4459s.
71 Anticorruzione, lo Spazzacorrotti e legge. Di Maio:"Lo aspetavamo dai tempi di mani pulite." Bonafede: "E' per I giovani", Il Fatto Quotidiano, dec 16, 2018. https://www.ilfattoquotidiano.it/2018/12/18/anticoruzzione-ok-definitivo-della-camera-allo-spazzacorotti-bonafede-e-legge-che-pensa-ai-giovani/4844833.
72 An exception to this may be considered in the case of increased civil liability of judges that was adopted in 2015 after more than two decades of lobbying from the center-right parties that started as a result of the Mani pulite framework. See Simone Benvenuti, The politics of judicial accountability in Italy: Shifting the balance, *European Constitutional Law Review*, 14(2), (2018), 369–393.
73 Violante, note 37 (Chapter 2), 115–116. Cf. Sondra Z. Koff & Stephen P. Koff, Italy from the First to the Second Republic, (2019), 43–44.
74 See Manzi, note 12 (Chapter 2), 107–113.
75 See an overview of the current Brazilian party finance legislation and its evolution at the website of the International Institute for Democracy and Electoral Assistance at https://idea.int/data-tools/country-view/68/55. This progress remains fragile and under threat from the current government.

76 Fabio Engelmann, The 'Fight Against Corruption' in Brazil from the 2000s: A Political Crusade through Judicial Activism, *Journal of Law and Society*, (2020), 13–14.
77 Interview of Deltan Dallagnol. In Lagunes & Svejnar (eds.) note 9 (Chapter 2) at 125.
78 Juiz das garantias fica de fora da pauta do STF para o primeiro semestre de 2022, ConJur, December 19, 2021 https://conjur.com.br/2021-dez-19/juiz-garantias-fica-fora-pauta-stf-semestre.
79 Brazil: Setbacks in the Legal and Institutional Anti-Corruption Frameworks, Transparency International Brazil, (2019), 8.
80 Paul Lagunes et al., President Bolsonaro's promises and actions on corruption control, *Revista Direito GV*, 17(2), (2021), 15–20.
81 Peluso Meyer, note 45 at 97.
82 See above, Chapter 2.
83 Lagunes et al., note 80 at 14–15.
84 Peluso Meyer, note 45 at 97.
85 Peluso Meyer, note 45 at 91.
86 The extensive communication of this association concerning Lava Jato may be found at the association's website at http://ajd.org.br/inicio/busca?searchword=lava%20jato&searchphrase=all.
87 Interview with a Brazilian academic, September 2021.
88 Carlos Henrique Vieira Santana & Marcela Nogueira Ferrario, Crafting Negative Partisanship in Brazil and the Rise of Bolsonaro, (2024). 10, https://preprints.apsanet.org/engage/apsa/article-details/66f1750312ff75c3a13838b1
89 Interview with a Brazilian academic September 2021; Interview with a Brazilian political scientist, September 2021.
90 Peluso Meyer, note 45 at 219–225.
91 Interview with a Romanian judicial activist, July 2021.
92 Interview with a Romanian judicial activist, July 2021.
93 Interview with a Romanian civil society activist, July 2021.
94 See an overview of the current Romanian party finance legislation and its evolution at the website of the International Institute for Democracy and Electoral Assistance at https://idea.int/data-tools/country-view/252/55; See GRECO reports dealing with party funding in Romania Council of Europe (2017). Addendum to the Second Compliance Report on Romania "Incriminations (ETS 173 and 191 GPC 2)" "Transparency of Party Funding", Strasbourg 20–24 March 2017.
95 Clara Volintiru, Clientelism and Cartelization in Post-communist Europe: The Case of Romania, Unpublished Ph.D. dissertation, 256–259.
96 Alexandra Iancu & Sorina Soare, Party membership in Romania: Political legitimacy, party finance and organisational changes, *Sociologicky Casopis*, 56(3), (2020), 315, 335–336; Claudia Marian, The Social Democrat Party and the use of political marketing in the 2016 elections in Romania, *Sfera Politicii*, 26, (2018), 70–82.
97 Generally, see Capussela, note 27 (Chapter 2).
98 Generally, see Miriam Golden & Lucio Picci, Proposal for a new measure of corruption, illustrated with Italian data, *Economics and Politics*, 17, (2005); Piercamillo Davigo, L'occasione Mancata (2021).
99 Nadia Fiorino, Emma Galli & Ilaria Petrarca, Corruption and growth: Evidence from the Italian regions, *European Journal of Government and Economics*, 1(2), (2012), 126–144. Also, see Raffaella Coppier, Mauro Costantini & Gustavo Piga, The role of monitoring of corruption in a simple endogenous growth model, *Economic Inquiry*, 51(4), (2013), 1972–1985. (Arguing that the effect of monitoring on economic efficiency was to a certain extent felt during and after Mani pulite in the north but not in the south of the country.).

100 Sandro Busso & Rocco Sciarrone. Alla ricerca della corruzione politica. In Sciarrone R. (ed.) *Politica e Corruzione Partiti e reti di affari da Tangentopoli a oggi*, (2017), 57–62.
101 Andrea Capussela, Political Economy of Italy's Decline, (2018), 17.
102 See Fisman & Golden, note 100 (Chapter 1) at 166.
103 Kenneth Dyson & Kevin Featherstone. Italy and EMU as a 'Vincolo Esterno': Empowering the technocrats, transforming the state. *South European Society and Politics*, 1(2), (1996), 272–299.
104 Roberta Rabellotti, Anna Carabelli & Giovanna Hirsch, Italian industrial districts on the move: Where are they going? *European Planning Studies*, 17(1), (2009), 19–41.
105 Grazio Sebastiana Corica & Vittorio Martone, I circuiti corruttivi nei livelli di governo in Sciarrone R. (ed.) *Politica e Corruzione Partiti e reti di affari da Tangentopoli a oggi*, (2017), at 151.
106 Luiz Fernando de Paula & Rafael Moura, Consequências econômicas da operação Lava-Jato. *Valor Econômico*, 28, (2019).
107 Padula, A.J.A. & Albuquerque, P.H.M. Government corruption on Brazilian capital markets: A study on Lava Jato (Car Wash) investigation, *Revista de Administração de Empresas*, 58, (2018), 405–417.
108 Nicolas Campos et al. The ways of corruption in infrastructure: Lessons from the odebrecht case. *Journal of Economic Perspectives*, 35(2), (2021), 171–190.
109 Arthur do Nasimento Ferreira Barros et al., Are politically connected firms in Brazil worried about anti-corruption disclosure? *Journal of Accounting in Emerging Economies*, 12(2), (2022), 300–317.
110 According to the data of World Bank available at https://data.worldbank.org/indicator/NY.GDP.MKTP.KD.ZG?locations=BR.
111 Generally, see Antonio M. Spilimbergo & Krishna M. Srinivasan, Brazil: Boom, bust, and the road to recovery, (2019).
112 Interview with a Brazilian academic, July 2021.
113 See above, Chapter 2.
114 Mungiu-Pippidi, note 33 (Chapter 2) at 107.
115 12 years of European economic growth, in just two maps, *World Economic Forum* June 18, 2019. https://www.weforum.org/agenda/2019/06/a-european-atlas-of-economic-success-and-failure; The Netherlands on the European scale 2019. https://longreads.cbs.nl/european-scale-2019/economic-growth/.
116 See Mendelski, note 6 (Chapter 2), n. 63.
117 How Romanian people Power took on Mining and Corruption, Foreign Policy, November 17, 2016, https://foreignpolicy.com/2016/11/17/how-romanian/people-took/on-mining-and-corruption-rosia-montana.
118 Corina Lacatus & Ulrich Sedelmeier, Does monitoring without enforcement make a difference? The European Union and anti-corruption policies in Bulgaria and Romania after accession, *Journal of European Public Policy*, 27(8), (2020), 1236–1255.
119 Irina Mădălina Doroftei, Measuring government favouritism objectively: The case of Romanian public construction sector, *European Journal on Criminal Policy and Research*, (2016), 399–413.
120 Map of Clientelism in Romania, Expert Forum, https://expertforum.ro/en/clientelism-map.
121 Sorin Nicolae Borlea, Sorin Nicolae, Monica Violeta Achim & Monica Gabriela A. Miron. Corruption, shadow economy and economic growth: An empirical survey across the European Union countries, *Studia Universitatis "Vasile Goldis" Arad–Economics Series*, 27(2), (2017), 19–32. A larger ethnographic study gathering the data on this evolution was presented by Roxana Bratu. Corruption, Informality and Enterpreneurship in Romania, (2017).
122 Davigo, note 53 (Chapter 3) at 19.

123 In the 1990s, the calculations of the Corruption Perception Index relied primarily on business people's and foreign investors' perceptions of the presence of corruption within a region.

124 See the variations of the CPI at https://tradingeconomics.com/italy/corruption-index.

125 Mungiu-Pippidi, A., & Dadašov, R, Measuring control of corruption by a new index of public integrity, *European Journal on Criminal Policy and Research*, 22, (2016), 415–417. https://doi.org/10.1007/s10610-016-9324-z.

126 See the variations of the WGI at https://db.nomics.world/WB/WGI?dimensions=%7B%22country%22%3A%5B%22IT%22%5D%7D.

127 See the variations of the ROLI for Italy at https://worldjusticeproject.org/rule-of-law-index/country/2019/Italy/Absence%20of%20Corruption/.

128 Global Integrity Report available at http://globalintegrity.org/wp=content/uploads/2-19/08/GIRScorecard2010_Italy_comments.pdf.

129 See the scores of Italian regions for the QoG index at http://qog01-p.gu.gu.se/shiny/users/xalvna/qog/eqi_map/. Also, see Nicholas Charron, Victor Lapuente & Monica Bauhr. Sub-national quality of Government in EU member states: presenting the 2021 European Quality of Government Index and its relationship with COVID-19 indicators. University of Gothenburg: The QoG Working Paper Series 2021, 4.

130 Fisman & Golden, note 100 (Chapter 1) at 204.

131 Alina Mungiu-Pippidi, The good, the bad and the ugly: Controlling corruption in the European Union. Advanced Policy Paper for Discussion in the European Parliament, 9, (2013); Special Eurobarometer 470 Corruption (2017).

132 Special Eurobarometer 470 Corruption, (2017), 60.

133 Picci & Vannucci, note 43 (Chapter 1) 52 at 55.

134 For the use of the word cleavage in political science (essentially describing the term as a specific type of conflict in democratic politics that is triggered by large-scale societal processes that lead to a social division concerning the recognition and the use of social norms), see Simon Bornschier, Cleavage Politics in Old and New Democracies, (2009) at www.livingreviews.org/lrd-2009-6.

135 Dallara, note 57 at 69–70 strongly argues that trust in the courts in Italy is lower than in other EU countries, following up with the data that this lack of support is more pronounced in those that are center-right voters.

136 Gherardo Colombo. Sulla corruzione abbiamo perso, ora tocca ai ragazzi. *Corriere Della Sera*, May 12, 2019, https://milano.corriere.it/19_maggio_12/gherardo-colombo-sulla-corruzione-abbiamo-perso-ora-tocca-ragazzi-7fad41ac-742b-11e9-a46f-84c039eb72db.shtml.

137 Chang et al., Legislative malfeasance and political accountability.

138 Amelia Cheatham, Lava Jato: See How Far Brazil's Corruption Probe Reached, Council on Foreign Relations (2021). https://www.cfr.org/in-brief/lava-jato-see-how-far-brazils-corruption-probe-reached.

139 Celso Rocha de Barros How Lava Jato Died—And What Comes Next, https://www.americasquarterly.org/article/how-lava-jato-died-and-what-comes-next/ (2020).

140 Corruption Perception Index, is available at https://www.transparency.org/en/cpi/2020/index/bra.

141 Latin American Public Opinion Project, cited as presented in Eduardo Carvalho Nepomuceno Alencar, Applying Structural Equation Modeling to Analyze the Mutual Causality between Corruption and Trust and the Impact of Lava Jato: Evidence from Brazil and Mexico, (2021), 6.

142 E. Gonzales-Ocantos, 2021. The Criminalization of Corruption in Latin America: Causes and Consequences of Lava Jato (unpublished manuscript, see the presentation at https://www.youtube.com/watch?v=C0SiWJ1QnDY between the 18- and 35-minute mark. Note that these focus groups were organized prior to the revelations

of the collusion between Dallagnol and Moro—it is reasonable to conclude that later surveying would have revealed even more division and skepticism.

143 Dallagnol terá que indenizar Lula em R$ 75 mil por entrevista do PowerPoint, LexLatin, 22 March 2022, https://br.lexlatin.com/noticias/dallagnol-indenizar-lula-75-mil-entrevista-powerpoint.

144 See the standings of Brazil on the World Justice ROLI at https://worldjusticeproject.org/rule-of-law-index/pdfs/2020-Brazil.pdf.

145 See the standings of Brazil on the WGI at http://info.worldbank.org/governance/wgi/Home/Reports by selecting Brazil from the drop-down menu.

146 See Latinobarometro data for Brazil in 2013 and 2020 to the question "Have you or anyone you know personally witnessed an act of corruption or bribetaking by a politician or government official in the past year?".

147 See the performance of Brazil at the IPI index at http://integrity-index.org/?yr=2019.

148 Kandis Scott, The European Union and romanian mentalitate: A case study of corruption, *Santa Clara Journal of International Law*, 3, (2005), 225.

149 Report *From the Commission to The European Parliament and the Council on Progress in Romania Under the Co-Operation and Verification Mechanism*, Romania: Technical Update, European Commission Com (2008), 494 final, 14.

150 One in five people in parts of EU pay bribes for healthcare, survey finds, *The Guardian*, June 15, 2021, https://www.theguardian.com/world/2021/jun/15/one-in-five-people-in-parts-of-eu-pay-bribes-for-healthcare-survey-finds.

151 Cristina Matiuta, The ICT and its uses: fighting corruption and promoting participatory democracy—the case of Romania. In Anna Visvizi & Miltiadis D. Lytras, (eds.) *Politics and Technology in the Post-Truth Era*, 159–169.

152 Andi Hoxhaj The EU Anti-Corruption Report a Reflexive Governance Approach, (2020), 133.

153 See the Romania standings on the index at the World Justice ROLI site https://worldjusticeproject.org/rule-of-law-index/pdfs/2020-Romania.pdf. Cf. Mendelski, note 189 (Chapter 2).

154 See the standings of Romania at the WGI at http://info.worldbank.org/governance/wgi/Home/Reports.

155 Global Integrity reports for Romania for the years 2006 and 2010 available at http://globalintegrity.org/resource/gir2006/report/Romania/ and http://globalintegrity.org/resource/gir2010/report/Romania/.

156 For the scores of Romania on the Index of Public Integrity see http://integrity-index.org/yr=2019.

157 For the scores of Romania on the QoG index see https://www.gu.se/en/quality-government/qog-data/data-downloads/european-quality-of-government-index.

158 To this point, at the height of the campaign, 93% of Romanians perceived corruption as an important problem that the country faces. See European Commission 2017. Special Eurobarometer 397 on Corruption. For mobilization of the Romanian population by the civil society organizations in anti-corruption protests see Ana Adi & Darren Lilleker, #rezist-Romania's 2017 Anti-corruption Protests: Causes, development and implications, (2017), 1.

159 Raluca Iacob. Brain drain phenomenon in Romania: What comes in line after corruption? *Revista Română de Comunicare şi Relaţii Publice*, 20(2), (2018), 53–78.

160 See above, Chapter 3.

161 Cf. Guarnieri et al., note 67.

162 In this book, I have not introduced the concept of the constitutional crisis, as it is here understood more as a consequence of the other actions of the Bolsonaro government than of Lava Jato proper. See Meyer, note 45 for a definition of the constitutional crisis in Brazil.

163 Cf. Tănăsescu, E. S., & Selejan-Gutan, B. *A Tale of Primacy*, Verfassungsblog, (2021).

164 Maria Popova & Vincent Post. Prosecuting high-level corruption in Eastern Europe, *Communist and Post-Communist Studies*, 51(3), (2018), 1–14.

5 Conclusion

5.1 Introduction

The two main theoretical approaches in corruption studies, principal–agent theories, and collective action theories, introduced in the first chapter of this book, demonstrated their value in explaining the emergence and development of judicial anti-corruption campaigns. In that sense, we can observe that judicial anti-corruption campaigns change the equilibrium of corruption within a society, and this effect has been observed in all three of the cases discussed herein. First, anti-corruption campaigns lead to a change in corrupt exchanges, with misuses that benefit political parties now being less likely to occur as changes to the party financing system have made standards in that area stricter. Second, anti-corruption campaigns impact the performance of political parties. In that sense, the impact of transparency and access to information about the practices of the government and the electoral parties leads to a change in the behavior of voters. Moreover, the campaigns become a cleavage, something over which the political parties and societies divide based on partisanship and how they perceive the role of the judiciary and its relationship to politics. The fact that this cleavage exists over time, as described in the cases of Italy and Romania, and is very likely to manifest itself in the case of Brazil proves that we should observe the campaigns as big-bang moments of legal, political, and societal mobilization against corruption. In particular, the evidence from Italy and Romania suggests that, despite the significant backlash against the campaign, the judiciary remains resilient and prepared to launch investigations against top-level officials and that the campaigns may (as we have seen in the case of Italy, even 27 years since its beginning) remain a rallying point for those willing to mobilize the people in an anti-corruption struggle.

Equally, the anti-corruption campaigns are (as the anti-corruption literature explained in Chapter 1) a big-bang moment for those who are willing to mobilize the people against the significant role of the judiciary in society. While they send a strong and inspiring message that mobilizes civil society, signaling that the days of impunity for the holders of the highest political offices are over, the change they bring is mirrored in the incremental reforms, meaning that it does not change the governance paradigm in society. In that sense, they

DOI: 10.4324/9781003334811-5

are not "game changers," representing more a light that would start the fire than the fire itself. This means that the long-lasting impacts of the campaigns exist but do not represent a point of no return for anti-corruption, especially not the one expected by the prosecutors as such, that is, the foundation of the political class in the case of Italy, the foundation of public morals in the case of Brazil, and the elimination of corrupt practices in the case of the Romanian political parties. In that sense, for those who would wish to consider them big bangs solely on the basis of their success, only the Brazilian campaign presents itself as a big flop, while the Italian and, in particular, the Romanian campaign seem more successful.

This is also evidenced by the failures of the reform projects, both legal and societal, initiated by the campaigns. The ten measures against corruption of the Brazilian public prosecutors, the Cernobbio proposal of the Mani pulite pool developed in cooperation with the academic community, and the proposals for legislative changes proposed by the Romanian DNA, have all failed without bringing the changes necessary to alleviate the fight against corruption for law enforcement agencies or the judiciary. More than this, both the prosecutors and the judiciary as a whole were faced with a backlash from the other two branches of government but also with an internal struggle over what the role of the judiciary within a society should be. Where the judicial councils and associations had more independence and power, as in Italy, the backlash made less of a success; where they had less power, such as in Romania, the conflict over the position of the judiciary led to a constitutional crisis, and where the constitutional crisis was created as a result of other political developments, such as in Brazil, the role of the judiciary became crucial in preventing further backsliding. Paradoxically, we may conclude that even this backlash proves the thesis that observing judicial anti-corruption campaigns as events stemming out of stronger constitutional entrenchment and judicial socialization appears more useful as an explanans than observing them as events that stem purely from the particularities of a legal culture.

5.2 Nature of the campaigns

This proves that the theoretical stance taken in Chapter 2, namely that anti-corruption judicial campaigns are closely linked to judicial reputation, is valid. The campaigns strengthened the reputation of the individuals but also the reputation of the judiciary as a whole. But, reputation is a two-way street. One direction is represented by the reputation of the individuals who engage in the campaigns in the most direct manner, and the other is the perception of reputation that the judges and magistrates have of the judicial branch of government to which they belong. In the cases I analyzed, the members of the judiciary not only accepted that their actions would have political consequences; they accepted these consequences and have, in the case of Brazil, explicitly shaped some of their activities to influence the outcome of the campaigns. As a result, the personal reputation of the prosecutors involved in the campaigns grew; they became internationally recognized anti-corruption crusaders awarded and recognized by the international anti-corruption community. These actors believed that they were fulfilling the role that the judiciary ought to have. But also, many key actors came to believe that the real power was elsewhere; Dallagnol, Moro, and di Pietro all started their political projects. The backlash against Kovesi perhaps did not lead her to start a political project. However, she has remained an essential figure for the political parties based on anti-corruption and a potential presidential candidate in the future.

If the campaigns were fierce and strong in the mobilization of anti-corruption discourse and activism, no less intense was the backlash against them. In all three cases, the negative effects on the judicial branch as a whole have been initiated through legislative changes, negative populist rhetoric that seeks to undermine the judiciary's reputation, and popular mobilization against anti-corruption. In all three of the cases, the judiciary responded differently but with the same goal of preservation of independence. In Italy, it was the mediating role of the judicial council and the judicial associations that prevented backsliding and allowed the magistrates to lobby for solutions that would preserve independence. In Brazil, the existing judicial associations and councils, while supportive of the misuse of power in anti-corruption investigations, have been—owing to their strong representation in the courts—equally engaged in preventing the authoritarian abuses under the regime of President Bolsonaro. In Romania, a true popular mobilization of the judges witnessed in the protests referred to in Chapters 3 and 4 uncovered a deep-seated generational division between the younger and older judges that occurred in the aftermath of the backlash against the judiciary. In all three of the countries, elements of civil society became active in preserving and promoting the legacy of the campaigns. Still, the reputation of the profession suffered in all three jurisdictions.

Thus, it is not surprising that the campaigns do not lead to a stable increase of public trust in institutions or actors such as the parliaments, political parties, or governments. Instead, the rise of institutional trust occurs vis-à-vis courts that become increasingly perceived as independent actors willing to tackle corruption. Even this effect is not evenly spread throughout the population, remaining mostly focused on the supporters of political actors that are perceived to have suffered the least through the campaigns. However, this increase of trust in the courts remains a long-term effect, as evidenced by the example of Italy discussed in Chapter 4. This means that, despite the strong challenges to the independence of the judiciary, the campaigns increase the overall standing of the courts and the demand for a judiciary that challenges the other two branches of government.

5.3 The rule of law challenges

As analyzed in Chapter 3, the actors leading the campaigns often "danced" on the edge of legality, sometimes overstepping this line. Most of this dancing was related to the collection of evidence of the existence of a corrupt pact between the briber and the bribee. In the case of Brazil, owing to the revelations of the investigative journalists, we have evidence to conclude that collusion, which overrides the lawful division of labor between the courts and the prosecutors, occurred. In the case of SRI's wiretaps in Romania and the agreements made between the SRI and the DNA, the division of labor was again violated, but this time between the intelligence agency and the judicial bodies. In the case of Italy, the magistrates did not violate the division of labor but faced an unprecedented willingness of the entrepreneurs to testify about the corrupt exchanges. That, however, allowed the prosecutors to freely classify the entrepreneurs as being victims of extortion and not active bribe offerors or persons induced to give bribes. As discussed in Chapter 4, this was not for nothing, as all three of the said actions have contributed to overall crime control and corruption control; however, in the case of Brazil and Romania, they have also contributed to a weakening of some other rule of law qualities, such as procedural guarantees. In that sense, Romania remained in the gray zone as the collection of evidence by SRI was legal but with huge possibilities for misuses that those opposing the campaigns often mentioned but rarely produced evidence for. In Brazil, on the other hand, the misuses concerning the process of Lula were of such a nature that they overshadowed the entire Lava Jato campaign, which was substantially bigger and more diverse than his process.

Furthermore, even if we accept that the procedural guarantees were limited, these actions by themselves do not prove that the political actors that were investigated were above suspicion. The collusion between Judge Moro and Dallagnol does not mean that the apartment kept for President Lula was indeed not a part of the award for some activities. It appears to us that their collaboration resembles what Seamus Miller called noble cause corruption.[1] The fact that a high number of persons were wiretapped or processed as those that reported corruption in Romania and Italy does not mean that there was no corrupt environment in which the corrupt exchanges were a part of a societal norm **and** a technique of governance.

If we can also blame the prosecutors for behaving in a strategically political way, we must also conclude that little evidence exists of this being done in direct co-ordination with the political actors. The defeat of their legal and political projects and a simple observation that it would be rather strange to pick the allies that would adopt none of their ideas seem to testify of that. Similarly, the allegation of a judicial revolution or a coup should be rejected; the judges and the prosecutors did not seek to govern the countries, appoint or remove their rulers,[2] or facilitate their economic transition. The rule of law crises that occurred and the legislative changes impacted by the campaigns were triggered by the desire of political actors within the two other branches of government to limit judicial independence and the reputation of the judiciary. Elements that are typically involved in the assessment of the rule of law quality of a national system that we discussed in Chapter 1 (clarity, stability, generality, prohibition of retroactivity, independence of the judicial institutions and the judicial review, access to justice, limitations to discretion of law enforcement agencies) were, generally speaking, less endangered by the campaigns than by the reactions to them. The violations that we may speak of concern the violation of the human rights of individual persons, either through the violation of their presumption of innocence or the fair trial standards. However, these two have come together most prominently in the case of Lava Jato—most notably in the case of ex-president Lula.

5.4 Impacts of the campaigns

Cynically speaking, the investigations would have achieved a more lasting impact had the prosecutors been less brave and principled. Had they decided not to attack Berlusconi (or at least, not frontally and very soon after he took office as the Italian Prime Minister) or to go around Lula (as was allegedly the case in the Mensalao investigation that preceded Lava Jato), the investigations would have been perceived as less polarizing. In the case of Italy (and with the benefit of hindsight), we could hypothesize that the frontal attack on Berlusconi was not an act of strategic thinking or conspiracy but motivated by the fear of prosecutors that the legacy of the campaigns would be undone immediately. In the case of Brazil, it appears that there was a certain degree of manipulation not so much from the prosecutors but from the side of Judge Moro, who (unsuccessfully) attempted to recreate what he perceived as the main success and the main lost opportunity of Mani pulite: communication with the media and a chance to change its political class. The prosecutors in Romania had no such choice, as the prosecutions of not only Nastase and Ponte as the highest-ranking figures of the PSD and the Romanian government, respectively, as well as many other important figures, seemed inevitable, possibly also requested at the political level by EU officials.

To what extent was the societal mobilization against anti-corruption successful? Symbolically, the citizens can see moments in which political figures previously considered untouchable are apprehended and prosecuted as a moment that demonstrates that the law applies to all and that there has come an end to impunity. As such, these moments are emotional, as they bring hope and, by themselves, resemble a bloodless revolution, which is one of the reasons why they are defined as collective action problems.[3] However, the campaigns seem to promise more than they deliver, a fact particularly visible in the two areas we touched upon in this book: the public narrative and the economic impacts of the campaigns.

All three cases examined reveal the public narrative, both for and against the campaigns, as the crucial aspect that determines the success of the campaigns, and their emergence in the public narrative. Given their coverage of the campaigns, we have seen that both the media and the judiciaries have understood this. The existence of news media outlets willing to report on the corruption crisis in all countries freely was crucial to the campaigns' impact. The practice of the prosecutors to leak information to the media and, in the case of Brazil, to use modern digital platforms to effectively communicate their findings bordered (and may have crossed) the guarantees of the presumption of innocence.

However, more important than this was the success of the discourse against the campaigns that were launched, the discourse that has been able to present the campaigns as politically partisan events organized not for the sake of corruption control but for the sake of political change and the control of secret power organizations; the pool of judges in Italy with mysterious connections to foreign services, the internationally supported prosecutors in Brazil, and the Securitatea successors in Romania. This narrative, as we have seen in Chapters 2 and 4, did not primarily seek to negate the corruption charges against political figures but rather to put them within a larger context of societal and political battles, which were—in their view—better led by those charged with corruption. To counter this with evidence such as those presented in Chapter 4, that the campaigns have contributed to better overall and regional governance in Romania, a more robust framework of corporate compliance and governance in both the public and private sectors in Brazil, and a transparent system of party funding in Italy, appears not to prevent the fears that the narrative raises. This is why the campaigns run a high risk of judicial populism.

Another field where the promise of anti-corruption campaigns falls short of expectations is economic development, where, as discussed in Chapter 4 and later in this conclusion, the effects were the most difficult to quantify and assess. Compared to what both the literature dealing with corruption and the very promise of the anti-corruption campaigns hold regarding the economic effects of the fight against corruption, the effects seem to be minor. This is surprising because if we accept the premise that the companies and other economic actors make their decisions based on a certain corruption equilibrium, then the change of this equilibrium must produce practical and observable consequences. From the compilation of the research on this topic that I have presented in Chapter 1 and the subsequent assessment in Chapter 4, we can safely exclude some of the major impacts of our three campaigns, such as the dramatic increase in economic growth or a more evenly spread regional growth. However, to what extent the campaigns have contributed to the breaking of monopolies within society, to what extent the campaigns have allowed new actors to enter the market, and in which sectors of the economy or at which geographical locations this happened remains unclear. We have seen that the campaigns have made a limited impact in making the investments in the Italian south more efficient and a somewhat stronger impact on the development of Romanian regions. Certainly, this is not to minimize that the campaigns did contribute to the increased efficiency of public procurement, more transparent party funding, increased compliance within the corporate sector, more certainty for foreign investors, and outsourcing of public services to private actors. But, for the average citizen, not too much has changed for the better, at least over a short period. Simply put, not too many impacts were visible and recognized or sought after by academic writers and researchers.

Bordering on conspiracy theories' discourse, the claims of the campaigns' opponents that the campaigns favored foreign capital are to be rejected as no concrete evidence concerning bias or collusion between the prosecutors (magistrates) and the exponents of global capitalism is to be found. Instead, what should be recognized is that the anti-corruption drive in all three countries coincided with the rise of global neo-liberal capitalism and has (in)directly favored global capitalism. The reason for this lies in the transitional nature of all three countries at the moment of the beginning of the campaigns. Italy of the early 1990s was living beyond its means, and its *classe dirigente* was unable to comply with the demands of the joint European market. Brazil's economic growth became unsustainable, and the country's recession was difficult to escape with the PT in power. Romania's establishment was heavily divided over its communist legacy and over the clashes between the socialist and liberal approaches to redistribution. In all three countries, the anti-corruption campaigns facilitated a drive toward less protectionism for the domestic economic actors.

Further research might be able to overcome some of the inadequacies. For example, it is much needed to quantify the number of those who have successfully offered goods and services to the government (before and after the campaigns or after the adoption of some anti-corruption program or measure) via public procurement and compare trends in this area. A promising avenue of research currently under development aims to tackle this problem by quantifying the effects of public procurement and connecting them to events such as changes in government.[4] Aiming to mark the entrance of new actors in the market, this research connects their entrance to political influence. However, this strain of research, focused purely on quantitative analysis, remains self-confined without a qualitative analysis that explores these actors contextualizing their role in the market and the wider society.

Important limitations also exist when we face the question of comparisons between countries. At the beginning of my research, I had hoped not only to compare the countries where the anti-corruption judicial campaigns happened but also a case where they did not, despite a comparable institutional setup, external factors, and levels of corruption. Indeed, a study that includes one such case would be richer and bring us additional insights. However, as I progressed with my research, I realized that significant data-collecting obstacles, such as collecting data regarding the work of the prosecutors (and possibly the archives of the national security services), would restrict progress. Bypassing that problem would require more time and resources than are available to me and would produce a work that would be more speculative. That is why this book, while valid for the cases it discusses, may remain less useful for explaining why the campaigns did not happen in other jurisdictions. However, as a predictor of their future occurrence and the problems related to the overall stability of the legal and political systems in which they occur, I believe this research contributes to the academic debate by filling an important gap left by the absence or inadequate comparison of the campaigns. For the examinations of the quality of the judicial systems, this means that judicial reputation, while useful as an explanans, does not necessarily provide us with an explanation of all the complexities governing the operations of a judicial system. As suggested in Chapter 2, I hope that by understanding the relationship between the anti-corruption campaigns as events that are critical junctures in shaping the legal, and in particular, the judicial culture of the countries, this book has contributed to an improved understanding of the concept of judicial reputation. Furthermore, the research adds to the comparison of the events that impact the rule of law and the separation of powers and to the research on the economic impacts of the judicial anti-corruption campaigns, which I find to be a surprisingly underexplored topic.

This leads us to a general problem of corruption studies: the lack of an interdisciplinary approach and its deficiencies where it exists. The indexes that aim to help us capture societal change sometimes deliver unexpected results, such as the measurements that Brazil has more integrity than before the Lava Jato crisis. As such, they appear superficial and based on criteria that fail to capture some of the more sophisticated concepts, such as integrity.

From a public policy standpoint, the campaigns and their aftermath have revealed a systemic weakness of the political party funding regulatory framework. The legislative changes and significant energy invested in the application and development of domestic (Italy and Brazil) and international standards in this area (Italy and Romania) have produced uncertain results. On the one hand, it is understood that no clear solution based solely on either public or private funding is possible. On the other hand, party funding regulation does not capture the extent of undue influence that the holders of political power may capture to advance their political projects. The contributions that the party funding regulation brings are more in the field of transparency; the implementation of regulation and financial reporting maps a sizable part of the financial contributions that make the party operational, revealing its support network. However, this transparency does not automatically translate into more accountability—a whole series of events that includes the role of the media, civil society, and the overall party preferences within a country stand between the process. In that sense, we observe that the principal–agent theory has considerable limitations, as citizens do not necessarily value transparency as much as the models predict they would. Instead, citizens base their political preferences on a number of factors that might or might not be in line with the legacy of the anti-corruption campaigns or their improvement. Also, they might not be in line with the principal–agent model, as the efficiency of the government observed by the citizens as principals might not necessarily be a concern for all of the citizens.

Which of the countries had the best campaign, how would we define the best campaign, where were the impacts most positive, and what factors did this depend on? We cannot offer clear answers to all of these questions. In terms of rule of law quality, there is no doubt that the Italian campaign, owing to the high degree of control exercised by the Court of Cassation and the CSM, had the best overall quality. This campaign brought a high degree of uncovering of the corrupt networks, the greatest number of voluntary confessions, and the greatest number of credible revelations that were to uncover the governing mechanism of the country. In terms of impact, however, the greatest advancement seems to have been made in Romania, as evidenced by its overall improvement in the quality of government, regulatory standards, and economic growth. However, the mostly successful backlash of the government and the parliamentarians against the judiciary and its power makes it the only one out of the three judicial systems that have exited the campaign significantly more constrained in the exercise of its independence than it was at its commencement. Despite being the most international of the three in the scope of the impact made outside of its boundaries, the Lava Jato campaign had limited impact outside of the specific sectors of the Brazilian economy and with a very doubtful positive impact even in the field of corruption control. Both the Brazilian and Romanian judiciaries were strengthened by the entrenchment of the esprit de corps, which could demonstrate its power in the campaigns to come. But in all three of the cases, the legislative framework has made that a less probable chance of occurring. This should not be understood to mean that there is no public demand for such a campaign. The increased specialization and criminalization of specific corrupt actions such as influence trading leave ample space for the qualification of diverse actions of the highest political actors as corrupt. With the general perception of corruption by citizens remaining high, there can be no doubt that a new campaign would also be highly popular, just as the three campaigns were or, to a certain extent, still are.

5.5 Avenues for further research

Several additional issues that I have identified in the campaigns deserve our attention at the end of this book. First is the issue of evidence of the perpetration of corrupt criminal acts. As we have seen, most of the problems raised in Chapter 3 have been directly tied to this problem. A part of the solution to this problem lies in the focus on the regulation of the status of whistleblowers as persons who are willing to report crimes and their preparation. While the solution used in the US, where most whistleblowers are rewarded for the revelations they make, might not be adequate for application in many other jurisdictions, the approach currently developed in Europe following the adoption of the EU Directive on whistleblowers would guarantee a gradual change of corporate culture that could contribute to the prevention and revelation of corrupt exchanges.

Second, there is the issue of corruption as a national security threat, an approach that, as discussed in Chapters 2 and 3, Romania took to legally involve the evidence collected by the SRI wiretaps in the criminal proceedings for corruption. In my view, the lesson learned from the Romanian example is that of a careful assessment of a genuine need for such an involvement of the intelligence agencies. In the case of Romania, it was the lack of trust in the police investigators and parts of the judiciary that prompted the desire to use the intelligence agency as the main collector of evidence of corruption. While this involvement guaranteed speedy evidence-gathering operations and the bypassing of corrupt officials, subsequent events clearly demonstrated the legal and political risks of the use of evidence gathered by the intelligence agencies in the criminal prosecution of corruption cases. Such activities break the traditional wall that existed between the intelligence agencies and the courts. Even in the absence of much concrete evidence for misuse, the case of Romania demonstrates that the intelligence agency and its reputation may endanger the credibility of the entire anti-corruption campaign when this campaign targets the highest political officials in the country. It appears that more restraint and caution in the exercise of intelligence measures, coupled with the reliance on money laundering prevention measures and the specialized investigatory units of the police, seem adequate to tackle the most serious crimes.

However, the fears of the power of transnational corruption to affect political developments in the countries lead contemporary actions of the states to further expand the field of national security to the field of corruption, as witnessed by the recent examples of the United States, which has done so in 2021. The expansion of the national security field to include acts of transnational corruption will naturally yield more surveillance activities over political actors, further exacerbating the vicious circle of anti-corruption and political conspiracy theories. This expansion will be fueled by the fears of the power of transnational corruption and legal definitions of corrupt acts that are always bound to be imperfect due to the contested nature of the term.

As we have seen, the judicial anti-corruption campaigns come with a number of problems regarding their legality, legitimacy, and the challenges to the entire judicial branch. As such, the literature on corruption sometimes negates their contributions to the fight against corruption altogether. Mungiu-Pippidi, as one of the most influential contemporary authors in the field of corruption, reduces Romanian judicial anti-corruption to populism, proposing instead vast preventive measures such as the control and analysis of public procurement patterns. Similar charges, as we have seen in Chapter 2, have been made regarding the Lava Jato campaign. I do not agree with this view, as I do not think that we should reject the anti-corruption campaigns altogether and focus on better preventive and reporting measures as the main tool against corruption. I have three main reasons for this stance. The first reason is that we still do not know enough about the transformative potential of these campaigns. The anti-corruption academic community does not study the campaigns or the prosecutions of political corruption—with the exception of Lava Jato—as much as it could and should, and its analysis is often only quantitative, leaving the more narratively prepared qualitative material to often partisan and partial journalists and commentators or dramatic TV series that, by their very nature, do not conform to the scientific standards of inquiry. I believe that more studies that would extensively research the transformation of societies would have the potential to shine a light on the aspects of the campaigns that are not entirely visible to the public eye. For example, the approach of Capussela to Italy, that is based on tracing the evolution of trust, while in my view perhaps too critical of the country (claiming that Mani pulite brought no result!), allows us to see how a corruption-related variable such as trust has shaped the

Italian economy, preventing, in the view of the author, a societal evolution toward a more universalistic and less particularistic approach to the concept of public good. More than just contributing to our knowledge on the transformation of societies, such studies would also tell us more about the specific developments of the causes of corruption within societies.

The second reason is that, while the value of preventive actions should be acknowledged as they make the job of the judiciary much easier, societies may not fully rely on their capacity to prevent wrongdoings from occurring. The very nature of corruption, which relies on quid pro quo transactions, will always provide opportunities to misuse public power. Thus, the capture of these preventive mechanisms will be (and in the cases of some Eastern European member states already is) as dangerous or even more dangerous than the capture of the judiciary. It is for these cases that we would have to accept that while the campaigns bring us many problems concerning legitimacy and legality, the very threat of a successful judicial campaign is enough to capture the public imagination and delegitimize the actions of political agents in power. This, especially because the recent approach of the EU and the US in sanctioning corrupt individuals as a primary means of dealing with those that have exploited the state capture, is another approach of extrajudicial solution to corruption that remedies the failures of preventive measures and state capture. However, growth in the usage of such measures will create perhaps much bigger problems than the judicial investigations ever have.

The third reason to oppose the discarding of the judicial anti-corruption campaigns is the constitutional conceptualization of the position of the judiciary as a separate branch of power. If we begin to expect that our prosecutors and judges should think strategically about ending their investigations before they come to their procedural end or if we believe that preventive mechanisms are systematically better positioned to deal with corruption, we are advocating a gradual dismantlement of the judicial power. The risk of judicial populism exists whenever the judges are doing something that is popular with a large part of the population, but the same is true for the actors in the other two branches of government.

Notes

1 Seumas Miller, Noble cause corruption in policing, *African Security Studies*, 8(3), 12–22.
2 As an exemption from this, it seems that evidence from the Intercept leaks suggests that Judge Moro had used his influence to prevent the extension of Lava Jato investigations to former Brazilian President Cardoso.
3 Cf. Huntington, note 66 (Chapter 1).
4 Fazekas & Toth, note 50 (Chapter 1).

Index

Pages in **bold** refer to tables and pages followed by “n” refer to notes.

FSC
www.fsc.org
MIX
Papier | Fördert gute Waldnutzung
FSC® C083411

Kolibri 360 GmbH
Ferdinand-Jühlke-Straße 7
99095 Erfurt, Deutschland
produktsicherheit@kolibri360.de